MULTIPLE-CHOICE & FREE-RESPONSE QUESTIONS WITH DBQ IN PREPARATION FOR THE AP EUROPEAN HISTORY EXAMINATION

(FIFTH EDITION)

Ellis A. Wasson, *Ph.D.*
Tower Hill School
Wilmington, DE

Preface

The purpose of this book is to give you some pointers on how best to approach the AP European History examination and to help you practice and review for that exam. There is an introductory section, review outlines, multiple choice questions, examples of essays, and two full-length sample exams.

Remember that the examination is always evolving. Check with your teacher about the most current information relating to the structure and content.

Based on almost three decades of teaching AP to students of wide-ranging ability as well as many years of grading the exam and serving on the committee that makes up the questions, I have tried to make this book as realistic as possible. However, you can ask your teacher to show you the actual published past exams issued by the College Board. My book and those questions should give you a good idea of what to be prepared for.

I have made a particular effort to include illustrations, charts, graphs, maps, cartoons, and quotations from historical documents, which you will find are a part of both the multiple choice and essay portions of the examination. Work hard to acquire the skills necessary to master these problems of interpretation. Remember, even the factual section of the examination is not a mere exercise in memorization. You are being tested on your ability to think critically. Good Luck!

All communications concerning this book should be addressed to:

D&S Marketing Systems, Inc.
1205 38th Street
Brooklyn, NY 11218

TABLE OF CONTENTS

AP European History

Survival Guide for Students

What are the big problems that face the world and what can I do to help? How do I distinguish between fact and opinion in learning about these issues (or when I'm buying a used car for that matter)? What do I believe in and why do I believe it? How can I express what I believe and what I have learned in a coherent and persuasive manner? These and many other questions can be at least partially answered by taking a course such as AP European History. Remember that you will be acquiring and honing skills of vital importance to success in college and in life. At the same time you will be learning about an important piece of the past.

It is fashionable at the moment to value all societies equally. In many ways this is a fair and reasonable approach to history. Every person should be equal; every society is deserving of respect. We should be familiar with the broad outline of all human development, and understand the basic beliefs of all large cultures. But Europe has a special place in the creation of the modern, technological society in which we live. Our language and our laws derive directly from the European experience. Philosophy, art, literature, economic theory, etc. are all part of this inheritance. The modern research university and modern mathematics and science come from Europe. If you wish to understand the good and the bad in American society you must first learn about Europe.

One used to hear much talk about "the Pacific Century", but the setbacks suffered by Asian economies in recent years have made people realize that some of the "hype" was misleading. China, India, and Japan are important to the world economy and American strategic thinking, but Europe is still the largest and the richest economic force in the world and will remain so for a long time. The future of Russia may well determine whether you personally will experience the terror and passion of war. The legacy of European imperialism in the Middle East helped to create the tragedy of September 11th and our recent military interventions in Iraq and Afghanistan.

To do well in this course you will have to commit yourself to hard work. Only dedication combined with intelligence can win you the highest score on the examination. But enjoy yourself. There is so much wonderful drama, so much grandeur and horror, so much that is human.

CONNECTING THE PAST

Five themes are helpful in connecting the mass of information that will threaten to overwhelm you unless some kind of organizational structure is imposed on it. Try to fit what you read into this model.

1. The rise and decline of great powers. This involves religion, the idea of the state, the conduct of war and diplomacy, the growth of nationalism, the development of economic systems, and the influence of great individuals on history.

2. The second theme is "equality vs. liberty." This balance remains as elusive today as it has always been. The growth and decay of ideologies and the conflict between them falls here. So too does the attempt to solve problems by reform and revolution.

3. The third theme is social structure and the transition from orders and estates to class. You must focus attention on the elites, middle level, and the lower orders or classes in the worlds of agriculture, urban life, and industrial society. By the way, do not make the mistake of confusing royalty with aristocracy. Often the interests of kings and nobles were diametrically opposed.

4. The fourth theme is the history of the family – perhaps the most fundamental of all historical issues, involving the relationships between men, women, and children and the history of the home and the work place. The family is the building block of society. By the way, historians are in constant conflict with each other on virtually every kind of issue, but no area is faster moving or more fraught with misinformation at the moment than this one. Textbooks never give enough space to the topic and are obsolete almost immediately when it comes to family history.

5. The fifth theme is the history of culture: the visual arts, music, literature, science, philosophy, etc. The creators of culture shape our views of ourselves and of society. It is impossible to exaggerate the importance of Luther, Newton, and Darwin. Few have so profoundly understood the human condition as Count Tolstoy or Jane Austen.

Warning: Western Europeans and Americans, since the time of the Enlightenment, have been subject to what historians call the fallacy of the "Whig interpretation" of history. This is the notion that history moves onward and upward in a progressive trajectory that is inevitable and for the best. Ironically, Adam Smith and Karl Marx both suffered from this delusion. One would have thought that World War I and World War II and the nuclear bomb would have cured us of the idea, but alas we still believe in happy endings. That is our privilege, but do not assume that in the past positive change was inevitable or that every reform was an advancement.

THE EXAMINATION

Your teacher should let you look at the booklet published by the College Board called "Advanced Placement Program Course Description: History" (make sure it is the latest edition, because changes are made regularly), called the "Acorn book" for short (see also: http://apcentral.collegeboard.com). In it an outline is provided of the material covered in the examination, the percentage of questions in each topic area and chronological range. Sample questions are also included. There are three parts to the examination: 80 multiple choice questions; a document-based essay; and two free-response thematic essays.

MULTIPLE CHOICE

You will have 55 minutes to answer 80 multiple choice questions covering the period 1450 to the present. It is important to remember that the questions are mixed up chronologically and in level of difficulty. Do not panic if you come to a couple of questions you cannot answer. There will be easier ones later. If you can eliminate several of the answers (called distracters), you should take a guess even if you are not absolutely sure about the correct answer. 1/4 point is deducted for incorrect answers; nothing is deducted if you leave the question blank; 1 point is given for a correct answer. Move rapidly through the questions. Do not pause for long on difficult ones. Skip them and come back if you have time at the end.

There are three crucial things to know about the multiple choice section.

1. You will do better if you practice. That is the point of this book. Your teacher should give you some opportunities to answer multiple choice questions during the year. Several sets of multiple choice questions from past exams have been published by the College Board. Use these to practice on in your final review for the examination.

2. There is no substitute for careful study and memorization. You cannot "wing it" and hope to do well on this section.

3. You can leave a significant number of questions unanswered or incorrectly answered and still get a five on the examination. No course will cover all the material. Many different textbooks are used to prepare students for this test. You are competing against your peers, not against a set standard, and the final grade is a kind of curve. The booklets of past exams that have been printed contain breakdowns of the scores. You will be relieved when you see them.

THE DOCUMENT BASED QUESTION
[THE DBQ]

This is the best part of the examination. You have a fifteen minute reading period to look over a dozen or so documents and forty-five minutes to write an essay answering a question about them. To do well you have to understand how to analyze historical documents – not just letters or speeches but also newspapers, statistical tables, cartoons, photographs, maps, diary entries, etc. You have to be able to develop a thesis, synthesize a variety of ideas, and write coherently. Taking into consideration the constraints of time and place, the document-based question successfully simulates what an historian does in practice.

No background knowledge is required. Some topics have been focused on issues that few if any students had ever heard anything about, such as the conflict between the Flemings and the Walloons in Belgium. If you encounter such a topic, do not panic. You are not expected to know anything about it and can earn a perfect score on the essay working entirely with the documents provided. Some topics have concerned subjects courses cover only briefly, such as the Spanish Civil War, while others are main-line topics such as the Terror during the French Revolution. In these cases you may bring in outside information, but make sure it is accurate. Errors count against you even if the data is not part of the documents provided in the test. Even with a main line topic, you can earn the highest score without bringing in outside information.

As you go through the documents, ask the five "W" questions: who, what, where, when, why? Why have the examiners put this document in the collection? What does it contribute? Can I connect it with another document? Is it a primary or secondary document? Should I take it literally or is it sarcastic or ironic in intent? What is the social, economic, and political background of the author of the document? Is the document intended for public consumption or is it a private letter or diary entry never intended to be seen by outsiders? Is it polemical or a reluctant admission of truth running counter to the interests of the author? What is the point of view or bias of the author? Be alert to the dates of the documents. Is there change over time in the course of the set?

The examiners are looking for a unified essay with a thesis. They expect an introduction, an argument based closely on the documents, and if time allows a conclusion. You must have a thesis. You must back up the thesis convincingly with evidence. You must demonstrate, at least in several cases, that you understand the point of view of the document. State this explicitly.

In the introduction restate the question in your own words to show that you understand it. Notice the command words in the question. Are you asked to discuss, to analyze, to assess, to compare? Make sure you do what is asked, not what you want. Make sure you answer all parts of the question. Good students can come to grief when they forget to answer all parts of the question.

In the body of the essay establish your thesis. Identify patterns in the documents. Group several documents together. Do not catalogue the documents in a laundry list. This is not an exercise in regurgitation. The readers have the documents right in front of them as they grade your exam. Do not waste time stating the obvious. The readers are interested in your analysis not in re-reading the documents in correct numerical order as paraphrased by you. If you find yourself going over each document in numerical order, stop! Put them in an order that fits your thesis. Assess the quality of the evidence; analyze and explicitly state the point of view of some of the authors. Try to mention every document. Stick to the documents. Do not over generalize. Note changes in opinion over time if that is explicit or implicit in the documents. Note nuances of language.

Avoid using contemporary standards to judge historical controversies. For example do not use feminist, anti-abortionist, civil rights, anti-communist ideas to analyze women's suffrage, population expansion, slave trade issues, or Bolshevism. Keep your personal political, social, and religious views to yourself. Try to be as impartial as possible.

Use a few quotations, if appropriate, but do not quote at length. Always identify the documents that you quote or cite. The best method is to abbreviate and put them in parentheses – for example "(docs. 3, 7, 10)".

Write a conclusion if you have time. The conclusion should not repeat the essay over again. Try to place the question in a new context, connect it with other historical events. Is there a lesson to be learned?

Practice is vital. You should go over old questions in class. Do this first verbally, analyzing documents and developing theses as part of a discussion. Then do some without time restraints. Finally, practice in a one hour time limit.

The College Board publishes actual answers written by students on previous years document-based questions. Ask your teacher to see these so that you can compare your work to those of your peers and see what grades they received.

In the heat of the moment, you may easily forget to do the things listed above. I have a simple mnemonic device that students find helpful. You may want to develop a better one of your own. Mine is based on the word for a French roll – BAGET(TE).

B   is for bias – make sure you analyze for point of view.

A   is for all – try to use all the documents.

G   is for group – make sure to group documents and not discuss every one individually.

E   is for evaluate – that is to analyze not just regurgitate.

T   is for thesis – make sure you have one.

If you write BAGET at the top of your paper and remember to follow those rules, you should write an excellent essay.

SCORING WITH "THE CORE"

In recent years the scoring of the DBQ has been based on a "core" set of standards. An essay is assigned one point for accomplishing six basic tasks. Only if all six are completed may up to an additional three points be granted. In other words you can write a brilliant essay and be given a mid-range score if you fail to carry out one of the "core" tasks.

The six "core" tasks are as follows:

1. Has an acceptable thesis that directly addresses the question.

2. Uses at least a majority of the documents.

3. Addresses all parts of the question.

4. Demonstrates understanding of the documents by using them to support the argument. (May misinterpret no more than one document.)

5. Analyzes point of view or bias in at least three documents.

6. Analyzes documents by organizing them in at least three groups.

If all six of these tasks are accomplished, then and only then may additional points be assigned based on the following "expanded core" points.

- Has a clear, analytical, and comprehensive thesis.

- Uses all or almost all documents.

- Addresses all parts of the question thoroughly.

- Uses documents persuasively as evidence.

- Shows understanding of nuances in the documents.

- Analyzes point of view or bias in at least four documents cited in the essay.

- Analyzes the documents in additional ways – additional groupings or other.

- Brings in relevant "outside" historical content.

Other qualities, such as unusually persuasive and precise writing style, for example, can also earn points. Even essays that achieve the full nine points do not need to accomplish all of the "extended core". The reader who evaluates the essay is given discretion to use his or her judgment in this area. No such freedom exists in assigning the "core" points.

THE FREE RESPONSE THEMATIC ESSAYS
[FRQs]

You will have to write two 35 minute thematic essays. One topic must be selected from each of two groups of three questions. My experience has been that there is always at least one question in each section that you have studied and can answer well. The crucial thing is not to panic. Also do not pick the question which seems so broad that you can bull your way through. The examiners will be looking for specific data in that answer, and if the data is not there, you will not get a good score. The two groups of questions are arranged to ensure that you have covered a broad chronological range and a variety of social, economic, cultural, and political themes. You cannot concentrate your review on one area or era and expect to be prepared.

Practice makes perfect. The way to learn to write essays is to write a lot of them. Going over previous years thematic questions and answering them verbally is also helpful. Making lists of the causes and consequences of the great events of European history is also a good way to review. You should have at you finger tips the causes of the French Revolution, the consequences of the Reformation, etc. It also does not hurt to know the provisions of the great treaties such as Westphalia or Versailles.

Analyze the question. What is it really asking. Pay special attention to the command words such as "analyze" or "describe" (which mean very different things). Answer all parts of the question. That sounds like advice to a simpleton, but I assure you brilliant essays are written by very able students that get poor scores because one of the instructions in the question was neglected. If a question asks you to talk about before and after some event, do both. If you are asked about 17th century France, do not talk only about Louis XIV, who reigned during the second half of the century. Henry IV, Richelieu, Mazarin, and the Fronde, all of whom preceded him, require mention as well. If you are asked to talk about the factory system and the domestic system, do not write only about factories.

Develop a thesis. This is hard to do in 35 minutes. It can be a quite simple one, but some organizing idea is necessary to give the essay coherence and make it stand out. Write an introduction that restates the question in your own words. This forces you to be alert to the whole question. Place the issue in its historical context. State your thesis. Try to grab the reader's attention.

In the body of the essay use vivid and effective examples to back up your thesis. Be logical. Acknowledge any major arguments that can be made against your case. You must demonstrate that you know about the topic. The answer must be meaty and well-documented.

Every good essay in real life has a conclusion, containing what I recommended in the previous section on the DBQ. In a 35 minute format you will probably not have much time to do this. At all costs avoid repeating your points in the last paragraph. If you are doing this, it must be because you had too little knowledge of the question and the reader will assume that is the case. Try to end by answering the question, "So what?" Nothing gives an argument more force than a good answer to that question.

Proof read if you have time. Amazing errors slip past you in the heat of writing. The clearer your handwriting the better. If you cross something out, do so thoroughly.

Spell key names and terms correctly. Writing about Napoleon "Bonepert" instead of "Bonaparte" creates distinct unease in the reader's mind. Much will be forgiven in terms of style and spelling, but confusing Louis XIV with Louis XVI will not be. Also, do not write Queen Elizabeth "the" I or speak about "peasants" in 19th century England. Such errors also set off alarm bells in the graders' heads.

You may be witty but not flippant. Make sure the reader is laughing with you and not at you. Hindsight has a way of making us feel superior towards the people of the past. Try to remember to put yourself in their places and you will sound less patronizing. Applying the word "stupid" to Wilhelm II of Germany, for example, is not a good idea. He made grave errors of judgment, but he was by no means an unintelligent man. Also avoid overly familiar relations with the great. Florence Nightingale should not be called "Flo" or even Florence nor Napoleon I "Nappy".

Try to use simple and direct language; avoid jargon. Use the active voice and the past tense. Keep track of your thesis at all times. Avoid wild generalizations. Nothing causes more rapid deterioration in your reputation in the grader's eyes than a statement such as "all rulers are stupid." The words "never," "always," "all," etc. are dangerous and almost never accurate. "Perhaps" and "probably" can sound wishy-washy but are usually more appropriate and safer.

Remember that writing is a process of selection. You are selecting ideas and facts from a huge mass of information and you are selecting words to make your other selection process vivid, lively, and persuasive. Keep it simple. Be creative. Do not repeat yourself. Good luck!

HOW TO USE THE OUTLINES

At the beginning of each chapter, I have provided an outline. These lists are intended to include the bare minimum of essential factual information needed to succeed on the AP European history exam. No outline can be totally complete. The exam is very comprehensive, and some information may be highlighted in a given year that does not appear in my outlines. In particular some of the names or terms in the "distractors" (incorrect answers) in the multiple-choice section can be pretty esoteric. But the vast majority of the multiple-choice questions will involve information contained in these outlines.

I have also included lists of causes and outcomes of major events. These lists are good preparation for answering the free response essay questions (FRQs). Rarely are questions framed in a way to evoke simple regurgitation of a list (e.g. "Discuss the causes of the Renaissance"). However, if the question – "Was the Reformation mainly an economic event?" – is asked, knowledge of all the possible causes of the Reformation will give a student the foundation on which to build a solid answer.

Do not wait until the night before the exam to read over these outlines. The best thing to do is to review over several weeks. Compare your class notes and textbook underlinings or outlines to the guides here. Write in missing or supplementary information either in the margins or in your notebook, whichever works best for you. Once you have a consolidated outline, work particularly hard to review the sections that you found most confusing or have forgotten the most about.

Inevitably, in outlines of this kind, broad, sweeping trends over many countries or centuries and some big themes do not emerge clearly. Many essay questions may at first glance seem not to relate directly to "answers" in the outlines. However, if you are asked to write an essay on female monarchs or types of revolutions, you will find plenty of examples in the outlines on which you can draw.

The selection and ranking of important of facts and events can be controversial among historians. In some cases even terms such as "Counter Reformation" vs. the "Catholic Reformation" or the English "Civil War" vs. "Revolution" divide historians into opposing camps. What is purveyed here is not "the truth" but a collection of information that will help you organize a vast amount of data as efficiently as possible for the purpose of spending three hours taking the AP exam. I have included items in my lists because while some historians and teachers would reject them many others see them as important. Your teacher will make you aware of areas where current controversy is lively.

The outlines are no substitute for a solid textbook, hard work, and a good teacher. They are intended for review purposes only and presuppose much additional information that students should already know. Nor will they always work as review mechanisms for tests given by individual teachers who emphasize issues and events that seem important to them but may not appear on the AP exam. (Every good AP teacher emphasizes certain aspects of the course in which he or she has special interests and expertise.)

Many of the dates provided here are not necessarily crucial to remember. They are provided in order to help you place people and events in chronological context. It is much more important to remember the **ORDER** in which things happen than the year. Nonetheless certain dates **must be memorized** both to provide a skeleton upon which to organize the rest of the chronology and because they mark crucial moments in the human story that we should never forget. **I have marked the ones that have great importance with an ***.

Chapter I
The Renaissance

The main characteristics of medieval life were a reliance on agriculture and the power of the Church. Rank and order were central to the social hierarchy that ranged from the Pope and Holy Roman Emperor at the top through kings and sovereign princes to the great nobles, lesser nobles, knights, merchants, artisans, independent peasants, laborers, and serfs. Massive poverty, overwhelming pandemics, illiteracy, and spirituality existed everywhere. Although a few Jews and Muslims lived on the fringes of society, virtually all people from Poland and Hungary westward were Roman Catholics. Feudalism was the principal system of political, social, and economic organization. Latin was the predominant written language among the literate, who largely came from the clergy. People tended to see themselves as part of large communities and organizations with little individual self-awareness, focused on life after death. Marriages were partnerships in which work was divided by gender, but the contribution of men and women were both critical to survival.

Change was fostered by the impact of the Black Death (1347), the increasing wealth of merchants who allied with monarchs against the great nobles, the Schism in the Church (1378-1417), the Crusades (1095-), and technological advances in navigation and weaponry (especially the invention of cannons).

THE FIFTEENTH CENTURY

FRANCE
Still internally fragmented by the 100 years war with England (1337-1453) with a powerful nobility that weakened the king.

SPAIN
Divided into numerous kingdoms including Castile and Aragon with the Muslims still in Granada until 1492. The marriage of Ferdinand and Isabella brought unity and strength, led to the conquest of the South, intensification of religious uniformity, and overseas exploration.

ENGLAND
The Wars of the Roses (c. 1455-85) kept the nobility preoccupied and divided and led ultimately to the growth of a strong monarchy under the Tudors (Henry VII 1485). Still a small, weak, and relatively unimportant country.

1

HOLY ROMAN EMPIRE (largely Germanic Federation)
Hopelessly divided with the power of the Emperor (from 1452 on always a Habsburg of Austria) deteriorating (outside his personal domains) after concessions to the seven **electors** and the hundreds of minor autonomous princes and bishops were made at each election.

ITALY
Fragmented into many states, of which the most important were: the Papal territories, Venice, Milan, Rome, Genoa, Naples, and Florence. It is here that the Renaissance developed.

THE RENAISSANCE

A period from the later 14th* to the mid 16th* century whose name "Renaissance" ("rebirth") first gained wide currency after its use by the 19th-century Swiss historian, Jacob Burckhardt. A rich flowering of culture and revival of Classical ideas and learning. However, some historians see more continuity than change. The effects of the Renaissance were largely confined to high culture.

Causes:

- Breakdown of feudalism and the rise of a market economy in northern Italy
- Great wealth produced by banking and trade
- Urbanization
- The Crusades brought back new wealth and ideas
- Enlarged merchant class, literate and with leisure
- Great Schism weakens the authority of the Church
- Classical revival accelerated by the influx of scholars bringing texts from endangered Byzantium and partly by the revived heritage of Latium (Constantinople conquered by the Ottomans 1453*)
- Individual geniuses interacting with each other, above all in Florence
- Absence of any single controlling authority in Italy and its physical location as a focus of trade with the Near East and Northern Europe

Central ideas:

- Humanism – liberal and secular learning, recovery and study of the Classical texts, secular eloquence
- Individualism – "man is the measure of all things" – focus on personal achievement
- Civic humanism – engagement in politics is noble and necessary
- *Virtù* – reaching for perfection, fully developed mind and body, shape own destiny
- Weakening of Church's authority, (but do not exaggerate this – the majority of great paintings of the Renaissance are based on religious themes; the Popes became principal patrons of humanists and artists after c. 1450)
- Materialism
- Importance placed on education, being refined, literate
- Balance, order, symmetry

- Use of the vernacular
- Increasing self-awareness – rise of study of history, "know thyself"
- Continued subordination of women
- Interest in individual merit/talent but continued social hierarchy
- City-state government
- Civic and individual patronage of the arts
- Limitless opportunities for human achievement
- Life in the present can be improved, not just in the hereafter

Great Figures:

- **Dante** – (d. 1321) vernacular literature; *Divine Comedy*
- **Petrarch** – (d. 1374) father of humanism; coexistence of Classical and Christian values, contempt for Scholasticism and admiration for ancient Rome
- **Boccaccio** – (d. 1375) pioneer of humanist studies; *Decameron*
- **Castiglione** – (d. 1529) education, good manners; *Courtier*
- **Brunelleschi** – (d. 1446) cathedral dome in Florence
- **Donatello** – (d. 1466) "living" sculpture, "David"
- **Pico della Mirandola** – (d.1494) *On the Dignity of Man*
- **Botticelli** – (d. 1510) female beauty, "Birth of Venus"
- **Da Vinci** – (d. 1519) universal man, art, science, "Mona Lisa", military designs
- **Michaelangelo** – (d. 1564) glorification of human body and spirit; Sistine Chapel ceiling; "David"
- **Raphael** – (d. 1520) "School of Athens" in the Vatican
- **The Medici** – bankers who ruled Florence, bourgeois who became royal, great patrons of the arts, ruthless and Machiavellian; Cosimo (d. 1464) and Lorenzo the Magnificent (d. 1492)
- **Machiavelli** – (d. 1527) author of *The Prince*, a guide to politics, admired the heroism and patriotism of the Romans
- **Pope Julius II** – (d. 1513) great patron of the arts, expels French invaders – "Warrior Pope"
- **Savonarola** – (d. 1498) Florentine religious reformer, preached against decadence

Outcomes:

- Weakening of the authority of the Church
- Modern frame of mind begins to emerge
- Critical and analytical outlook encouraged
- Revival of Classical style, ideas, and texts
- Revival of the study of Classical Greece and its language accelerates
- Huge body of great art created employing new techniques to achieve realism such as perspective
- Greater interest in exploring unknown areas of the globe
- Improved technology and greater interest in science
- Encourage individualism over corporatism

- Man is glorified
- Creation of modern business functions and techniques including double-entry bookkeeping
- Rapid growth in the printing and distribution of books; moveable type printing press – Gutenberg c. 1450
- From the 1520s **Mannerism** emerged in Italy as the dominant new style in art
- In the 17th century the arts developed in the **Baroque** style, extravagant, heavy, elaborate, stresses tensions and contrasts, eventually develops in the 18th century into Rococo (emphasized power and authority, St. Peter's; Versailles)

NORTHERN RENAISSANCE

The ideas of the Italian Renaissance spread northward gradually in the fifteenth and sixteenth centuries, reaching France, the low countries, England, Poland, Hungary, and Germany, finally penetrating to Scandinavia. The Renaissance had less impact in Spain and little at all in Russia.

Characteristics:

- Less secularizing than the Italian Renaissance
- Christian humanism
- Spreads Classical ideas and texts
- Expansion of education, greater literacy
- Great art, especially produced in the Netherlands
- Gutenberg's printing press (1450s)
- Rise of vernacular literature, greater sense of national feeling

Great Figures:

- **Erasmus** (d. 1536) – reconciled Classical and Christian values, believed in the freedom of human will, critical scholarship, resists the Reformation
- **Thomas More** (d. 1535) – English author of *Utopia*, resists English Reformation: social liberal, theological conservative
- **Dürer** – (d. 1528) German painter and engraver
- **Fuggers** – German banking family of international scope
- **Shakespeare** (d. 1616) – great English playwright
- **Rubens** – (d. 1640) great Flemish Baroque artist
- **Rembrandt** – (d. 1669) Dutch painter of unsurpassed sensitivity and penetration

Photo used by permission, © 2004 www. Ancient-Empires.com

1. Painting and sculpture during the Renaissance were characterized by which of the following?

    (A)   Reliance on Gothic themes and styles
    (B)   cold and one-dimensional depictions of myths
    (C)   human body presented in naturalistic terms
    (D)   inaccurate and unrealistic representations
    (E)   exclusively secular themes

2. "I say that, in my opinion, in a Lady who lives at court a certain pleasing affability is becoming above all else, whereby she will be able to entertain graciously every kind of man with agreeable and comely conversation suited to the time and place and to the station of the person with whom she speaks."

The author of this passage was

    (A)   Galileo
    (B)   Botticelli
    (C)   Machiavelli
    (D)   Castiglione
    (E)   Colleoni

3. Late Medieval universities focused their curricula on which of the following sets of offerings?

   (A)   law, theology, and medicine
   (B)   physics, mathematics, and chemistry
   (C)   literature, sociology, and architecture
   (D)   art history, political science, and history
   (E)   poetry, creative writing, and government

4. In 1500 what proportion of the European population lived in towns of more than 10,000 inhabitants?

   (A)   six percent
   (B)   thirty percent
   (C)   fifty percent
   (D)   sixty percent
   (E)   seventy-seven percent

5. "Canon law" is a term that applies to

   (A)   military recruitment
   (B)   diplomatic negotiations
   (C)   civil suits
   (D)   eccelsiastical affairs
   (E)   jury selection

6. The three orders of people in medieval Europe consisted of

   (A)   clergy, nobles, and peasants
   (B)   professions, bourgeoisie, and peasants
   (C)   clergy, bourgeoisie, and peasants
   (D)   soldiers, clergy, and nobles
   (E)   royalty, nobles, and clergy

7. All of the following were major figures in the "Northern" Renaissance EXCEPT

   (A)   Thomas More
   (B)   Geoffrey Chaucer
   (C)   Nicholas Copernicus
   (D)   Christopher Marlow
   (E)   Erasmus

8. "For of men one can, in general, say this: They are ungrateful, fickle, deceptive and deceiving, avoiders of danger, eager to gain."

This quotation typifies an essential underpining of the work of which of the following authors?

(A)   Castiglione
(B)   Petrarch
(C)   Machiavelli
(D)   Bruni
(E)   Palladio

9. History, moral philosophy, and eloquence were described by Renaissance writers as

(A)   topics to be avoided at all costs in dinner table conversation
(B)   necessary skills for all educated women
(C)   the liberal arts
(D)   Scholastic precepts
(E)   the foundation of good theology

10. Skeptical criticism of documents and texts during the Renaissance led to which of the following?

(A)   the refusal by the pope to grant Henry VIII's divorce from Catherine of Aragon
(B)   created a repproachment with Arab universities
(C)   the unconditional support of new scholarship by the papacy
(D)   made Spain the center of European scholarship
(E)   called into question the authenticity of important documents such as the "Donation of Constantine"

Alinari/Art Resource, NY

11. This building, constructed in Rome in 1502, incorporates all of the following Classical elements most admired in Roman architecture by Renaissance thinkers EXCEPT

    (A)   a dome
    (B)   a spire
    (C)   columns
    (D)   symmetry and balance
    (E)   Tuscan capitals

12. Which of the following was NOT incorporated into the kingdom of Spain by Ferdinand and Isabella?

    (A)   Portugal
    (B)   Castile
    (C)   Navarre
    (D)   Aragon
    (E)   Granada

13. The most important innovation in warfare in the fourteenth and fifteenth centuries was the

    (A) the crossbow
    (B) Greek fire
    (C) siege cannon
    (D) cavalry
    (E) barbed wire

14. During the Renaissance wealthy women

    (A) enjoyed much greater freedom at home and work
    (B) did not gain any significant loosening of restrictions placed on them
    (C) were encouraged to study law and medicine
    (D) married earlier and had more children
    (E) were never allowed to study the humanities or theology

15. French kings established a "Gallican" church in the late fifteenth century and early sixteenth century in order to

    (A) give the pope more influence in France
    (B) win the friendship of the English Tudors
    (C) enhance economic growth
    (D) launch a new crusade
    (E) gain tighter royal control over the church

16. Which of the following was considered most appropriate for the study of women in fifteenth-century Italy?

    (A) science
    (B) military arts
    (C) rhetoric
    (D) mathematics
    (E) religion

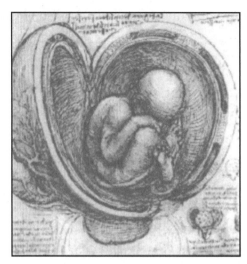

The Royal Collection © 2004, Her Majesty Queen Elizabeth II

17. These drawings are the work of

    (A)   Petrarch
    (B)   da Vinci
    (C)   Rembrandt
    (D)   Bruni
    (E)   Donatello

18. One of the most characteristic literary innovations of the Renaissance was?

    (A)   autobiography
    (B)   biography
    (C)   homilies
    (D)   the novel
    (E)   poetry

19. The great Renaissance writer, Petrarch, believed strongly in the importance of studying

    (A)   theology
    (B)   science and technology
    (C)   medicine and law
    (D)   military tactics and strategy
    (E)   Classical poetry and rhetoric

20. Terms connected with medieval and early modern commercial life in urban centers include all of the flowing EXCEPT

    (A) apprentice
    (B) journeyman
    (C) cartel
    (D) masterpiece
    (E) guild

21. Beginning in 1452 which family traditionally gained election as Holy Roman Emperors?

    (A) Medici
    (B) Valois
    (C) Habsburg
    (D) Wittlesbach
    (E) Hohenzollern

22. The Renaissance style of painting may be characterized by which of the following descriptions?

    (A) flat and linear
    (B) naturalistic
    (C) abstract
    (D) dark and brooding
    (E) narrow range of colors

Europe, A HISTORY by Norman Davies, © 1993 by Norman Davies.
Used by permission of Oxford University Press, Inc.

23. This map depicts

    (A) Spain under Ferdinand and Isabella
    (B) Habsburg possessions in the Mediterranean
    (C) Italy during the Renaissance
    (D) cities that converted to Lutheranism
    (E) the Risorgimento

24. Which of the following was a leading city state during the Renaissance?

    (A) Budapest
    (B) Seville
    (C) Athens
    (D) Milan
    (E) Bordeaux

25. "The art of printing is very useful insofar as it furthers the circulation of useful ... books, but it can be very harmful if it is permitted to widen the influence of pernicious works. It will therefore be necessary to maintain full control over the printers so that they may be prevented from bringing into print writings which are antagonistic to the Catholic faith."

This statement was most likely authored by

(A)   Pope Alexander VI
(B)   Henry VIII of England
(C)   John Hus
(D)   William Tyndale
(E)   John Wyclif

No testing material on this page.

Chapter II

The Reformation

The Protestant Reformation was a revolution in the Christian church that split Western Europe into Catholic and Lutheran communities, and ultimately led to the fragmentation of Protestantism into many sects. Humpty Dumpty fell off the wall and could never be put back together again.

Causes:

- Challenge to Papal authority and Catholic teaching by the German monk, Martin Luther, (95 Theses, 1517*) deriving from theological objections and personal crisis of faith
- Use of Luther's break by some of the German princes to challenge the authority of the Catholic Holy Roman Emperor
- Economic discontent among the wealthy in Germany over sending money to Rome (Tetzel and indulgences)
- Economic and social discontent among the peasantry (price inflation)
- Weakness of authority of the Holy Roman Emperor
- New critical spirit encouraged by the Renaissance
- Weakness of the Papacy due to the Great Schism and poor leadership
- Corruption in the Church: simony, nepotism, sale of indulgences, pluralism, and vice among the Church hierarchy
- Henry VIII's desire to gain firmer control over the state in England
- Greater emphasis on individualism in relationship with God (due both to the late medieval movement towards mysticism and the Renaissance)
- Attacks by Turks and French on territories of the Emperor
- Invention of printing press allows rapid dissemination of religious news and tracts
- Rise of capitalistic spirit that emphasizes personal restraint and pursuit of wealth

Theology:

- Lutheran core –
    priesthood of all believers
    authority of scripture alone
    justification by faith alone (by God's grace)
- Luther's criticism of corruption in the Church – salvation cannot be bought and sold
- Overthrow of Papal authority
- Bible translated into the vernacular (Luther's German Bible)
- More radical critics –
    no transubstantiation (Eucharist)
    no altars, stained glass, statues, relics

15

pulpit in center front of church

no central aisles, incense

no fasts or pilgrimages

no bishops

predestination

reduced number of sacraments

emphasis on teaching (sermons) and text (scripture) as center of worship

clergy do not stand between God and man

clergy can marry

no Purgatory

- English Reformation – King head of the Anglican Church (1534)
- The Catholic Reformation (Counter Reformation)

  Inquisition

  Council of Trent

  Society of Jesus: teachers and missionaries
- Anabaptists' attempt to create a perfect Christian community, brutally suppressed by Catholics and Protestants

Great Figures:

- **Jan Hus** (d.1415) – Bohemian reformer, burned at stake
- **Martin Luther** (d. 1546) – first leader of the Reformation
- **Ulrich Zwingli** (d. 1531) – challenges transubstantiation
- **John Calvin** (d. 1564) – radical Protestant, develops idea of predestination, establishes "theocracy" at Geneva
- **Charles V** – (r. 1520-58) Holy Roman Emperor, but also ruler of Spain, the low countries, Austria, Bohemia, part of Italy, and an empire in the Americas. Leader of the Catholic party. Ultimately abdicated 1556 and divided his empire between his brother (HRE, Austria-Hungary) and his son, Philip II (Spain, Italy, the Netherlands, and the new world)
- **Ignatius Loyola** (d. 1556) – founds Jesuit Order

Events:

- **Diet of Worms** (1521) – Luther called to defend himself, put under imperial ban
- **Peasants' War** (1525) – Luther supports princes when they suppress social and economic uprising
- **Schmalkaldic League** (1531) – German Protestant alliance against Charles V and Roman Catholics
- **Act of Supremacy** (1534) – Anglican Church established in England
- **Peace of Augsburg** (1555*) – *cuius regio, eius religio* (he who rules, his will be the religion), but excludes Calvinists and Anabaptists; victory to the Lutherans, weakens HRE

- **Council of Trent** (1545-63) – Counter Reformation – ends pluralism and enacts other clerical reforms to end corruption in the church; reaffirms traditional doctrine, papal authority, the vulgate (Latin) Bible, clerical celibacy
- **College of Propaganda** established to propagate faith for Catholics

Outcomes:

- Destruction of the single institution common throughout Europe – the end of a united Christendom
- Brutal and bloody wars of religion both between nations and within France and Germany
- Fierce religious persecutions, especially in Spain
- Disappearance of most remaining authority of the Holy Roman Emperor in Germany, sovereign princes rule more independently
- Italy, Spain, Austria, Hungary, Poland, and Southern Germany remain Catholic
- England became Anglican, Scotland, Switzerland, and Holland were Calvinist, Northern Germany and the Baltic were Lutheran
- France split between Catholics and Huguenots, although Catholics predominated; tries to keep Germany divided religiously
- Counter Reformation – refreshes and strengthens traditional Catholic theology – founding of new orders, esp. Jesuits, emphasis on education
- Religious, political, and social conflicts become intermingled
- Encourages growth of capitalism by emphasis on thrift, sobriety, search for material success as a sign of Grace, moral discipline, and individualism
- New value placed on family and marriage
- More companionate marriage but patriarchic households
- Challenged the Cult of the Virgin and woman seen as "the Temptress"
- Males remain dominant in Protestant clergy, and women lose autonomy where monastic life is curtailed
- Emphasizes need for education of both sexes in order to study scripture
- Overthrow of the Latin vulgate in Protestant countries, and the firm establishment of modern German and English languages based on Luther's translation of the Bible and the King James Bible and Cranmer's (d. 1556) *Book of Common Prayer*
- Encouragement of settlements in Massachusetts and elsewhere to escape religious persecution
- More tolerance for Jews
- Confiscation of church and monastic lands enriches rulers and elites
- Kings of France and Spain gain tighter control of the Catholic church (Gallican Church)

1. "We...take it for granted that you will release us from serfdom as true Christians, unless it should be shown us from the Gospel that we are serfs."

This statement was written by

(A) French peasants in 1789
(B) Turkish peasants in Asia Minor
(C) English peasants under Henry VIII
(D) conquered Aztecs in Mexico
(E) German peasants in the 1520s

2. Luther's ideas and the spirit of the Reformation were spread by all the following EXCEPT

(A) hymns such as "A Mighty Fortress is Our God"
(B) woodcuts and illustrations
(C) reformers appearing before the Pope in person
(D) translations of the Bible into vernacular languages
(E) university debates and curricula

3. Roman Catholics, Lutherans, and Calvinists shared all the following EXCEPT

(A) wariness about new astronomical discoveries
(B) hostility to using human bodies for anatomical research
(C) refusal to permit women to take a more active role in religious life
(D) active persecution of those who did not share their beliefs
(E) belief in transubstantiation during the Eucharist

4. The Reformation encouraged literacy and education

(A) so that people could read the scriptures
(B) due to Luther's interest in poetry
(C) because the Roman Catholic church denounced education
(D) due to Luther's belief in social equality
(E) because it began in Florence

5. Who among the following was not a member of the family of Henry VIII of England?

(A) Catherine de Medici
(B) Catherine of Aragon
(C) Mary I
(D) Edward VI
(E) Elizabeth I

6. The Protestant Reformation encouraged all of the following changes in the status of women EXCEPT

   (A)   more companionate marriage where partners were respected
   (B)   more grounds for divorce if husbands violated the laws of marriage
   (C)   nunneries as a means of escape from wife beating
   (D)   more sensitivity by husbands to the needs of wives
   (E)   better education for women

7. Among the following groups in France during the sixteenth century which contained the largest proportion of Protestants

   (A)   clergy
   (B)   peasants
   (C)   aristocracy
   (D)   guild members
   (E)   paupers

8. The saying "Erasmus laid the egg that Luther hatched" refers to

   (A)   the Renaissance
   (B)   civic humanism
   (C)   the Reformation
   (D)   Mannerism
   (E)   the baroque style

9. "Christians should be taught that, if the Pope knew the exactions of the preachers of Indulgences, he would rather have the basilica of St. Peter reduced to ashes than built with the skin, flesh and bones of his sheep."

   This passage was contained in which of the following?

   (A)   Thomas More's *Utopia*
   (B)   Erasmus's *In Praise of Folly*
   (C)   Loyala's *Spiritual Exercises*
   (D)   Joan of Arc's speech from the stake
   (E)   Luther's "95 Theses"

10. Calvinists disapproved of central aisles in churches because they

   (A)   divided the worshipers in two
   (B)   allowed for ceremonial processions
   (C)   used up floor space
   (D)   encouraged debates about theology
   (E)   drew attention away from the altar

11. The accomplishments of Queen Elizabeth I of England included all of the following EXCEPT

    (A)   established peace and stability
    (B)   aided Protestants in the Netherlands
    (C)   defeated the Armada
    (D)   created long-term financial security for the monarchy
    (E)   more extensive conquest of Ireland

    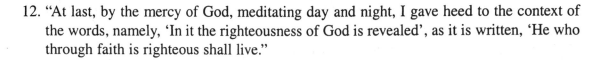

12. "At last, by the mercy of God, meditating day and night, I gave heed to the context of the words, namely, 'In it the righteousness of God is revealed', as it is written, 'He who through faith is righteous shall live."

    This passage was written by

    (A)   Pope Julius II
    (B)   Martin Luther
    (C)   Baldassare Castiglione
    (D)   Leonardo da Vinci
    (E)   John Tetzel

13. The Peace of Augsburg (1555) left unresolved which issue?

    (A)   the place of Calvinism in the religious settlement
    (B)   the border divisions of Scandanavia
    (C)   the Italian frontier with Switzerland
    (D)   the restoration of Catholicism in France
    (E)   the religious missions in South America

14. Which of the following held that the communion service was merely symbolic of Christ's presence at the ceremony?

    (A)   Pope Leo X
    (B)   Martin Luther
    (C)   Ulrich Zwingli
    (D)   Charles V
    (E)   Frederick the Wise

15. Calvinism became an influential force in all of the following countries EXCEPT

    (A)   Spain
    (B)   Scotland
    (C)   the Netherlands
    (D)   France
    (E)   Switzerland

16. The "Revolt in the Netherlands" during the second half of the sixteenth century was caused by all of the following EXCEPT

    (A)   resentment of Spanish interference in Dutch government
    (B)   the shortcomings of William the Silent's leadership
    (C)   Calvinists resisting Catholic rule
    (D)   desire for economic independence from Spain
    (E)   encouragement from England

17. Northern Christian humanists such as Erasmus of Rotterdam

    (A)   were unwilling to renounce papal authority totally
    (B)   condemned the papacy in the strongest terms
    (C)   focused only on questions of aesthetics
    (D)   were the key leaders of the Reformation
    (E)   expressed tolerance for Russian Orthodoxy and Islam

18. Among Martin Luther's most important beliefs were all of the following EXCEPT

    (A)   justification by faith
    (B)   authority of scripture
    (C)   priesthood of the believer
    (D)   denunciation of indulgences
    (E)   the seven sacraments

19. Ignatius Loyola is noted for all of the following EXCEPT

    (A)   founded the Jesuit order
    (B)   urged ecumenical embrace of all Protestant sects
    (C)   believed in a military style leadership for his religious order
    (D)   extreme Catholic orthodoxy
    (E)   intense devotional writings

20. Which among the following territories was not among the Habsburg possessions ruled by the Holy Roman Emperor Charles V?

    (A) Spain
    (B) Austria
    (C) The Netherlands
    (D) Mexico
    (E) Sweden

21. The new interpretation of the Protestant religion enunciated by John Calvin in Geneva was characterized by

    (A) intellectual rigor
    (B) elaborate rituals
    (C) emotional mysticism
    (D) revulsion at harsh punishments
    (E) acceptance of transubstantiation

22. "Live according to the Gospel and the Word of God...without...any more masses, statues, idols, or other papal abuses."

    This ruling was made by

    (A) Anglicans
    (B) Calvinists
    (C) Lutherans
    (D) Jesuits
    (E) Carthusians

23. Among the corrupt practices in the Roman Catholic church that weakened its moral authority during the middle ages were all the following EXCEPT

    (A) simony
    (B) pluralism
    (C) multiple popes
    (D) the Vulgate
    (E) nepotism

24. The Peace of Augsburg (1555) represented the end of Emperor Charles V's hopes to

    (A)   defeat the Turks in Hungary
    (B)   contain French aggression in the Rhineland
    (C)   force Henry VIII to marry his sister
    (D)   restore Catholicism in all parts of Germany
    (E)   regain his title as Holy Roman Emperor

No testing material on this page.

Chapter III

Expansion and War

Brutal civil and international conflicts arose over religion. Emperor Charles V fought to restore his authority and uphold the Church in Germany and failed. Princes fought to gain power. Religious people fought to destroy the "devil's work" – for or against religious reform. France and the low countries were torn apart by war.

The **English Reformation** was precipitated by the Pope's refusal to grant a divorce to Henry VIII. Queen Catherine was Charles V's aunt. Henry's new Anglican Church kept largely to Catholic doctrine, but with the King replacing the Pope as Head of the Church. Henry's son, **Edward VI**, encouraged more advanced Protestant theology, but he died young (1553). His sister, **Mary I** (Bloody Mary), restored Catholicism and married the great defender of the Roman faith, Philip II of Spain. She also died after a brief reign, and was succeeded by **Elizabeth I** (r. 1558-1603) – a *politique* – who balanced a personal predilection for Catholic theology with Protestant rule because it made her succession legitimate and pleased her subjects. She was able to sustain a permanent Protestant settlement in England. Philip II tried to reclaim his throne and overthrow Anglicanism with the **Armada** (1588*) and failed. Elizabeth sponsored revolt against Philip's rule in the Netherlands. She executed the Catholic heir to the throne, her cousin, **Mary Queen of Scots** (d. 1587).

Many aristocrats converted to Protestantism in France, and the Queen regent, **Catherine de Medicis**, although she initially tried to balance competing religious claims, ultimately sanctioned the **St. Bartholomew's Day Massacre** (1572) of Protestants in an attempt to secure the triumph of the ruling dynasty in the midst of civil war. This event created massive fear across the continent. Eventually, the throne fell to the **Huguenot** (Calvinist) leader, **Henry IV** (of Navarre) (r. 1589-1610), founder of the Bourbon dynasty, a *politique*, who converted to Catholicism to retain the throne and please the majority of his subjects. However, he granted toleration to Protestants (**Edict of Nantes** 1598*). He strengthened the monarchy and the economy.

Philip II of Spain (d. 1598) tried to centralize the power of the monarchy and restore Catholicism in Europe. He built a great monastery, which also served as his residence – **El Escorial**. He fought a long war to suppress Protestantism in the Netherlands and failed. William the Silent (of Orange), a *politique*, organized powerful resistance to Spanish/Catholic rule and helped found the United Provinces in the northern half of the low countries. England sent troops to support the Dutch. Although Philip successfully annexed Portugal, defeated the Turks in a contest for control of the Mediterranean (Battle of Lepanto – 1571), and reaped great riches from the Americas, his incapacity to delegate and his religious obsession led to disaster.

The **Thirty Years War** (1618-48) precipitated by religious and national conflict in Bohemia turned into a massive civil war in Germany, in which France, Denmark, and Sweden also played a notable role. It started as a religious war with political overtones and ended as a political war with religious overtones. The Protestant King Gustavus Adolphus of Sweden carved out a large empire in Northern Germany but died in battle (1632). The war eventually turned into a struggle for power between Austria and France. The population and economy of Germany suffered tremendous losses. The struggles of the 17th century also ended the dominance of the Mediterranean states and economy in European affairs. Amsterdam emerged as the great financial center.

Treaty of Westphalia (1648*):

- Calvinism recognized as a co-equal religion with Catholicism and Lutheranism and Catholic claims to Protestant territory were abandoned in the HRE
- Austria emerged as separate from the HRE and became the focus of Habsburg rule
- Bavaria emerged as the leading Catholic power in S. Germany
- Switzerland was unified into cantons
- The United Provinces were officially recognized as a Protestant independent state
- Sweden gained territory in northern Germany
- France emerged as the "superpower" of Europe
- Germany lost virtually all central authority and the over 300 states became virtually sovereign
- Brandenburg-Prussia, the leading Lutheran power in N. Germany emerged as stronger
- The Modern European state system emerged

The Witchcraft Craze

Magic was still a powerful force in the 16th and 17th centuries. Persecution of mainly female "witches" peaked in the century after 1550. The anxieties of the religious conflict, war and destruction, and individuals or communities taking advantage of the weak and the old led to the upsurge, predicated on misogyny and superstition. Midwives were particularly vulnerable because infant mortality was so high. Eventually the elites themselves felt threatened (no one was safe from accusation) and the new level demanded for legal evidence fostered by the Scientific Revolution brought trials to an end.

AGE OF EXPLORATION

Europeans began to look outwards and explore unknown coasts in search for trade and wealth. Prince Henry the Navigator of Portugal sponsored early voyages in the 15th century, Ferdinand and Isabella of Spain after 1492, and Elizabeth I of England in the 16th century.

Causes:

- Monarchs desired expanded territory and income
- Merchants sought trade routes to India and China in order to avoid trading through middlemen in the Middle East, especially after the fall of Christian Byzantium (1453)
- Renaissance ideas fostered a spirit of inquiry and adventure and encouraged pursuit of individual goals and fame
- New technology in construction and operation of sailing ships
- Adventurers sought fame and fortune
- Missionaries sought to convert the non-Christians

Events:

- **Dias** rounded Cape of Good Hope 1487; DaGama to India 1497-99
- **Columbus** to the Caribbean 1492*
- **Treaty of Tordesillas** (1494) divided the world between Spain and Portugal (Portugal gets Brazil and the Indies) brokered by Pope, ignored by other powers
- **Magellan** circumnavigated the globe 1519-22
- **Cortes** took Aztec Empire 1519-21
- **Pizzaro** conquered the Incas 1531 – Potosi silver mine 1545
- **Jamestown** settlement 1607*
- **Mayflower** voyage 1621

Outcomes:

- Immense influx of precious metals and spices, and later silk, tea, coffee, chocolate, tobacco, and porcelain
- The rise of the slave trade between Africa and the Americas
- Price rises in Europe (inflation) partly due to the vast amount of new gold and silver and inefficient use of those metals; owners of land profit; bourgeois "rentiers" rose more rapidly into the upper classes through purchase of land
- Great new understanding of geography and the shape of the world
- Oceans ceased to divide the world and become highways
- The Commercial Revolution – changes in investment and production – rise of the **domestic system** – new industries, new banking practices
- Rise of the East India Companies 1600 onwards
- Rise of the economic idea of **mercantilism**
  a) export more than you import
  b) trade as much as possible with colonies, taking in raw materials and exporting manufactured goods
  c) state sponsors manufacturing ventures
  d) accumulate as much gold and silver as possible
  e) object was to increase national revenue by increasing national wealth

- Encounters with unknown cultures of high levels of civilization that did not practice Christianity or even monotheism; opened European mind to new ways of seeing and criticism of traditional institutions and values
- New foods such as the potato and tomato brought to Europe while the horse and guns were brought to America
- Exchanges of diseases between continents, small pox in particular wiping out large proportions of some aboriginal peoples
- Promotion of capitalism, encouragement of new forms of investment and insurance
- Vast Portuguese empire
- Spain acquired most of South and Central America, some of N. America, islands and ports in the Caribbean and Africa, and the Philippines
- The Dutch acquired the Cape of Good Hope, islands in the Caribbean, trading rights in Japan, and much of the East Indies (from Portugal)
- England expanded in North America from the coast inwards and gradually took islands in the Caribbean, Atlantic, and Pacific, parts of India and eventually Australia and Canada
- France acquired Canada, and moved through the interior down the river systems; islands in the Caribbean, parts of India
- Most other European nations did not get much out of the scramble for colonies, although the Swedes made headway at first in America, the Danes got a few islands, and Russia expanded inexorably east and southwards, eventually taking Alaska and part of California

© Robert Frerck/Odyssey/Chicago

1. El Escorial, Philip II of Spain's new palace north of Madrid built between 1563 and 1584 was

   (A)   a center for entertainment and pleasure
   (B)   built with the profits of the conquest of England
   (C)   a monastic center of militant Catholicism
   (D)   never completed
   (E)   built to please his wife, Elizabeth I of England

2. The rivalry between the Guise, Montmorency, Bourbon, and Valois families during the sixteenth century was focused on

   (A)   control of the French throne
   (B)   the Holy Roman Emperorship
   (C)   papal elections
   (D)   who would marry Catherine de Medici
   (E)   colonial policy in North America

3. Which of the following was NOT a food brought to Europe from the New World in the sixteenth century

   (A)   potato
   (B)   chocolate
   (C)   tomato
   (D)   chili peppers
   (E)   apples

4. In the fifteenth century Portuguese explorers first reached which of the following new territories previously unknown to Europeans

   (A)   Australia
   (B)   The Philippines
   (C)   Cape Horn
   (D)   Cape of Good Hope
   (E)   Florida

5. European diseases that decimated non-European populations in the sixteenth and seventeenth centuries included all of the following EXCEPT

   (A)   measles
   (B)   typhus
   (C)   small pox
   (D)   bubonic plague
   (E)   cancer

6. The Peace of Westphalia concluded in 1648 accomplished which of the following?

   (A)   brought an end to the major wars of religion
   (B)   gave Spain to France
   (C)   eliminated Holland from the map of Europe
   (D)   made Britain the dominant power in Europe
   (E)   dissolved the Holy Roman Empire

Map: The Holy Roman Empire from A HISTORY OF MODERN EUROPE: FROM THE RENNAISANCE TO THE PRESENT by John Merriman. Copyright © 1996 by John Merriman. Used by permission of W. W. Norton & Company, Inc.

7. This map shows the extent of the Holy Roman Empire in

    (A)   1300
    (B)   1400
    (C)   1450
    (D)   1600
    (E)   1650

8. Early trade between Portugal and India during the fifteenth century included such items as

    (A)   cinnamon, pepper, and rubies
    (B)   pinewood, gold, and chrome
    (C)   china, cloves, and slaves
    (D)   silver, rum, and sugar
    (E)   coal, glass, and fish

9. "My enemies object that I have 'established liberty of conscience.' I confess that the glow of fires in which so many poor Christians have been tormented is not an agreeable sight to me, although it rejoices the eye of the duke of Alba and the Spaniards."

    This passage was written by

    (A)   Mary Queen of Scots
    (B)   Mary Tudor
    (C)   Philip II
    (D)   William of Orange
    (E)   the Duke of Parma

10. The weakness of the Spanish economy during the sixteenth century was characterized by all the following EXCEPT

    (A)   excessive taxation to support military power
    (B)   spiraling inflation caused by the importation of precious metals
    (C)   repudiation of royal debts
    (D)   slack growth in manufacturing
    (E)   lack of good ports

11. Philip II was married to which of the following

   (A)   Elizabeth I of England
   (B)   Mary Queen of Scots
   (C)   Mary I of England
   (D)   Catherine de Medici
   (E)   Christina of Sweden

12. During the seventeenth century Russian landowners

   (A)   were completely exterminated as a class by the Tsar
   (B)   fled en masse to Germany
   (C)   held no power in the state
   (D)   enserfed the peasantry
   (E)   assassinated Tsar Peter the Great

13. The portion of South America called Brazil came under permanent control of Portugal because

   (A)   Pope Alexander VI divided the non-Christian world into Spanish and Portuguese zones
   (B)   Portugal defeated Spain in war and took Brazil as its reward
   (C)   the English granted Brazil to Portugal
   (D)   Brazil was the first place discovered in the "New World"
   (E)   the native population asked Portugal to save them from Spanish rule

14. The most important force causing a continuation of the conflict during the "30 Years War" (1618-1648) was

   (A)   the fundamental incompatibility between Scandinavian and Mediterranean cultures
   (B)   religious antagonisms
   (C)   intervention by the Russians
   (D)   the fight to control North America
   (E)   a revolt by the peasantry against the aristocracy

From THE RISE AND FALL OF THE GREAT POWERS by Paul Kennedy, copyright © 1987 by Paul Kennedy.
Used by permission of Randon House, Inc.

15. This map shows the

    (A)   conquests of Philip II
    (B)   possessions of Charles V
    (C)   Calvinist centers
    (D)   merchant republics
    (E)   allies of England

16. Which of the following did NOT die a violent death during the religious and political struggles in France during the sixteenth and seventeenth centuries?

    (A)   Henry II
    (B)   Henry III
    (C)   Henry IV
    (D)   the duke of Guise
    (E)   Catherine de Medici

17. Most of the victims of the witchcraft persecutions of the seventeenth century were

    (A)   wealthy merchants
    (B)   poor, single women
    (C)   prosperous peasants
    (D)   town officials
    (E)   female clergy

18. Monarchs and statesmen called "politiques", who put the security of the state ahead of religious prejudice included all of the following EXCEPT

   (A)   Elizabeth I of England
   (B)   Henry IV of France
   (C)   Cardinal Richelieu of France
   (D)   Charles II of England
   (E)   Louis XIV of France

19. "It will be a service to the Church of great consequence to carry the gospel into those parts of the world [that are pagan] and to raise a bulwark against the kingdom of Antichrist which the Jesuits labor to rear up in those parts."

   This passage was written by

   (A)   a puritan emigrant to New England
   (B)   Bartolmé de Las Casas
   (C)   Henry IV of France
   (D)   Ignatius Loyola
   (E)   Pope Sixtus V

20. The Treaty of Westphalia (1648) helped to ensure all of the following EXCEPT

   (A)   German Calvinists gained the same rights as those previously granted to Lutherans
   (B)   Dutch independence was recognized
   (C)   Spain and Portugal were united
   (D)   emergence of France as the dominant continental power
   (E)   Sweden acquired West Pomerania

21. The declining power of the Holy Roman Emperors during the late middle ages and early modern period was due in part to

   (A)   the authority the papacy gained because of the Reformation
   (B)   the succession of several female heiresses
   (C)   a series of imcompetent and insane rulers
   (D)   authority was traded away to gain election to the crown
   (E)   too little attention was paid to Austrian colonies

22. The seventeenth-century French leader, Cardinal de Richelieu,

    (A)   pursued an exclusively Catholic foreign policy
    (B)   treated rebellious nobles too leniently
    (C)   worked hard to strengthen royal absolutism
    (D)   encouraged traditional regional loyalties
    (E)   always respected the rights of Huguenots

23. Which of the following was not a possession of Philip II?

    (A)   Spain
    (B)   the Netherlands
    (C)   Mexico
    (D)   Naples
    (E)   Austria

Scala/Art Resource, NY

24. This Baroque statue by Bernini of the Ecstasy of Saint Theresa embodies the chief qualities of the style

    (A)   theatricality and movement
    (B)   rational responses to irrational forces
    (C)   cold and emotionless contemplation
    (D)   secularism and objectivity
    (E)   humor and lack of seriousness

No testing material on this page.

Chapter IV

Britain, France, Spain, and Holland

Great Britain emerged as a richer and more influential nation during the seventeenth century. The Scottish **Stuart dynasty** succeeded to the English throne (though the countries were quite separate except for the union of the crowns). Mary Queen of Scots' Protestant son, James VI, became **James I** (authorized "King James" version of the Bible 1611) of England on the death of his childless cousin and last Tudor, Elizabeth I (the "Virgin" Queen) in 1603. He and his son, **Charles I** (1625-49), attempted to strengthen the power of the monarchy at the expense of Parliament and believed in the Divine Right of Kings. This led to civil war in 1641 and the execution of Charles I, the first occasion in modern history when a monarch was put on trial and executed for crimes against his people. Parliament was largely supported by small landowners, merchants, and Puritans, in London and the South. The King found more support among the high aristocracy, Anglicans, and in the North and Wales.

The Civil War (1641-49*)

Causes:

- Monarchs could not acquire enough tax income to operate the government, especially in times of war – plus large debt left by Elizabeth I
- Parliament attempted to force the monarch to accept religious, foreign, and other policy initiatives in exchange for more income – fear of absolutism and Catholicism
- Charles I attempted to rule without Parliament
- Conflicts in Scotland and Ireland provoked crises in England
- Archbishop Laud imposed strict "high" church Anglican doctrine and practice in England and Scotland
- Charles I imposed "illegal" tax – ship money
- Charles I seen as sympathetic to Catholics in Ireland, has a Catholic wife
- Charles I pursued foreign and domestic policies that provoked Puritan opposition in Parliament led by Pym
- Charles I punished opponents brutally and failed in attempt to arrest Pym
- Resentment against "corruption" at Court, granting of monopolies and other favors to aristocrats close to the throne
- Possible resentment by lesser gentry towards richer elites
- Character of Charles I – in many ways a decent man in private – who lacked political skill and came to be seen as dishonest and unreliable

Events:

- Petition of Right (1628)
- Scots invaded England 1638
- Charles I rallied supporters against Parliament 1641
- "Roundheads" (Parliament)/ Cavaliers (Royalists)
- Charles I executed 1649*
- Cromwell (died 1658) – New Model Army, Lord Protector
- The Restoration – Charles II, a *politique*, returned 1660

Outcomes:

- "Commonwealth" established by military force by **Oliver Cromwell**, who became Lord Protector (r. 1649-58)
- Once the war began Cromwell emerged as a major historical figure of great political gifts
- Parliament gradually diminished and ignored
- Country ruled by dictatorship enforced by military rule
- Puritan restrictions against the arts and entertainment
- Toleration granted to the Jews
- Successful war against the Dutch and building of a strong navy
- Rebellions in Ireland suppressed brutally and land taken from Catholics and given to a new Protestant elite
- Radical groups such as the Levelers, Diggers frightened elites
- Restoration of the monarchy with little retribution or constitutional change (1660)
- Restoration of the Anglican religion as the state church

The Glorious Revolution (1688*-89)

Causes:

- Incompetence of **James II** (r. 1685-88), who antagonized his own supporters; absolutist policy
- Birth of a son to James II, who unlike his Protestant sisters, ensured an unending succession of Catholic rulers in a Protestant state
- King's friendly treatment of Catholics in Ireland
- Fear of an alliance between the King and Louis XIV of France (secret Treaty of Dover did exist)
- Ambition of **William of Orange** (r. 1689-1702), husband of James's daughter, **Mary**, and stadholder of the Netherlands to gain military strength to defeat Louis XIV and save Holland from conquest
- The brutality used in the suppression of opposition to James II
- Decision by great aristocrats that the King could not be trusted and that they were the true guardians of the nation
- Declaration of Indulgence – can the King suspend laws of Parliament on his own authority?

Outcomes:

- Succession of the Protestant joint monarchs **William III** and **Mary II** (1689)
- All future monarchs must be Protestant
- Alteration of legitimate line of succession by Parliament destroys idea of "Divine Right"; succession to Crown now lay with the legislature not the royal family
- Defeat of James II and the Catholic forces in Ireland at the Battle of the Boyne, Protestants set to rule Ireland
- **Bill of Rights** enacted to protect individual liberties; prevent arbitrary royal acts
- Ascendancy of Parliament dominated by the great landowners
- Emergence of Whig and Tory parties
- Victory of the United Provinces over France and the building of alliances that would halt the expansion of Louis XIV to Holland and Spain
- The Netherlands much weakened by its "victory"
- Parliament pursued an imperial and commercial policy that promoted trade and mercantile interests
- Union of English and Scottish parliaments (1707)
- Succession in 1714 of the German Hanoverian dynasty after the death of the last Stuart, Queen Anne

France took a different course from that of England in the 17th century. Monarchs were more astute and successful in gaining and retaining power. Henry IV, Louis XIII's great minister Cardinal Richelieu, and above all King Louis XIV (r. 1661-1715) centralized power in their hands and gradually weakened the power of the nobility. The latter group was much larger than the equivalent in England, and few individuals were as rich as many of the great dukes and earls across the Channel. During the **Fronde** (1648-53) the nobles tried to reassert their authority, but failed. The Estates General, the French equivalent of the English Parliament, did not meet at all between 1614 and 1789. Under the "Sun King" France enjoyed a golden age in culture under absolutism.

Louis XIV's success was due to:

- Political acumen and hard work – single-minded focus on his goals
- Effective use of bourgeois "intendants" or local officials who owed their careers to the King
- Appointment of able ministers such as **Colbert**
- Ideological underpinnings of absolutist rule supported by **Bishop Bossuet**
- Successful economic policies including building canals, improving roads and ports, and state sponsored enterprises, mainly due to Colbert
- Focus on military reform, and exerting greater control over the army (Louvois and Vauban), uniforms, etc.
- Use of the **Court at Versailles** to weaken powerful nobles
    - a) the "place" to be for fun
    - b) source of favors and rewards
    - c) rituals emphasizing royal stature – "*lever*"
    - d) under the King's watchful eye

Louis XIV's failure was due to:

- He loved war too much – pursuit of expensive military campaigns that did not yield true value to France or ended in defeat
- He reigned too long (60 years) and grew old and tired
- His weakening of the nobility separated them from their estates, left them without a sense of duty or purpose, and built up resentment and desire to rule without a sense of responsibility or experience to do so
- Colonial policy that did not include plans for large settlement by French people
- Leaving a successor who was less fit to rule (Louis XV)
- Suppression of Jansenists
- **Revocation of the Edict of Nantes** (1685*) led to the expulsion of many talented Huguenots who went to Germany, the Netherlands and Britain where they prospered and helped their new countries in commerce and war
- Excessive ambition in hoping to combine the French and Spanish empires under his sole rule
- Left his successors ever worsening financial problems due to inefficient taxation

War of the Spanish Succession (1701-13)

- Louis succeeded in placing his grandson **Philip V** on the Spanish throne after the death of the last Habsburg
- **The Peace of Utrecht** (1713-14*) provided:
    a) if the Bourbon line failed in France, the Spanish line could not succeed to both crowns
    b) England gained Gibraltar, which gave it control over access in and out of the Mediterranean (becomes British "lake")
    c) Savoy acquired Sardinia (dukes now kings)
    d) Spanish territory in Italy (Milan, Naples, Sicily) passed to Austria
    e) Spanish Netherlands (Belgium) acquired by Austria
    f) France ceded Newfoundland and Nova Scotia to Britain (which gave the latter control over the mouth of the St. Lawrence River and hence the interior of N. America)
    g) Dutch independence secured
    h) Elector of Brandenburg recognized as King (Prussia)
    i) *Asiento* (trading privileges) granted to British in Spanish colonies
- French preeminence in Europe blocked, although it retained conquests along the northern border
- Dutch weakened and decline from the status of a great power
- Great Britain poised to become a global great power

1. The Dutch penchant for paintings of still lifes and domestic interiors indicates that during the seventeenth century they

   (A)   set great importance on home life, family, and material success
   (B)   rejected religious values and interests
   (C)   lacked interest in the world outside of Holland
   (D   did not have many skilled painters
   (E)   emulated England in all cultural matters

2. Mercantilist economic policies can best be described as

   (A)   a "bullionist" approach to building self-sufficiency
   (B)   *laissez-faire*
   (C)   avoidance of imperial responsibilities
   (D)   leaving everything up to the actions of individual merchants
   (E)   hostile to innovation

3. The success of such a small country as the United Provinces during the seventeenth century was due to all of the following EXCEPT

   (A)   banking and credit facilities in Amsterdam
   (B)   colonial possessions
   (C)   creation of productive agriculture through drainage and new techniques
   (D)   religious toleration
   (E)   strong, absolutist monarchy

4. King Charles I of England was executed by order of Parliament in 1649 because he

   (A)   had become a Roman Catholic
   (B)   went back on promises previously made
   (C)   tried to assassinate Oliver Cromwell
   (D)   made an alliance with Spain
   (E)   pusued an unsuccessful colonial policy

© MUSEE DE LA MARINE/Mask of Apollo, God of Light

5. This image was the personal emblem of

    (A)   Charles II of England
    (B)   William III of England
    (C)   Maria Theresa of Austria
    (D)   Louis XIV of France
    (E)   William the Silent of the United Provinces

6. "We forbid our subjects of the so-called Reformed religion to assemble any more for public worship."

    This decree was issued by

    (A)   Henry IV of France
    (B)   William III of England
    (C)   Louis XIV of France
    (D)   Charles II of England
    (E)   James II of England

7. The policies of Charles II of England after the Restoration (1660) were aimed at

    (A)   exterminating all opponents of Charles I
    (B)   making Scotland Catholic again
    (C)   establishing Ireland as an independent state
    (D)   trying to put the clock back to 1640
    (E)   eliminating his Catholic brother from the succession

8. The English society known as the Quakers, founded in the mid-seventeenth century, were

   (A) political revolutionaries
   (B) pacifists
   (C) millenarians
   (D) competitors with the East India Company
   (E) sufferers from palsy

9. All of the following were causes of the English Civil War during the mid-seventeenth century EXCEPT

   (A) religious divisions
   (B) conflict over taxation
   (C) a Scottish invasion
   (D) dispute over the division of power between the king and parliament
   (E) the character of Oliver Cromwell

10. During the seventeenth century marriage among ordinary people

   (A) the wife was totally subservient to the husband
   (B) dominated by the wife
   (C) often ended in divorce
   (D) was rarely contracted until both parties were in their thirties
   (E) was a partnership

11. Charles I of England faced a revolt against royal authority led by

   (A) Parliament
   (B) the Anglican church
   (C) a renegade governor of Ireland
   (D) French agents
   (E) Prince Rupert

12. "No one person [henceforward] whatsoever shall or may have, or hold the office, style, dignity, power, or authority of king of the said kingdoms and dominions, or of them, or of the Prince of Wales."

   This law was enacted in

   (A) Holland in 1648
   (B) England in 1649
   (C) England in 1688
   (D) France in 1613
   (E) France in 1653

13. "The Pyrenees exist no longer!" was a phrase summarizing what change in the political landscape of Europe due to the wars of Louis XIV?

   (A)   the Peace of Utrecht allowed a Bourbon king to ascend the throne of Spain
   (B)   Italy was united into a single nation
   (C)   a Hohenzollern prince became King of Spain
   (D)   Switzerland became neutral
   (E)   the Peace of Westphalia reestablished Portugal as independent

14. Reasons for the decline of Holland in the later seventeenth century included all the following EXCEPT

   (A)   lack of technological innovation
   (B)   excessive military spending
   (C)   impact of war on shipping and agriculture
   (D)   defeat by England
   (E)   conquest by France

15. The Glorious Revolution of 1688 in England accomplished which of the following?

   (A)   restored King James II to the throne
   (B)   created religious toleration for both Catholics and Protestants
   (C)   unified Ireland, Scotland, and England
   (D)   weakened the monarchy and strengthened parliament
   (E)   the Elector of Hanover heir to the British throne

16. Among the mercantilist policies implemented by Jean-Baptist Colbert were all of the following EXCEPT

   (A)   establish new industries
   (B)   improve roads and build canals
   (C)   increase internal tariffs
   (D)   found the French East India Company
   (E)   increase efficiency of tax collection

17. The civil revolt known as "the Fronde" that shook France between 1648 and 1653 was

   (A)   led by nobles of the sword trying to regain lost influence
   (B)   organized by the bourgeoisie to resist encroachments of the crown
   (C)   precipitated by agents subsidized by the king of England
   (D)   a peasant revolt centered in the South
   (E)   used by Louis XIV to overthrow Mazarin

18. "I am the martyr of the people." Which of the following made this statement just before he was beheaded?

    (A)   Oliver Cromwell
    (B)   Emperor Charles V
    (C)   Martin Luther
    (D)   King Charles I
    (E)   King James II

19. Which of the following banned the maintenance of a standing army in time of peace?

    (A)   the Bill of Rights of 1689
    (B)   the *Cahiers de doléances*
    (C)   the Edict of Nantes
    (D)   the Petition of Right
    (E)   the Declaration of Pilnitz

Print Collection, Miriam and Ira D. Wallach Division of Art
Prints, and Photographs, The New York Public Library
Astor, Lenox, and Tilden Foundations

20. This illustration appeared in which of the following books?

    (A)   William Shakespeare's *Hamlet*
    (B)   Miguel de Cervantes' *Don Quixote*
    (C)   Thomas More's *Utopia*
    (D)   Thomas Hobbes' *Leviathan*
    (E)   Isaac Newton's *Principia*

21. The term "United Provinces" was used to describe

    (A) East and West Prussia
    (B) Scotland, England, and Wales
    (C) Castile, Aragon, and Navarre
    (D) the Thuringian states
    (E) the northern part of the Netherlands

22. In the first half of the seventeenth century the hub of the business world in Europe was located in

    (A) Vienna
    (B) Amsterdam
    (C) Paris
    (D) Rome
    (E) St. Petersburg

Musée du Louvre, Paris

23. This portrait of Louis XIV of France by Hyacinth Rigaud was commissioned by the king to

    (A) express the grandeur and power of monarchy
    (B) start a new fashion in clothing
    (C) commemorate his granting of religious toleration
    (D) express his fundamentally modest character
    (E) exemplify Colbert's campaign to reduce the costs of government

24. "Divine Right" monarchy was a term used to refer to

    (A)   a king's power derived from God
    (B)   the Pope's authority over bishops
    (C)   kings must be ordained priests
    (D)   the rights of subjects under a king
    (E)   kings descended from Christ

No testing material on this page.

Chapter V

State Building

In the later 17th and early to mid-18th century a number of great powers began to enter periods of decline, others emerged, and some held their own. Not all the causes for this situation applied in every case. Roughly this was the situation.

Winners	Mixed	Losers
Britian	Austria	Spain
Prussia	France	Poland
Russia		Sweden
		Holland
		Holy Roman Empire
		Ottoman Empire

Winners:

- Strong leadership
- Strong central government, effective bureaucracy
- Effective sources of income
- Flexibility
- Diversified economies
- Large, modernized armies/navies
- Monarchy and aristocracy work out a mutually satisfactory relationship

Losers:

- Poor leadership
- Weak governmental institutions
- Rigidity
- Fragmented regions, intense local loyalties
- Narrowly focused economies
- Ineffective cooperation between monarchs and nobles

SPAIN

- Virtually no exports or manufacturing
- Resources of empire depleted
- Empire too far flung and fragmented to be ruled successfully by the system in place
- Poor leadership both from Habsburg and Bourbon kings
- Massive noble class many of whom were poor, not interested in government, and rigidly old fashioned (Hidalgos)
- Profligate spending of national resources without adequate returns

POLAND

- Perhaps the most disastrously organized state in Europe
- Dysfunctional elective monarchy
- Dysfunctional parliament (diet) – *liberum veto*
- Surrounded by ravenous and powerful states with no natural frontiers for protection
- Nobility too numerous (8% of population) and mostly poor
- Antiquated agricultural system and little commerce
- Gradually gobbled up by neighbors in a series of **"Partitions"** 1772, 1793, 1795

SWEDEN

- Empire too far flung
- Weak economy cannot sustain huge army
- Nobility and monarchy in conflict
- No successful ruler after Gustavus Adolphus (d. 1632)
- Recklessness of Charles XII (d. 1718) – defeated by Peter the Great of Russia – Battle of Poltava (1709)

HOLLAND

- Regional identities very strong
- Religious divisions
- Stagnation of industries
- London replacing Amsterdam as European economic center
- Exhaustion and damage after prolonged conflicts with England and France
- Dutch East India Co. pushed out of India
- Weak leaders after the death of William III
- Stadholdership still elective and cumbersome and powers limited by the jealousy of the mercantile elite
- British outstrip in naval technology and trade competition

HOLY ROMAN EMPIRE

- Central institutions, including the emperorship crippled
- Habsburgs increasingly focus on their Austrian territories
- War of the Austrian Succession (1740)
- Divided into over 300 mini-states, with big states such as Prussia trying to expand territories at the expense of others
- Economy and population devastated by 30 Years War
- Divided religiously and culturally

OTTOMAN EMPIRE

- Complicated and inefficient system of succession
- Too fragmented and far flung
- Deep conservatism strangled innovation
- Bordered aggressive Russia and Austria
- Over-reached selves in attempted conquests of central Europe (at gates of Vienna 1529 and 1683)

AUSTRIA

- Affairs of HRE divert attention from essential issues
- Female heir of Charles VI (d. 1740) leads to sacrifices made in the **Pragmatic Sanction**
- Ottoman Sultan conquers southern territories and reaches Vienna 1683
- Frederick the Great seizes the rich province of Silesia in 1740
- Hungary regained 1687, but the nobles remained restive under Habsburg rule
- Habsburgs continue to hold their empire together, and gain territory from Poland and in Italy and the Balkans
- Habsburgs do well in the War of Spanish Succession (1701)
- Most of the population Roman Catholic
- Protestant nobles removed and land used to reward nobles to the Habsburgs
- Strong lines of internal communication
- Some innovation and growth in the economy

FRANCE

- Weak leadership in last years of Louis XIV and under his successors. Corruption and vice at Court
- Mississippi Bubble hurts economy and undermines central banking structure (1720). Hard to organize credit
- Costs of wars high; leads to huge public debt
- Indecisiveness in deciding about who was their most serious enemy – leads France to compete on sea and land against multiple enemies – divided resources and led to losses
- Clumsy censorship weakens respect for government without stifling criticism
- Nobility want power, are given it by the Regent Orleans (d. 1723), but largely ineffective

- Large resources and many effective government officials, but antiquated, cumbersome, unproductive tax system; inefficient budgetary and accounting apparatus
- Innovative society with a large and influential intelligentsia
- Valuable colonial empire
- Strongest army in Europe
- Paris the grandest city in Europe – huge popularity of French language and culture

BRITAIN

- More tightly held together after Union with Scotland 1707
- Parliamentary system and a largely free press allowed public opinion to play a significant role in shaping policy
- Absence of a standing army and the Bill of Rights forced monarchs and Parliament to rule rationally and help build commercial prosperity
- Economy and central banking system weathers South Sea Bubble crisis (1720)
- London became the money market of Europe
- Navy gained supremacy at sea around the world
- Empire expanded and prospered
- Aristocrats governed responsibly and effectively
- Flexible economy and politicians – gifted leadership: William III, Marlborough, Walpole, the Pitts, etc.
- **Robert Walpole** (d. 1745) first "prime minister" (1721-42)
- Social and political system open to men rising by merit

PRUSSIA

- Exceptional leadership from several members of the Hohenzollern dynasty
    a) the "Great" Elector Frederick William (d. 1688)
    b) King Frederick I (d. 1713)
    c) King Frederick William I (d. 1740)
    d) King Frederick II the "Great" (d. 1786)
- Added territory that contained resources, urban populations, and commercial and manufacturing activity in the Rhineland and Silesia
- Exceptionally strong army disproportionate to the size of the state
- Strong royal bureaucracy organized to support the army
- Rulers enjoyed large income aside from taxes
- Society tolerant in religion and welcomed French Huguenots
- High literacy rate
- Strong cooperation between **junker** landowners and monarchs
- Becomes a major European state under Frederick II

RUSSIA
- No influence of the Renaissance or Roman Catholic Church
- Time of Troubles (1604-13), a period of chaos followed by the establishment of the Romanov dynasty
- Vast size, resources, and population
- Peasants effectively enserfed during 17th century (1649)
- Vigorous leadership from Peter the Great, Elizabeth, and Catherine the Great (some intervals of weak leadership) – Peter's system of succession faulty
- Frequent peasant uprisings weaken state
- Strong absolutist government developed Peter the Great's (r. 1682-1725) achievements
    a) took Baltic territories from Sweden, pushed south to Black Sea
    b) built St.Petersburg – access to the West
    c) Westernization of manners, customs, society
    d) built strong modern army and navy
    e) imposed strict control over nobility (boyars)
    f) destroyed opposition – Old Believers/ streltzy
    g) gained tight control over the Church
    h) built economy
- Became a major European state

1. The partitions of Poland 1772 -1795

   (A) created three independent Polish states
   (B) eliminated Poland as an independent state
   (C) divided Poland between Sweden, Finland, and Lithuania
   (D) divided Poland between Austria, Saxony, and Sweden
   (E) divided Poland between Russia, Hungary, and Austria

2. Tsar Peter the Great reformed the Russian army in order to

   (A) gain access to the Baltic coast
   (B) conquer Siberia
   (C) defend against an invasion by France
   (D) provide employment for the peasantry
   (E) invade Germany

3. During the nineteenth century the "United Kingdom" in the British Isles consisted of all of the following EXCEPT

   (A) England
   (B) Brittany
   (C) Wales
   (D) Scotland
   (E) Ireland

4. During the eighteenth century landowning aristocrats exercised the greatest political influence in

   (A) Russia
   (B) Italy
   (C) Spain
   (D) Prussia
   (E) Poland

5. Emperor Charles VI of Austria negotiated the "Pragmatic Sanction" of 1740 in order to

   (A) ensure his daughter, Maria Theresa, could inherit the crown
   (B) establish his dominion over the Holy Roman Empire
   (C) conclude a peace with France
   (D) absorb Prussia into his empire
   (E) unify Italy

6. The decisive battle by which the British won Canada from the French was fought at

    (A)   Trafalgar
    (B)   Plassey
    (C)   Quebec
    (D)   Yorktown
    (E)   Waterloo

7. Typically the largest expenditure item in the budget of an eighteenth-century state excluding interest on the national debt was

    (A)   military
    (B)   royal palaces
    (C)   civil service
    (D)   subsidies for the poor
    (E)   education

8. The Ottoman Empire went into serious decline in the eighteenth century for all the following reasons EXCEPT

    (A)   they fell behind in military organization and technology
    (B)   their domains were so widespread it was hard to maintain communication and control
    (C)   imperial officials became increasingly corrupt
    (D)   no regular system for succession to the throne was developed
    (E)   conversion of the sultans to Christianity

9. The Hanoverian dynasty, made Kings of England in 1715, came from

    (A)   Russia
    (B)   Germany
    (C)   Italy
    (D)   France
    (E)   Sweden

10. Peter the Great revised the method by which landowners in Russia held noble rank based on

    (A)   size of their estates
    (B)   service to the state
    (C)   military courage
    (D)   length of pedigree
    (E)   residence in Moscow

11. Put the following in the correct chronological order from earliest to latest

   (A)   War of the Austrian Succession, War of the Spanish Succession, Seven Years War

   (B)   War of the Spanish Succession, War of the Austrian Succession, Seven Years War

   (C)   Seven Years War, War of the Spanish Succession, War of the Austrian Succession

   (D)   War of the Spanish Succession, Seven Years War, War of the Austrian Succession

   (E)   Seven Years War, War of the Austrian Succession, War of the Spanish Succession

12.

Number of Ships of the Line

	1739	1779	1790	1815
Britain	124	90	195	214
France	50	63	81	80
Spain	34	48	72	25
Russia	30	40	67	40

This table indicates that

   (A)   Russia consistently improved the size of its navy
   (B)   Britain always had twice as many ships as any other country
   (C)   Spain was never primarily a naval power
   (D)   Britain was the dominant naval force among the great powers
   (E)   Britain bankrupted itself on naval spending

Scala/Art Resource, NY

13. This scene set in Venice portrays the

    (A)   great flood of 1723
    (B)   poverty and despair prevelent after the War of the Spanish Succession
    (C)   wealth of a great port city
    (D)   Gothic architecture predominant in Northern Italy
    (E)   lack of seagoing vessels that made it impossible for Venice to trade over long
          distances

14. Sweden faded as a great power during the seventeenth and eighteenth centuries due to

    (A)   a series of incompetent rulers
    (B)   over-commitment to a colonial empire in North America
    (C)   expansion of Russia
    (D)   internal religious divisions
    (E)   alliance with Russia

15. "The Victory which the king of Poland hath obtained over the Infidels, is so great and so compleat that past Ages can scarce parallel the fame; and perhaps future Ages will never see any thing like it."

This passage comes from an account of the defeat of the

(A)   Turks at Vienna
(B)   Russians at Poltava
(C)   Prussians at Leuthen
(D)   French at Blenheim
(E)   Dutch at Utrecht

16. Among the principal characteristics of seventeenth and eighteenth-century absolutist states were all the following EXCEPT

(A)   large standing armies
(B)   development of constitutions
(C)   weakening of the nobility
(D)   strong centralized bureaucracies
(E)   close association of the church and monarchy

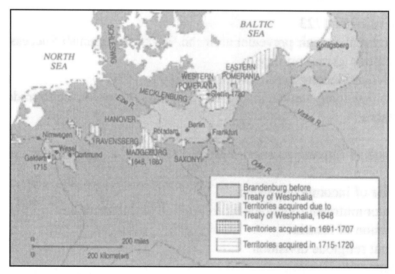

from *A HISTORY OF MODERN EUROPE: FROM THE RENNAISANCE TO THE PRESENT* by John Merriman. Copyright (c) 1996 by John Merriman. Used by permission of W. W. Norton & Company, Inc.

17. This map illustrates the expansion of territory between 1644 and 1720 of what dynasty?

(A)   Hohenzollern
(B)   Orange
(C)   Habsburg
(D)   Bourbon
(E)   Stuart

18. Tsar Peter the Great of Russia

    (A)　supported the Old Believers
    (B)　took special pride in the achievements of his son and heir
    (C)　conquered Constantinople
    (D)　established the first Duma
    (E)　admired Western technology

19. States that grew strong and prospered during the eighteenth century possessed all of the following EXCEPT

    (A)　strong leaders
    (B)　efficient tax system
    (C)　centralized bureaucracy
    (D)　reduced friction between nobles and monarchs
    (E)　large navies

20. In Prussia during the eighteenth century which of following was the only class permitted to own most agricultural land?

    (A)　nobles
    (B)　bourgeoisie
    (C)　peasants
    (D)　serfs
    (E)　artisans

21. Prussia was able to expand successfully during the seventeenth and eighteenth centuries because of all of the following EXCEPT

    (A)　a series of able rulers
    (B)　willingness of the nobility to subordinate itself to the crown
    (C)　a large navy
    (D)　creation of an army out of proportion to the size of the state
    (E)　a strong centralized bureaucracy

No testing material on this page.

Chapter VI

The Eighteenth Century

Struggle for Global Power

Britain emerged as enormously successful politically and economically during the course of the 18th century, in spite of the loss of the American colonies in 1783. Robert Walpole and William Pitt the Elder helped develop success in trade and empire. Two attempts by the Stuarts to restore their rule (supporters were called **Jacobites**) failed in 1715 and 1745. Britain's principal rival, France, was formidable but chose the wrong strategy and was crippled by ineffective leadership.

The **War of the Austrian Succession** (1740-48) and the **Seven Years' War** (1756-63) engaged most of the great powers. Prussia seized Silesia (nearly doubling its size and wealth in one stroke) and succeeded in holding it against all comers – at one point Frederick the Great was fighting France, Austria, and Russia simultaneously. Even possessing interior lines of communication, British subsidies, and a king of military genius almost failed to be enough. Fortunately, the succession of Tsar Peter III in Russia (1762) led to the latter's withdrawal from the war. The French strategy of fighting both in a major continental war and in a global conflict overseas proved beyond its powers and led to a huge debt, loss of India (Battle of Plassey 1757 – Robert Clive) and Canada, and serious decline in prestige.

THE ANCIEN REGIME

The old regime is a term used to describe European society in the 17th and particularly the 18th century, before the French Revolution.

Characteristics:

- Emphasis on tradition and established rights and privileges
- Hierarchy, ranks, orders, rigid social conventions
- Aristocracies assertive
- All countries monarchies except for Switzerland, Venice, and the Netherlands
- Agricultural economy, life governed by scarcity and the seasons
- Family economy – few large scale economic units
    a) all members of the family work
    b) father is the head
    c) marriage crucial to economic stability

    d) role of women – bring dowry, economic partners of the men, raise children, housework

    e) high infant mortality rate, high birth rate

- Change is slow, most people find it difficult to imagine a different social or political organization
- Large numbers of servants
- Massive poverty
- Many children born out of wedlock; foundling hospitals
- More commercialized sex
- In the East serfdom – Russia, Prussia, Austria-Hungary (*robot* – compulsory unpaid labor)
- In the West more complex rural social structure with independent landowning peasants, sharecroppers, wage laborers, scavengers – in England few peasants, mostly wage laborers
- Most land owned by the Crown, church, aristocrats, and rich merchants
- Aristocracies divided into many levels – the smallest and richest in England, the largest and poorest in Poland
- Growing literacy, especially in Prussia, France and England, but majority of the population still uneducated
- Comparatively small armies fighting wars with limited objectives and few battles (although those were very bloody)
- Violence endemic
- Religion still very important, both among followers of traditional, organized Catholic and Protestant churches, and new upwellings such a John Wesley's "Methodism" (later 18th c.); Quakers
- Rise of popular, often "emotional" and pietistic Movements – reactions to "rationalist" religion
- Bourgeoisie increasingly prosperous in Western Europe, consumers on a large scale, interested in "polite" manners and culture
- Great age of classical music: Mozart (d. 1791), Haydn (d. 1809); Beethoven (d. 1827)
- Rise of the novel: Richardson's *Clarissa* (1747); Fielding's *Tom Jones* (1749)

Challenges:

- Cities growing larger
- Population expanding rapidly
- Increasing secular spirit
- Bourgeois wealth increases to great size
- The Enlightenment
- Separation between high and low cultures growing

- Separation between East and West Europe increasing
- Industrialization and new technologies
- The American Revolution
- Global economy
- Emergent nationalism
- Easier and more rapid travel
- Increasing literacy

1. The most important difference between the British "parliament" and the French "parlements" was

    (A)   only the French parlements had a property qualification for membership
    (B)   the first was primarily a legislature and the second judicial courts
    (C)   the first limited royal power and the second did not
    (D)   only the French parlements could declare war
    (E)   only the British parliament required noble birth for membership

The Pierpont Morgan Library/Art Resource, NY

2. This cartoon entitled "The Female Politicians" (1770) portrays the artist's view that women

    (A)   are unfit for government responsibilities
    (B)   were the cause of the French Revolution
    (C)   are more vigorous than men as defenders of civilization
    (D)   should be given the vote
    (E)   are more concerned about clothes than politics

3. Nobles were least important politically and socially during the eighteenth century in which of the following regions and countries?

    (A)   England and Italy
    (B)   Spain and Germany
    (C)   Switzerland and Holland
    (D)   Poland and Austria
    (E)   Russia and Prussia

4. Between the sixteenth and eighteenth centuries peasants in Poland, Bohemia, Hungary, and Russia

    (A)   enjoyed more propsperity and independence
    (B)   were losing their rights and freedoms
    (C)   escaped from the *robot*
    (D)   migrated to the West in massive numbers
    (E)   were granted democratic control over village life

5. Which country was not engaged in trade in the East Indies during the eighteenth century?

    (A)   Great Britain
    (B)   The Netherlands
    (C)   France
    (D)   Portugal
    (E)   Germany

6. The British House of Commons in the eighteenth century was

    (A)   a bicameral body appointed by the king
    (B)   an elective chamber composed largely of landowners
    (C)   modeled on the Estates General in France
    (D)   elected by full manhood suffrage
    (E)   largely ceremonial in function

7. Tom Paine's book, *Common Sense*, published in 1776

    (A)   was an attack on the British monarchy
    (B)   denied the existence of natural rights
    (C)   advocated Enlightened absolutism
    (D)   was the precursor of the Farmer's Almanac
    (E)   urged a compromise solution between the British government and the rebellious colonies

8. The British lost the thirteen American colonies because of all the following reasons EXCEPT

    (A)   aid to the rebels from France
    (B)   overextension of British military resources
    (C)   political divisions within the British political elite
    (D)   the courage and persistence of George Washington
    (E)   George III's incompetent generalship

9. Agricultural yields in England increased significantly during the eighteenth century due to

   (A)   enclosure acts that consolidated land into fewer hands
   (B)   application of chemical fertilizers
   (C)   an increased number of farm laborers
   (D)   use of soldiers to help plant and harvest crops
   (E)   the subdivision of estates into the hands of small holders

10. The "bubbles" in England and France during the first half of the eighteenth century were

   (A)   a source of increased middle class wealth
   (B)   caused by inflated prices on the stock exchanges
   (C)   balloon experiments
   (D)   so beneficial that the Bank of France became the most important financial institution in Europe
   (E)   humanitarian relief to the poor

Yale Center for British Art, Paul Mellon Collection, USA/Bridgeman Art Library

11. This eighteenth-century picture of an English family suggests that

   (A)   girls were treated better than boys
   (B)   children were seen as miniature adults
   (C)   men and women dressed alike
   (D)   aristocrats lived simply
   (E)   the upper classes had no intellectual interests

12. Which of the following was NOT a significant industrial innovator during the English industrial revolution of the eighteenth century?

   (A)   James Watt
   (B)   Henry Cort
   (C)   Richard Arkwright
   (D)   Matthew Boulton
   (E)   Thomas Malthus

Kenwood House, London, UK/Bridgeman Art Library

13. This painting of an eighteenth-century countess and her son conveys

   (A)   the importance of women in government
   (B)   affectionate relations between parents and children
   (C)   influence of impressionism
   (D)   the simplicity of eighteenth-century clothing
   (E)   the relative poverty of the British aristocracy

14. During the early modern period single women

   (A)   married as soon as they could
   (B)   led independent lives much as women do today
   (C)   were never accused of witchcraft
   (D)   could become Protestant ministers
   (E)   served in government offices as secretaries

15. Before 1789 French peasants were subject to all of the following impositions EXCEPT

    (A)   manorial courts
    (B)   the *robot*
    (C)   the *corvée*
    (D)   the *taille*
    (E)   the *gabelle*

16. Which of the following lists of qualities was most important to eighteenth-century noblemen?

    (A)   honor, courage, good manners
    (B)   thrift, piety, chastity
    (C)   obedience, solemnity, perspicacity
    (D)   intelligence, bookishness, kindness
    (E)   caution, education, religious devotion

17. Peasants formed what proportion of the French population during the eighteenth century?

    (A)   10%
    (B)   30%
    (C)   40%
    (D)   75%
    (E)   95%

© Mary Ann Sullivan, Bluffton University

18. This house built by the Earl of Burlington in 1725 epitomizes what style that English aristocrats of the eighteenth century admired?

    (A) Gothic grandeur
    (B) Romantic sensitivities
    (C) Classical symmetry
    (D) Baroque emotionalism
    (E) Mannerist excess

19. The most profitable commodity traded across the Atlantic Ocean during the eighteenth century?

    (A) gold
    (B) rice
    (C) rum
    (D) slaves
    (E) silver

20. "The law locks up both man and woman
    Who steals the goose from off the common,
    But lets the greater felon loose
    Who steals the common from the goose."

    This stanza from Oliver Goldsmith's *Deserted Village* (1770) refers to

    (A) rivalry between peasants
    (B) rivalry between husbands and wives
    (C) heavy taxation on geese
    (D) the enclosure movement
    (E) establishment of new serfdom in England

21. During the eighteenth century Russian serfs were

    (A) at the mercy of their owners and could be bought and sold like slaves
    (B) were tied to particular plots of land
    (C) enjoyed more and more freedom as the eighteenth century progressed
    (D) were cowed into submission and never revolted
    (E) were similar in all respects to French peasants

22. Which of the following was the largest city in Europe during the eighteenth century?

    (A) Berlin
    (B) Moscow
    (C) London
    (D) Vienna
    (E) Lisbon

23. Members of the upper class in England and France in the eighteenth century were more and more concerned with

    (A) religion and magic
    (B) soccer and rugby
    (C) business careers and marketing
    (D) tourism in the Indian ocean and Pacific
    (E) privacy and comfort

24. Provision for the pauperized poor in England during the eighteenth century was made

   (A)   exclusively through charities
   (B)   through government payments
   (C)   was provided in prisons only
   (D)   in any parish the poor person chose
   (E)   to encourage emigrant to the continent

25. Thomas Malthus predicted in 1798 in his *Essay on the Principle of Population* that

   (A)   wages were controlled by an "iron law"
   (B)   the agricultural gains of the eighteenth century were fraudulent
   (C)   population would decline drastically in the second half of the nineteenth century
   (D)   population would expand beyond the capacity of agriculture to feed the people
   (E)   England would become larger than Germany by 1815

No testing material on this page.

Chapter VII

The Scientific Revolution

During and after the Renaissance a gradual expansion of scientific knowledge and understanding about the physical world began to take place. Astrology became astronomy. Progress was more rapid in some fields than others. The supreme achievement was Newton's synthesis of earlier work that led to a profound understanding of the mechanics of the universe: gravity, interplanetary motion, and a sense of mastery over the mysteries of nature that unleashed the modern world. Many Catholic and Protestant leaders united in their criticism of the initial scientific advances.

Great Figures:

- **Copernicus** – (d. 1543) heliocentric solar system which challenged the Ptolemaic earth-centered theory
- **Brahe** – (d. 1601) Danish astronomer who collected massive amounts of accurate data at his observatory
- **Kepler** – (d. 1630) Brahe's assistant, who used the data to develop mathematical laws predicting the elliptic orbits of the planets
- **Galileo** – (d. 1642) invented the telescope, law of inertia, mathematical uniformity of motion
- **Newton** – (d. 1727) invented calculus, studied optics, laws of gravity, argued strongly for religion, key figure in establishing the **Royal Society** (1662) as the premier scientific organization in Europe
- **Bacon** – (d. 1626) human improvement was the practical purpose of science, empirical research, scientific method, induction
- **Descartes** – (d. 1650) analytical geometry, scientific method, deduction, *cogito ergo sum* – "I think, therefore I am" – renounce all previous assumptions and go back to the drawing board
- **Pascal** – (d. 1662) combine reason and science with faith
- **Harvey** – (d. 1657) blood circulation
- **Boyle** – (d. 1691) laws of gases

Outcomes:

- A new skepticism and the application of mathematics to the study of nature
- Empiricism and the scientific method
- A new view of the universe – the world is not random or chaotic
- Mankind gains a new sense of mastery of its own fate, we can penetrate the mysteries that surround us
- A new self-confidence and the **idea of progress**

73

- A new emphasis on manners, delicacy, rational behavior; popular culture gradually tamed
- Awe and fear at the vastness and impersonal nature of the universe
- New technologies to help with mining, navigation, construction, ballistics – stimulus to business and trade
- Weakening of superstitions (belief in witchcraft) and of irrational traditions, more emphasis on merit than blue blood
- Increased emphasis on education and research
- Microscope, telescope, accurate maps, etc.
- Increased weakening of organized religion, new skepticism in biblical studies, more toleration
- Laws more rational and just, rules for evidence in court more rigorous
- New understanding of natural law
- Attempts increase to relieve poverty and "improve" the poor
- A number of women become scientists and intellectual leaders (Paris salons important 17th and 18th centuries)

Cultural developments:

- **Cervantes** – (d. 1616) *Don Quixote*, satire of chivalric romance
- **Shakespeare** – (d. 1616) conservative, patriotic, psychological penetration
- **Milton** –   (d. 1674) *Paradise Lost*, man responsible for his own fate
- **Bunyan** – (d. 1688) Puritan piety
- **Hobbes** – (d. 1679) man is base and materialistic, life brutish and short, to preserve order accept the will of a strong central authority – *Leviathan*
- **Locke** – (d. 1704) *tabula rasa* – man is a blank slate – the natural human state is perfection, purpose of government is to cultivate human goodness, rebellion may be necessary under seriously unjust or incompetent rule, constitutions – the rational way to construct governments, property owners (stake-holders) rule. "Life, Liberty, Property."

1. The greatest achievements of seventeenth century science were largely confined to

   (A) biology, chemistry, and medicine
   (B) physics, astronomy, and mathematics
   (C) geography, medicine, and anthropology
   (D) chemistry, psychology, and engineering
   (E) botany, zoology, and optics

2. The world of scholarship and research societies responded in what way to the achievements of women scientists during the seventeenth and eighteenth centuries?

   (A) welcomed with delight
   (B) accepted with some reservations
   (C) rejected except in one or two cases
   (D) ignored completely
   (E) supported capital punishment for women involved in science

3. "The greatest good that in any form of government can possibly happen to the people in general is scarce sensible in respect of the miseries and horrible calamities that accompany a civil war or that dissolute condition of masterless men."

   The author of this passage was

   (A) Oliver Cromwell
   (B) John Locke
   (C) John Milton
   (D) John Pym
   (E) Thomas Hobbes

4. The Royal Society was founded in 1662 by King Charles II to

   (A) encourage the arts and culture
   (B) honor military achievement
   (C) improve scientific knowledge
   (D) expand science teaching in secondary schools
   (E) confer Nobel prizes

Alinari/Art Resource, NY

5. The room depicted above was most likely located in

   (A)   Versailles Palace near Paris
   (B)   El Escorial near Madrid
   (C)   the royal observatory near London
   (D)   Erasmus's rooms at Cambridge University
   (E)   Petrarch's villa near Florence

6. Sir Isaac Newton's discoveries included all of the following EXCEPT

   (A)   differential calculus
   (B)   the theory of universal gravitation
   (C)   first spring operated clock
   (D)   calculation of the average density of the earth
   (E)   all colors are composed of a mixture of the primary colors

7. "The men of experiment are like the ant, they only collect and use; the reasoners resemble spiders, who make cobwebs out of their own substance. But the bee takes a middle course: it gathers its material from the flowers of the garden and of the field, but transforms and digests it by a power of its own."

This passage argues for the importance of

(A) the utility of hard work
(B) Scholasticism
(C) algebraic analysis
(D) zoology and botany and a combined science of biology
(E) examination of empirical evidence to advance science

Image Select/Art Resource, NY

8. This engraving shows the solar system as conceived by which among the following astronomers?

(A) Kepler
(B) Boyle
(C) Newton
(D) Copernicus   *orbits are circules*
(E) Pascal

9. Francis Bacon's method of scientific enquiry called induction embodied which of the following concepts?

(A) move from general principles to a logical conclusion
(B) systematic observation and experiment leading to generalizations
(C) astrology
(D) an updated form of Scholasticism
(E) Cartesian dualism

10. In the seventeenth century medical advancements were hindered by religious objections to

   (A)   professional schools for doctors
   (B)   printing books
   (C)   experimenting with medicines
   (D)   alchemy
   (E)   dissection of human bodies

11. "Cogito ergo sum" – I think, therefore I am – was the basis of a new approach to scientific thinking developed by

   (A)   Paracelsus
   (B)   Ptolmey
   (C)   Galen
   (D)   Copernicus
   (E)   Descartes

12. Among the most important advances of the Scientific Revolution were all of the following EXCEPT

   (A)   discovery of the spherical nature of the globe
   (B)   emphasis on empirical research
   (C)   invention of the telescope
   (D)   development of the scientific method
   (E)   invention of calculus

13. "I profess to learn and teach anatomy not from books but from dissections, not from the tenets of philosophers but from the fabric of nature."

This passage was written by

   (A)   Isaac Newton
   (B)   William Harvey
   (C)   Vlad the Impaler
   (D)   Denis Diderot
   (E)   Rene Descartes

14. The most serious conflict facing great thinkers of the seventeenth century, such as Newton and Pascal, was

   (A) understanding the role of the king in national politics
   (B) resolving the dilemma between Christianity and Islam
   (C) replacing the scientific method with irrational thinking
   (D) rejecting mathematics inplace of alchemy
   (E) reconciling scientific discoveries with Christian teaching

15. The medieval conception of astronomy was based upon what fundamental assumption about the universe?

   (A) geocentric
   (B) heliocentric
   (C) cosmological
   (D) typological
   (E) gravitational

16. Who among the following was NOT an important astronomer?

   (A) Galileo
   (B) Vesalius
   (C) Copernicus
   (D) Brahe
   (E) Kepler

Mauritshuis - The Hague

17. All of the following are true about this painting EXCEPT

    (A) painted by Rembrandt
    (B) shows the importance of science
    (C) event took place in Holland
    (D) the participants had no understanding of methods of infection
    (E) depicts the first appendectomy

18. "Nature ... is inexorable and immutable; she never transgresses the laws imposed upon her, or cares a whit whether her abstruse reasons and methods of operation are understandable to men."

    This passage best embodies the spirit of

    (A) Galileo
    (B) Savanarola
    (C) Aquinas
    (D) the Lollards
    (E) Brahe

Image Select/Art Resource, NY

19. This is a drawing of

    (A)   an astronomer
    (B)   a chemist
    (C)   a physician
    (D)   a barrister
    (E)   an alchemist

20. "I may well presume, most Holy Father, that certain people, as soon as they hear that in this book about the Revolutions of the Spheres of the Universe I ascribe movement to the earthly globe, will cry out that, holding such views, I should at once be hissed off the stage."

This passage was written by

    (A)   Vesaliusyy
    (B)   Bacon
    (C)   Copernicus
    (D)   Descartes
    (E)   Cervantes

21. John Milton's *Areopagitica*, published in 1644, was

    (A)   a call for the return of the Stuarts
    (B)   an attack on Cromwell
    (C)   a plea for freedom of speech
    (D)   an argument for religious toleration
    (E)   an analysis of predestination

No testing material on this page.

Chapter VIII

The Enlightenment

The Enlightenment consisted of the spread of ideas during the 18th century that grew out of the spirit of the Scientific Revolution. Emphasis on rational thought (the Age of Reason), secularism, and the spread of education and knowledge (the Age of Improvement). These ideas were articulated and spread by the **philosophes**, writers and thinkers interested in improving the world. Paris salons, often led by women, help spread ideas among the elite.

Great Figures:

- **Locke** – (d. 1704) with Newton the real father of the Enlightenment; a more original and creative philosopher than most *philosophes*. Promoted more rational government and an understanding of human psychology
- **Voltaire** – (d. 1778) deism, freedom of thought, popularized Newton, secularizer, historian
- **Montesquieu** – (d. 1755) climate and circumstances affect types of government, separation of powers good
- **Diderot** – the *Encylopédie* (1751-72)
- **Rousseau** – (d.1778) politics, education, psychology, feelings, the *Social Contract*, the general will
- **Beccaria** – (d. 1794) criminologist, against torture
- **Adam Smith** – Scottish *physiocrat* (economist), advocated *laissez faire* economics (least possible state intervention), *The Wealth of Nations* (1776), the "invisible hand"
- **Hume** – (d. 1776) Scottish Enlightenment, religion is mere superstition
- **Kant** – (d. 1804) German Enlightenment, *Critique of Pure Reason*, categories of understanding

Enlightened Absolutism (Despotism) is a term used to describe the rule of a number of monarchs who more or less attempted to incorporate some of the ideas of the Enlightenment into their governments. One can argue that far from being "reformers" or liberals, they were enhancing their own power. Frederick the Great set up state run elementary schools so his soldiers would be better able to follow orders. Louis XV and Louis XVI of France also presided over enlightened reforms but were not creative forces. Monarchs in smaller countries often emulated the reforms of the great figures.

Characteristics:

- Building canals, improving infrastructure, promoting commerce
- Enacting legal codes – which could actually enhance absolutist power by abolishing traditional privileges and rights
- Encouraging educational institutions

- Secularization, religious toleration
- Weakening the power of the church
- Increase revenues of state
- Centralize power, codify laws
- Build up military power
- Abolish or diminish use of torture
- Monarch is the "servant" of the state

Great Figures:

- **Maria Theresa** – (d.1780) Empress of Austria, fails to regain Silesia, but holds the rest of the empire together; devout Catholic; moderate reformer; improved economy, alleviated serfdom
- **Frederick (II) the Great** – (d. 1786) King of Prussia, started the War of Austrian Succession; consorts with *philosophes*; codified laws; frees Crown serfs
- **Joseph II** – (d.1790) Emperor of Austria; impatient and furious reformer; equal taxation; toleration; free press; Jewish nobles; improves commerce; suppressed monasteries; German language to be universal; secret police; land to serfs
- **Leopold II** – (d. 1792) Emperor of Austria, rolls back many of Joseph's reforms to reduce outrage of nobles, but a moderate reformer in his own right
- **Catherine (II) the Great** – (d. 1796) Empress of Russia, codified laws; consorts with *philosophes*; expands Russian territory to south and west; puts down Pugachev's Rebellion; has a French *philosophe* educate her grandson; allows nobles more power over serfs and in status

Reigning Houses of Europe:

- Scotland   Stuart (Stewart) – merged with England 1603
- England   Tudor 1485-1603
                    Stuart 1603-1714
                    Hanover 1714 – (becomes Windsor 1917)
- France   Valois to 1589
                    Bourbon 1589-1792 1814-30
                    Orleans 1830-48
                    Bonaparte 1804-1815 1852-1870
- HRE   Habsburg to 1806
- Austria-Hungary   Habsburg to 1918
- Prussia   Hohenzollern to 1918
- Germany   Hohenzollern 1871-1918
- Russia   Rurik to 1604
                    Romanov 1613-1917
- Spain   Habsburg 1516-1700
                    Bourbon 1700-1931 1975-
- Italy   Savoy 1861-1946
- The Netherlands   Orange 1572-(as elected stadholders until 1796)

1. Francois Quesnay, Anne-Robert Turgot, and Adam Smith were all leading figures in the development of Enlightenment ideas relating to

   (A) foreign policy
   (B) economics
   (C) civil law
   (D) psychology
   (E) religion

2. "Love childhood; encourage its sports, its pleasures, its loveable instincts.... As soon as children can appreciate the delights of existence, let them enjoy it."

   This passage was most likely written by a

   (A) junker aristocrat
   (B) Jesuit priest
   (C) Russian serf
   (D) French philosophe
   (E) Calvinist merchant

3. The leading philosophes of the French Enlightenment shared all the following beliefs EXCEPT

   (A) the concept of a republic of letters
   (B) unorthodox ideas about religion
   (C) the idea of progress
   (D) censorship of books was wrong
   (E) a vision about the best form of government

4. Voltaire was most outspoken and vehement in his denunciation of

   (A) Great Britain
   (B) the French Academy
   (C) the Roman Catholic church
   (D) modern science
   (E) Frederick II of Prussia

5. The philosophe least in step with the principal ideas of the Enlightenment was

   (A) Montesquieu
   (B) Voltaire
   (C) Diderot
   (D) Rousseau
   (E) Beccaria

6. "The punishment of death is pernicious to society, from the example of barbarity it affords…. Is it not absurd, that the laws, which detest and punish homicide, should, in order to prevent murder, publicly commit murder themselves?"

This passage was most likely to have been written by which of the following?

(A)   Cesare Beccaria
(B)   John Calvin
(C)   Pope Julius II
(D)   Peter the Great
(E)   Montesquieu

7. The English philosopher, John Locke, believed that individuals were born

(A)   corrupt and evil, which schooling and law could only restrain and contain
(B)   blank slates on which the environment and education imposed patterns of behavior
(C)   already imbued with a mixture of goodness and holiness
(D)   genetically programmed to pursue a particular walk of life
(E)   sinful but capable of redemption

8. Classical economic theory developed by Adam Smith and others put an emphasis on

(A)   increasing the number of monopolies
(B)   accumulating large reserves of gold
(C)   nationalizing industry
(D)   freeing the economy from restraints
(E)   heavy taxation

9. Enlightened monarchs were LEAST likely to do which of the following?

(A)   surrender royal prerogatives
(B)   improve education
(C)   reduce the power of the church
(D)   correspond with the philosophes
(E)   reform legal codes

10. The Classical economists argued that the state owes all of the following to its citizens EXCEPT

    (A)   protection against invasion
    (B)   enforcement of the laws
    (C)   supervison of contracts
    (D)   maintenance of public works
    (E)   support for the poor

11. John Locke in his two *Treatises of Government* argued that the chief goal of a system of government ought to be

    (A)   the protection of property
    (B)   an end to all war
    (C)   upholding the king
    (D)   the preservation of Roman Catholicism
    (E)   support for schools

12. Who among the following was NOT a French finance minister during the eighteenth century?

    (A)   Necker
    (B)   Terray
    (C)   Turgot
    (D)   Pitt
    (E)   Calonne

13. The Russian nobility regained power lost under Peter the Great when Catherine the Great was forced to turn to them for help during

    (A)   Pugachev's rebellion
    (B)   the Polish civil war
    (C)   the revolt of the True Believers
    (D)   the Prussian invasion
    (E)   the Orlov Conspiracy

14. Emperor Joseph II of Austria failed in his attempts to reform his country because he

    (A)   lacked the ruthlessness necessary to create a secret police force
    (B)   failed to win the support of the nobility
    (C)   was unwilling to dissolve the monasteries
    (D)   failed to abolish the *robot*
    (E)   agreed with his mother's opinions

15. Which among the following was the most influential publication of the eighteenth century?

   (A) *Hard Times*
   (B) *No Exit*
   (C) *In Praise of Folly*
   (D) *The Prince*
   (E) *The Encyclopedia*

16. Which state during the eighteenth century practiced the greatest toleration towards Catholics, Lutherans, Reformed Jews, and Calvinists?

   (A) Prussia
   (B) Russia
   (C) Italy
   (D) England
   (E) France

17. Spanish royal policy led to which of the following developments in the eighteenth century?

   (A) complete collapse of the colonial structure in central and south America
   (B) significant administrative reforms and some economic revival
   (C) renewed Spanish dominance in European affairs
   (D) military victories over the Ottomans
   (E) break up of Catalan and Basque regions from the rest of Spain

18. What terms best describe the interests of French courtiers and Versailles during the second half of the eighteenth century?

   (A) didactic and serious
   (B) religious and mystical
   (C) elegant and frivolous
   (D) harsh and grim
   (E) bourgeois and rural

19. It is reported that Louis XV of France said: "After me the deluge." He meant by this

   (A) France would be a great naval power by the end of his reign
   (B) his ministers were geniuses
   (C) France faced a financial and political crisis that could not long be avoided
   (D) morality would decline after his death
   (E) he feared God would take revenge on France for its pride and power

20. "Deism", as advocated by the philosophes, was supposed to be all of the following EXCEPT

    (A)   based on reason
    (B)   led to moral behavior
    (C)   did not restrict freedom of thought
    (D)   deduced from empirical evidence
    (E)   strictly Roman Catholic

21. The Classical economist and demographer, Thomas Robert Malthus, argued that

    (A)   population inevitably outpaced agricultural production
    (B)   industrialization would reduce population growth
    (C)   sale of birth control devices should be encouraged by the government
    (D)   poverty could be eliminated through communal living
    (E)   the death penalty should be abolished

No testing material on this page.

Chapter IX

The French Revolution

Convulsed France and Europe between 1789* and 1815*. Although urban workers and peasants played important roles at certain moments in the revolution, it was initially provoked by a struggle between the royal government and the *parlements*, noble-dominated courts that were used to resist increased taxation and encroaching monarchical power. Nobles continued to play a key role in the early stages of the revolution, and even Napoleon was a minor noble. All revolutions since have been influenced by the events in France during these years. Controversy among historians over interpretations of the Revolution has been vigorous. Disciples of Marx saw the Revolution as a triumph of the bourgeoisie over the second estate.

Chronology is key in understanding the French Revolution. Make sure to understand the sequence of the events.

Causes:

- Incompetence of Louis XVI
- Distrust and hatred of Queen Marie Antoinette
- Series of poor harvests in the 1780s
- National humiliation in war leading to the loss of India, Canada, and Atlantic trade
- Bankruptcy of the government due to war debts and inability to tax the nobility sufficiently (nobles paid some taxes)
- Tax farming system encouraged extreme measures in collecting taxes, but rendered less income to the state than direct collection would have
- Noble resistance to being taxed and fear of renewed royal incursion on their privileges
- Example of the American Revolution
- Ideas and criticisms of the Enlightenment
- Ineffective censorship
- Unpopularity of the Court nobility who often were detached from management of their estates
- Tension between bourgeoisie and nobility
- Unpopularity of church hierarchy and privileges
- Resentment of nobles remaining feudal privileges – *banalités*
- Heavy tax burdens on the poor – the *taille*, etc.
- Rising cycle of extreme rhetoric and violence, especially once war was declared, made the revolution veer towards an extreme path to dictatorship
- Decade-long recession

Great Figures:

- **Louis XVI** – (r. 1774-92) nice man out of his depth and incapable of the ruthlessness necessary to suppress a rebellion
- **Marie Antoinette** – (d. 1793) inept and insensitive to public opinion and a foreigner (Austrian)
- **Necker** – (d. 1804) royal financial official
- **Tom Paine** – English defense of the Revolution – *The Rights Of Man* (1791)
- **Olympye de Gouges** – *The Rights of Women* (1791)
- **Mary Wollstonecraft** – *Vindication of the Rights of Women* (1792)
- **Edmund Burke** – English critic – *Reflections on the Revolution* in France (1790) – profound case for caution in political reform
- **Marat** – Jacobin leader, murdered by counter-revolutionary woman 1793
- **Danton** – (d. 1794) Jacobin leader; executed by Robespierre
- **Robespierre** – (d. 1794) Jacobin leader; becomes head of the Committee of Public Safety and for a while the dictator of France: incorruptible and a monster
- **Pitt the Younger** – (d. 1806) British organizer of alliances against the forces of revolution and Napoleon
- **Napoleon Bonaparte** – (r. 1799-1815) revolutionary general who supported the Directory and then overthrew it

Terms/Events:

- **Estates General** – called in 1789 for the first time since 1614. Used by monarchy to try to resolve the financial crisis. Clergy, nobles, commoners vote separately
- **Tennis Court Oath** – 1789 Third Estate and some others declare selves a National Assembly
- **Bastille** – 1789 crowd attacks symbol of royal authority in Paris
- **The Great Fear** – 1789 agrarian insurrection
- **Declaration of the Rights of Man and Citizen** – 1789 National Assembly charts new society
- **Émigrés** – princes and nobles who fled France to raise foreign opposition and assistance
- **Sans-culottes** – shopkeepers and artisans in Paris who periodically placed pressure on the legislature
- **Constituent Assembly** – (1789-91) drew up new constitution: unicameral legislature; limited monarchy; all new personnel for new assembly; active and passive citizens
- **Civil Constitution of the Clergy** – (1790) church nationalized and clergy became employees of the State; deeply antagonized the Pope, the clergy, the King, and many good Catholics of all classes; key factor in escalation of the revolution
- **Le Chapelier Law** – (1791) against organized labor, typical of bourgeois attitudes of revolutionaries in legislature
- **Assignats** – bonds issued by government, later used as currency; over issue led to high inflation
- **Jacobins** – radical revolutionaries
- **Girondins** – more moderate than Jacobins, advocates of war with Austria
- **Enragés** – extreme radicals, the "Mountain" party

- **Levée en masse** – use of large numbers of fervidly patriotic troops to overcome disadvantage in training and organization of anti-revolutionary armies; precursor of Napoleon's mass armies
- **Flight to Varennes** – (1791) Royal family attempted to escape
- **Declaration of Pilnitz** – (1791) Leopold II of Austria promised to participate in an anti-revolutionary war, hedged by qualifications that made the promise worthless; used as an excuse for war by revolutionaries
- **National Convention** – (1792) new legislature; declared war on Austria; committed to spread revolution abroad
- **Brunswick Manifesto** – (1792) invading Austrians promised revenge if royal family harmed; helped rally support for the revolution
- **September Massacres** – (1792) first mass executions due to war scare; precursor of the Terror
- **The Vendée** – (1793) counterrevolutionary uprising in west central France; brutally suppressed by Robespierre
- **The Terror** – (1793-94) organized to suppress counter-Revolution; spiraled out of control and eventually destroyed Robespierre; 70% of the victims were from the lower orders; use of guillotine
- **The Committee of Public Safety** – (1793-94) organized the Terror; led by Robespierre
- **The Thermidorian Reaction** – (1794) reaction to the extremism of Robespierre; ended the Terror; established the Directory
- **The Directory** – (1795-99) continued revolution in a more conventional way; led by bourgeois; new constitution; continued the war

Outcomes:

- Overthrow of the monarchy; execution of the King and Queen
- Wealth and power of the nobility seriously weakened
- Peasants secured tenure to much land
- Secularization of the state (at one point France was de-Christianized and a state religion worshipping "reason" was established)
- France divided into new administrative structure
- Introduction of the metric system
- Revisions to the calendar (10 day week did not last)
- Reform of family, divorce, and property law; end of Primogeniture
- More equality before the law
- Two competing ideas of the state – libertarian and monolithic – left France unstable and unreconciled
- Indiscriminate use of political violence
- Radical reorganization of the military
- Expansion of borders, wars of the Revolution
- Rise of Napoleon
- Prolonged political and constitutional instability in France
- Egalitarian ideals entered the mainstream of Western political practice
- Great Britain emerged as the only global superpower

NAPOLEON

One of the most complex and astonishing figures to bestride the European stage. Bred in a minor Corsican noble family, he rose due to opportunities afforded young officers during the French Revolution. He seized control of the state in 1799 in a military coup, declared himself Emperor in 1804, conquered much of Europe, and was finally defeated and exiled in 1815*. He conquered the Netherlands, Italy, Dalmatia, Switzerland, Germany, Poland, Spain, Portugal, and placed a French marshal on the throne of Sweden. He invaded Egypt and Russia.

Terms/Events:

- **Invasion of Egypt** – (1798) Bonaparte's crazy expedition that ended in disaster, which he claimed was a victory
- **Coup d'État 1799** – Bonaparte overthrew the Directory
- **Consulate** – (1799-1804) Bonaparte dictatorship
- **Concordat** – (1801) restored partial independence of Catholic Church
- **Josephine** – the love of his life; jettisoned when she could not produce a male heir
- **Austerlitz** – (1805) Napoleon defeated Austria and Russia; enabled him to demolish HRE
- **Continental System** – (1807) economic warfare against the British; failed to stop British trade and alienated French allies
- **Bonaparte Family** – Napoleon's brothers and sisters, placed on various thrones
- **Jena** – (1806) Prussian army defeated and Prussia itself mortally endangered
- **Pitt the Younger** – (d. 1806) British Prime Minister who organized coalitions against Napoleon
- **Admiral Nelson** – victor at the Nile and Trafalgar, Britain's greatest naval commander
- **Trafalgar** – (1805) Admiral Nelson destroyed the French and Spanish fleets, making invasion of Britain impossible, and placing the British navy in an unchallengeable position for a century
- **Alexander I** – Tsar of Russia, at first Napoleon's ally at Tilsit (1807), then an organizer of his defeat
- **Talleyrand** – French diplomat, first for Napoleon and then at Vienna for Louis XVIII
- **Burning of Moscow** – (1812) Napoleon's invasion of Russia failed, catastrophic retreat
- **Battle of Nations** (Leipzig) – (1813) Napoleon defeated and driven back to Paris, abdicated and sent to Elba
- **100 Days** – (1815) Napoleon returned from Elba, overthrew Louis XVIII, fought the British and Prussians
- **Waterloo** – (1815*) Napoleon defeated by Wellington in Belgium, abdicates, sent to St. Helena
- **Wellington** – drove French out of Spain, defeated Napoleon at Waterloo, later British Prime Minister

- **Louis XVIII** – in 1795 threatened retribution for revolution, which blocked a restoration; more moderate in 1814 when he was restored; accepted parliamentary government, Napoleonic Code, abolition of feudalism, etc.
- **Metternich** – Austrian Chancellor, helped organize Napoleon's defeat and then presided at Congress of Vienna (1815); flexible, conservative, shrewd
- **Castlereagh** – British Foreign Secretary, top negotiator at Vienna

Outcomes:

One way to look at the Napoleonic era is to assess the degree to which the Emperor was an enlightened ruler as opposed to a despot.

"Enlightened"

- Encouraged a spirit of nationalism at home but inadvertently aroused powerful anti-French nationalism in Spain, Italy, Britain, Russia, and Germany
- Napoleonic Code (paternalistic and authoritarian)
- Abolished serfdom
- Ended the Holy Roman Empire
- Promoted soldiers and officials by merit
- Abolished guilds
- Held plebiscites, imposed constitutions
- Chose title "Emperor of the French" (not of France)
- Provided political stability
- Built infrastructure
- Left many revolutionary reforms in place
- Sold Louisiana to USA
- Gained Vatican recognition of the Republic 1801
- No tax exemptions by birth
- Created Bank of France
- Established new school system
- Ended traditional practices and noble privileges in conquered territories
- Ended restrictions on peasants
- Spread metric system

"Despotic"

- Secret Police, censorship (Fouché)
- Murdered duc d'Enghein, Bourbon prince though an innocent man, in order to prevent disloyalty among his followers
- Placed brothers on thrones of Holland, Spain, and Westphalia and other members of the family in Italy
- Created a new hereditary nobility
- Crowned self Emperor (1804); dictatorial
- Constantly at war, massive casualties and suffering
- Married a Habsburg Archduchess

- Restored Catholic Church to a privileged position
- Civil Code restricted women's rights, reasserted patriarchal values; guilty till proved innocent
- Self-glorification

Congress of Vienna – 1814-1815*

Peace conference ending the wars of revolution. Established a general peace in Europe that lasted a century. It evoked little bitterness in France, ended long colonial rivalries. Issues of Germany and Poland were deferred. It restored the balance of power.

- Bourbons restored in France
- Napoleon exiled and his heir taken to Vienna, where he died
- Quadruple Alliance (Austria, Prussia, Russia, Britain) to last 20 years
- British confirmed in possession of South Africa (taken from the Dutch)
- Britain gained possessions in the Mediterranean and West Indies
- France rapidly restored to company of great nations
- Germany left divided among a much reduced (39) number of small states with little central authority
- The Netherlands and Belgium combined into a large buffer state to contain France
- Austria regained Tuscany and Lombardy and also absorbed Venice
- Spanish, Portuguese, and Sicilian monarchies restored
- Polish-Saxon Question: Alexander I wanted to be king of a reunited Poland in exchange for giving Saxony to Prussia. France, Austria, and Britain resist. Russia and Prussia only gained a fraction of their desired goals
- Sweden gained Norway
- Sardinia gained Nice and Genoa
- Slave trade condemned
- Agreement to hold future congresses of the great powers to resist revolutionary ferment
- Holy Alliance formed by Alexander I vaguely in favor of peace and religion (Russia, Prussia, Austria – Britain does not join)

1. The Quadruple Alliance established at the Congress of Vienna in 1814 included all the following countries EXCEPT

    (A)   Austria
    (B)   Russia
    (C)   Prussia
    (D)   Great Britain
    (E)   France

2. On the night of August 4, 1789 members of the French National Assembly renounced exclusive rights to hunt game, collect manorial dues, crush grapes, and bake bread. The members who made these renunciations were members of which of the following groups?

    (A)   bourgeoisie
    (B)   peasants
    (C)   nobles
    (D)   clergy
    (E)   sans-culottes

3. Louis XVIII guaranteed all of the following after the resumption of Bourbon rule in 1814 EXCEPT

    (A)   Bonaparte family could keep their titles
    (B)   an elected legislature
    (C)   religious freedom
    (D)   the Napoleonic Code
    (E)   equality before the law

4. The Committee of Public Safety was established during the French Revolution in order to

    (A)   create a new republican order
    (B)   restore the monarchy
    (C)   set up savings banks
    (D)   defend against Jacobin terror
    (E)   protect the Pope on his visit to Paris

5. "It is our duty, as well as our interest, to retard, if we cannot avert, the return of a more contentious order of things: and our insular situation places us sufficiently out of the reach of danger to admit of our pursuing a more generous and confiding policy."

This is a summary of the policy pursued at the Congress of Vienna by which nation?

(A)   Great Britain
(B)   France
(C)   Prussia
(D)   Russia
(E)   Italy

6. The "Thermidorean Reaction" of 1794 accomplished which of the following?

(A)   elected Napoleon Emperor of the French
(B)   invaded Britain
(C)   restored the Bourbon monarchy
(D)   overthrew the Committee of Public Safety and established the Directory
(E)   became more radical than any previous government

7. Napoleon Bonaparte's social origins were

(A)   Parisian *sans-culottes*
(B)   Girondin bourgeois
(C)   Corsican noble
(D)   Burgundian peasant
(E)   West Indian merchant

From Western Civilization, 3rd edition, by J.J. Spielvogel © 1997.
Reprinted with permission of Wadsworth, a division of Thomson Learning.

8. This map depicts the borders of Europe in

    (A)   1768
    (B)   1788
    (C)   1790
    (D)   1795
    (E)   1815

9. A Marxist historian would argue that the French Revolution

    (A)   was the inevitable result of a bourgeois challenge to the old regime
    (B)   was ineffective due to bourgeois apathy
    (C)   lost its purpose once Christianity had been abolished
    (D)   achieved nothing due to the restoration of the monarchy
    (E)   failed to establish capitalism in France

10. All of the following were true about the *assignats*, paper money issued by the national assembly early in the French Revolution, EXCEPT that they

    (A)   lost much of their value due to a lack of confidence
    (B)   were backed by the value of confiscated church land
    (C)   primarily benefited purchasers of lands as mortgages lost value due to inflation
    (D)   were later issued without anything of value backing them up
    (E)   were first issued to pay compensation to aristocratic families for those who had been guillotined

11. Which of the following inventions was first tested in 1792?

(A) printing press
(B) pistol
(C) hot air balloon
(D) passenger railway
(E) telegraph

12. The civil code enacted by Napoleon in 1804 did all of the following EXCEPT

(A) left workers legally subordinate to their employers
(B) reaffirmed the patriarchal nature of the traditional family
(C) abolished primogeniture
(D) formed a basis for civil law copied in many countries
(E) granted special privileges to the aristocracy

13. Napoleon Bonaparte came to power in 1799 by which of the following means?

(A) coup d'etat
(B) free election
(C) appointment by the pope
(D) as a puppet of the English government
(E) at the request of the Directory

14. The ideals of the French Revolution were encapsulated in the phrase

(A) property, power, aristocracy
(B) equality, humanity, Godliness
(C) liberty, equality, fraternity
(D) justice, honor, socialism
(E) Robespierre, Bonaparte, Bourbon

15. "The Concert of Europe" was a phrase used to describe

(A) a musical event held each year at Salzburg
(B) an alliance against Russia made by Peter the Great
(C) an alliance system of the first half of the nineteenth century
(D) Napoleon's empire
(E) the papal alliance formed to support Roman Catholicism

16. The Woman's March on Versailles October 5, 1789 was a crucial turning point in the French Revolution because it

    (A)   placed the King and Assembly under the pressure of the Paris crowd
    (B)   was embraced and supported by the King and Queen
    (C)   was a peace offering to the monarchy after the storming of the Bastille
    (D)   was arranged by Robespierre
    (E)   forced the renunciation of feudal privileges

17. The "Great Fear" of July 1789

    (A)   refers to the royal family's flight to Varennes
    (B)   prompted the Declaration of Pillnitz
    (C)   consisted of peasant uprisings in rural France
    (D)   was the response of the *sans-culottes* to the Brunswick Manifesto
    (E)   led to the Pope's excommunication of the French nation

18. The Bastille in Paris was stormed on July 14, 1789

    (A)   in order to capture the royal family
    (B)   to defend against Austrian invasion
    (C)   to free the Marquis de Lafayette
    (D)   to seize arms to defend against royal reprisals
    (E)   to secure a prison for disloyal nobles

19. "The Declaration of the Rights of Man and Citizen" proclaimed all the following EXCEPT

    (A)   the emancipation of women
    (B)   universal suffrage
    (C)   protection of rights of property
    (D)   religious toleration
    (E)   an elective legislature

20. Voting in the Estates General called in 1789 to address the impending financial crisis

    (A)   took place by per capita count
    (B)   by estate
    (C)   national referendum
    (D)   *liberum veto*
    (E)   only nobles had the right to vote

21. The King's primary opponents in the struggle at the beginning of the French Revolution were the

    (A)   nobles
    (B)   clergy
    (C)   industrial workers
    (D)   artisans
    (E)   peasants

22. The Estates General convoked in 1789 by Louis XVI was the first meeting of the legislature in France since

    (A)   1485
    (B)   1614
    (C)   1715
    (D)   1785
    (E)   1788

23. The problems of the French monarchy in the late eighteenth century included all of the following EXCEPT

    (A)   uncooperative parlements
    (B)   inability to tax the nobility effectively
    (C)   popular hostility to the Queen
    (D)   lack of a consistent policy on the part of the King
    (E)   no male heir

24. The "Tennis Court Oath" that was taken by the members of the new National Assembly at Versailles in 1789

    (A)   began the revival of the Olympic Games
    (B)   avowed loyalty to absolutism
    (C)   defied royal authority
    (D)   was taken only by the clergy
    (E)   proposed the institution of state terror

Chapter X

The Nineteenth Century - I

[NOTE: The review material applies to Chapters X and XI]

THE INDUSTRIAL REVOLUTION

Historians disagree about the origins of this phenomenon, and especially about when it can be said to have begun. The conventional date is circa 1780*. There is also disagreement about the number of "stages" – first, second, etc. Again the conventional wisdom is that textiles and railways composed the first stage and electricity, chemicals, etc. was the base of the "second" one. One also has to remember that much pre-industrial activity (the domestic system, for example) continued long into the "industrial" era. Britain was the epicenter of the first Industrial Revolution and stayed in the lead until the late 19th century. However, some technologies spread very rapidly, such as the railways, even to countries that were otherwise very slow to change. Belgium followed Britain, then Northern France, the Rhineland, Silesia, and eventually Bohemia, Northern Italy, and the USA. Although pockets of industrialization developed elsewhere, such as around St. Petersburg in Russia or Belfast in Ireland, many areas remained primarily agricultural until the 20th century.

Causes:

- Agricultural Revolution – increased productivity and created large amounts of excess capital. Food for an expanding population and money for increased investment
    a) Occurred first in England and Holland due to methods of landownership that encouraged investment and entrepreneurship
    b) New technologies – seed drill
    c) New breeding techniques with animals
    d) New fertilizer, new crops, and crop rotations
    e) Enclosure – more workers mobile
    f) Investments in canals, transportation
- Population growth – more labor and consumers
    a) small pox vaccination
    b) greater availability of food – potato, corn
    c) increased job opportunities
- Stable political system – encourages long term investment, property secure
- Strong central banking system for capital allocation
- Abundant resources, especially coal and iron ore
- No place far distant from navigable waterways
- Low taxation

- Inventive geniuses – Hargreaves, Cartwright, Arkwright, Watt (d. 1819), Stephenson (d. 1848)
- Colonial system provides additional markets
- Britain largest free trade area in Europe
- Aristocracy open to entrepreneurship
- Experienced business and merchant class
- Abundant capital from slave trade, the *asiento*, and world trade generally

Terms/events:

- Waterframe – (1769) revolutionary method of making cotton thread
- Textile industry – first area of industrialization
- Steam engine – applied first to pumps in mines, then driving machinery, then railways
- Liverpool-Manchester railway 1829
- Manchester – "shock city" of growth and innovation

Outcomes:

- Movement of population from countryside to large cities – Manchester, Birmingham, Leeds, Sheffield
- Gradual impoverishment of domestic weavers
- Regimentation of life – no longer responsive to seasons or hours of sunlight, the factory whistle: long working hours, boring and dangerous work even by small children
- Boom – bust cycles become dramatic
- End of famine in industrialized societies
- Poor housing, alienation from support of local village life
- Gradual improvement of living standards and wages after 1840s
- Cheap, easily cleaned, quick-drying clothing (cotton)
- Eventually hours reduced, child labor regulated, schooling increased
- Clergy/churches slow to keep up with urban growth
- Industrial fortunes eventually began to match aristocratic ones
- Railways – post 1830*
    - a) national time
    - b) national newspapers distributed rapidly
    - c) food, goods transported cheaply and rapidly
    - d) suburbs – commute by train
    - e) vacations/tourism – travel by train, even the poor
    - f) social leveling – all classes travel in same way, suitable clothes for train travel similar for all
    - g) professional sports – teams can travel, scores rapidly disseminated
    - h) huge increase in employment both to build the tracks, bridges, viaducts, stations, and make the rolling stock and to operate the system with engineers, conductors, porters, clerks, etc.
    - i) stimulated other industries – demand for steel and coal, rapid and cheap transportation of raw materials and finished goods
- Expanded material culture, new industries

- Global trade expanded

ROMANTICISM

Revival of Gothic fantasies, nostalgia for traditional verities and irrational feelings began in the early to mid-18th century in response to the prevailing rationalism of the Enlightenment and were further stimulated by the horrors of the "rationalist" reforms and terror of the French Revolution and the ugliness and brutality of the Industrial Revolution. The peak of the movement lay c. 1780-1830. It was expressed in literature, religion, architecture, music, painting, poetry, and philosophy.

Characteristics:

- Value sincerity, authenticity, and toleration
- Value emotions, religion
- Mysticism, spirituality
- Revival of the Gothic (medieval) style
- Harmony with, not control over nature
- Interest in the past, history
- Sensuality, eroticism
- Nationalism
- Worship of nature
- Interest in folklore, folksongs, folktales
- Reaction against materialism

Great Figures:

- **Rousseau** – (d. 1778) the *philosophe* never entirely comfortable as an Enlightenment figure. Saw society as corrupt in nature, gave children more freedom to develop, uniqueness of each person
- **Kant** – (d. 1804) German sought to reconcile enlightened rationalism with human freedom, immortality, and God
- **Goethe** – (d. 1832) German writer and poet, deep spiritual struggles, feelings beyond polite society, improvement of mankind, reason cannot save us
- **Caspar David Friedrich** – (d. 1840) German painter, Gothic scenes of loneliness and abandonment, beauty of nature
- **J. M. W. Turner** – (d. 1851) English painter, moves almost to abstract style to convey emotions, natural beauty
- **Beethoven** – (d. 1827) German composer, powerful, emotional, sweeping music
- **William Blake** – (d. 1827) English poet and artist, materialism and injustice of society cause receding imagination and spirituality
- **Wordsworth** – (d. 1850) English poet, loss of child-like vision
- **Lord Byron** – (d. 1824) English poet, personal liberty, heroic motivation, died fighting for Greek independence
- **Mary Shelley** – (d. 1851) *Frankenstein*
- **Fichte** – glorification of great persons, the world the creation of mankind; German culture superior to others (1808)

- **Herder** – (d. 1803) German, revival of folk culture; national character or *Volkgeist*; cultural nationalism
- **Hegel** – (d. 1831) German, all cultures are equally necessary, each contributes to the dialectic – thesis, antithesis, and synthesis

REACTIONARY CONSERVATIVISM

Many see the period after the French Revolution as an age of reaction, of which some later Romantics can be seen as a part. Certainly, the Congress of Vienna put many things back the way they were. However, even Metternich implemented some imaginative and non-traditionalist policies.

Conservatives:

- Support monarchy, the church, and the aristocracy
- Active government, intervention in the economy
- Paternalistic
- Single national religion
- Censorship
- Generally they feared nationalism and liberalism
- Upheld hierarchy, the military, and "honor"
- Some were Romantics
- "Burkean" distrust of rapid change
- Supporters generally upper class or clerical

Congress of Aix-la-Chapelle 1818 – Allies withdraw forces from France; international force against changes by violence discussed; Atlantic slave trade discussed

Congress of Troppau 1820 – Russia, Austria, Prussia agreed to suppress revolution in Naples. Britain refused to agree to collective international action

Congress of Verona 1822 – intervention in Spain authorized and no support for Greeks against the Ottomans

RUSSIA
Although raised by *philosophe* tutors, and at first a reformer, Tsar Alexander I became a conservative, especially after 1822. His domestic policies were increasingly reactionary after 1803. He pressed at Vienna for a "Holy Alliance" of monarchs against modernity. He was succeeded in 1825 by even more reactionary Nicholas I (d. 1855), who suppressed the **Decembrist** revolt. Russia moved into an era of autocratic rule not matched in any Western state; Polish revolt suppressed in 1830

AUSTRIA

Leopold II's successor, Francis II, along with the dynamic and far-sighted Metternich charted a conservative course. The latter worked against constitutionalism and nationalism, dual threats to Habsburg authority. Press censorship and secret police were implemented. The **Carlsbad Decrees** (1819) suppressed student liberalism and nationalism. The "Congress System" established at Vienna helped suppress rebellions in Spain and Italy

GREAT BRITAIN

Lords Liverpool and Castlereagh pursued a conservative foreign policy (although they withdrew from the Congress System); at home they suppressed movements for reform (**Peterloo** and the **Six Acts** 1819); growth of Methodism dampens protest from below; Luddites suppressed

FRANCE

Louis XVIII restored in 1814 and again in 1815 tried to pursue a moderate course, and left a considerable amount of Napoleon's reforms intact. However, **Charles X** (1820-30) tried to turn the clock back. His extreme conservatism provoked a revolution that placed a cousin, **Louis Philippe**, Duc d'Orleans on the throne in 1830*

SPAIN

Ferdinand VII was restored to the throne in 1815, dissolved the Cortes, and ruled as an absolute monarch. French intervention during a revolt in 1823 saved his throne. Revolutions in Latin America won independence from Spain in 1820s

ITALY

Remained divided. Austrian intervention in 1822 and 1826 to repress revolts

PRUSSIA

Monarchy, aristocracy, and military restablized after Jena. Radical reforms by Scharnhorst and Gneisenau strengthen the army, Stein and Hardenberg strengthen the state, serfdom lessened; German nationalistic movements suppressed

OTTOMAN

Greek independence movement starts 1821; Russo-Turkish War; Battle of Navarino – Turks defeated: great powers recognize Greek independence 1829; other Balkan states recognized as autonomous; Turks weaker and weaker

LIBERALISM, REFORM, AND REVOLUTION

Revolutionary uprisings motivated by nationalism and liberalism did break out during the 1820s and 30s with varying degrees of success.

Liberalism is a term first used in the 1820s to convey the following:

- Enlightenment values of rationalism and freedom of the individual
- Distrust of the military
- Republicanism or constitutional, limited monarchy
- Dislike hereditary privilege and many distrust aristocracy
- Belief in constitutions
- Distrust of religious organizations and clerical powers
- A secular state
- Free speech and free press
- Anti-slavery (Britain abolished trade 1807 and slavery in the empire in 1834)
- Legal equality
- Promotion by merit
- *Laissez-faire* economics, anti-tariffs

Supporters largely middle class, businessmen, etc. Many accepted Benthamite concepts of "Utilitarianism" (greatest good for the greatest number). The most influential statement of Classical Liberalism was made by John Stuart Mill, *On Liberty* (1859)

Feminism emerged in the early 19th century and intertwined at points with socialism and liberalism. Mill wrote on the subject. Carried on the ideas of Wollstonecraft and de Gouges. The fight for political rights was more characteristic of England and the French focused on social, cultural, and legal rights.

Nationalism is a term that came to describe aspirations for national independence or unification. It threatened to break up multi-national empires such as Austria and pull together fragmented states such as Germany and Italy. Nationalists believed that true nations usually shared:

- Common history
- Historic geographical area
- Common language
- Common religion
- Shared culture
- Common enemies

Nationalists in particular countries tended to overlook inconvenient historical events and inconvenient problems with religion or language differences. They locked onto a vision of history that suited their ideological position. Nationalism tended to go beyond patriotism into the realm of arrogance and hatred. It gave a "moral" underpinning to racism.

- Greek Independence (1820s) – Nationalist (Greek Orthodox) uprising against Ottoman (Islamic) rule. Successful due to intervention by Russian and British forces.
- South America (1820s) – Nationalist and liberal uprising against Spanish rule – successful due to weakness of the mother country after Napoleonic wars. Brazil broke free from Portugal (1822) but retained Portuguese emperor

- Spain (1822) – unsuccessful liberal revolt against Ferdinand VII, put down by French
- Decembrist revolt (Russia 1825) – uprising led by officers exposed to liberal ideas while visiting the West 1814-15. Occasioned by confusion over the succession after the death of Alexander I. Ruthlessly suppressed by Nicholas I
- Poland (1830) – nationalist uprising against Russian control, suppressed by Nicholas I
- Belgium (1830) – successful nationalist revolt against rule by the Dutch
- France (1830*) – successful liberal revolt against Charles X, established liberal constitutional monarchy under Louis Philippe (Orleans) – "July Monarchy"
- Reform Act of 1832* (Great Britain) – liberal (Whig) party led by aristocrats imposes liberal reform of the electoral system doubling the number of voters and giving representation in Parliament to industrial cities; eliminate many "rotten" boroughs. Other reforms including reduction in use of capital punishment

THE INDUSTRIAL AGE

During the mid-19th century industrialization gradually spread beyond Britain to other parts of Europe. Life for the majority of laborers in Western Europe began to change as larger and larger numbers moved to the cities and entered urban life. However, many people remained on the farms and millions of others worked as servants and not in factories. Particularly difficult times were encountered in the "Hungry 40s" when potato blight provoked a catastrophic famine in Ireland and food crises in many continental countries. Wages were low and living conditions harsh in the cities. Gradually, from that time forward things began to improve.

Pros and cons of industrial urban life.

Pros	Cons
<ul><li>more opportunities to advance</li><li>more social activities</li><li>greater marriage opportunities</li><li>more personal freedom</li><li>eventually higher wages</li><li>eventually better schooling</li><li>more things to buy</li><li>eventually a political voice for men</li><li>professional police force set up</li><li>cheaper clothes and goods</li></ul>	<ul><li>loss of a sense community</li><li>loss of a sense extended family support</li><li>unhealthy and confined living spaces</li><li>factory regimentation/boring work</li><li>boom/bust – much unemployment</li><li>injuries and death with machinery/mines</li><li>lack of sense of accomplishment</li><li>more prostitution</li><li>urban crime increases</li><li>women less partners with men/more subordinated</li></ul>

Urban women were less subject to community restrictions and in the early Industrial Revolution entered the work force as independently paid (though at lower wages than men) agents. However, as men earned more, it became financially possible for husbands to become the sole breadwinner in the family. This meant that women could spend more time raising their children and on housework, but it also gave men a more securely dominant position in the home.

Competing philosophies developed as responses to the industrial capitalist system as it emerged. These included Classical Economics, Socialism, Anarchism, and Marxism (and also, eventually, Fascism).

Classical Economics:

Embraced Adam Smith's philosophy of *laissez-faire*. Further developed by the demographer **T. R. Malthus** (d. 1834). The latter argued that food production increased at an arithmetic rate and unchecked population at a geometric rate. Since food production only expanded slowly, its growth rate imposed a check (along with disease, war, etc.) on population growth. Artificially enhancing the food supply only created long-term problems in population expansion. Another economist, **David Ricardo** (d. 1823) built on this work to argue that raising wages, which would allow workers to buy more food and thus produce more children, would create an over-supply of workers driving down the market rate for wages and eventually unemployment. Fewer workers raised wages. (**Iron Law of Wages**). This gave employers a philosophical basis to keep wages as low as possible as a "kindness" to workers. The English **New Poor Law** (1834), though admirable in the sense that the government did not rely purely on charity to support the helpless, indigent, and old, as many continental countries did, was harsh in its treatment of the poor for Ricardian reasons. The British government's inhumane response to the Irish Famine in the 1840s was also to some degree based on this thinking, although it did abolish the **Corn Laws** (1846 – [corn = wheat], tariffs that artificially kept the price of food high to protect agricultural profits) as a means of making cheaper food available.

Malthus was wrong in the short term. It did become possible to increase food production much more rapidly than he thought. However, in the 20th century worry began about population again outstripping the food supply. Ricardo was wrong about parents producing an increasing number of children as their wages went up. This turned out not to be the case.

Socialism:

Early in the 19th century "Utopian" socialists began to espouse the idea that a humane society must emphasize the needs of the community over the selfishness of individuals. The critique began of Classical economic theory and the practical, cruel outcomes of industrial capitalism. **Saint Simon** (d. 1825) urged that private wealth be put under greater administrative control. **Fourier** (d. 1837) popularized the idea of utopian communities and more liberated social mores. **Robert Owen** (d. 1858) also set up separate communities and encouraged paternalistic management. **Louis Blanc** recognized the potential of the state as an employer of labor.

Eventually socialists all moved towards the notion that redistribution of wealth through the agency of the state was necessary to create more humane and workable societies. Socialists varied from those who wished to do this by democratically elected legislatures imposing taxation on the rich to radical revolutionaries who wished to kill all rich people and establish a dictatorship of factory laborers. Virtually all were republicans.

"Christian Socialism" (F. D. Maurice in England) Fatherhood of God with the Brotherhood of Man.

Anarchism:

An offshoot of the revolutionary spirit engendered by socialism. At first more of a theoretical device to critique government and society, suggesting the reduction of regimentation as possible and emphasizing decentralization of power. Towards the end of the 19th century it inspired terrorist attacks on authority figures including kings, empresses, parliaments, and a president of the USA.

Marxism:

The most influential socialist philosophy that eventually became a doctrine that ruled nearly half of humanity in the 20th century and was responsible for deaths of as many as 100 million people. **Karl Marx** was a middle-class German writer, who lived most of his adult life in England supported by journalism and subsidies from the profits of a Manchester factory owned by his cohort **Friedrick Engels**. They jointly wrote *The Communist Manifesto* (1848*).

Marxism (or Communism) was based on the notion that the basis of life is class struggle (**dialectical materialism**); the dialectic (see Hegel above) drove history. The triumph of bourgeois capitalism that Marx incorrectly identified with several historical events in the 17th and 18th centuries (such as the English Civil War and the French Revolution) created industrialization, which for the first time gave mankind the opportunity to have abundance. It was no longer necessary to struggle for scarce wealth because machines could give everybody a good life. At the same time capitalism would **inevitably** concentrate resources in fewer and fewer hands until the **proletariat** (industrial working class) would be able to overthrow the rich and exterminate them in a bloody revolution. The rich would resist, sincerely believing for instance in the system of laws they had established to protect their property and in the religion they had had taught to the workers (as a kind of drug) which emphasized submission and rewards in the next world. Society could then be reordered to eliminate the spirit of competition. Even the institutions of the state such as the police, would wither away since crime was a product of unequal distribution of material goods. History would cease since class struggle would no longer be necessary. Near the end of his life Marx acknowledged it might be possible to achieve change in advanced societies by peaceful means.

Marx was wrong about almost everything he wrote except that capitalism is cruel. Above all, it became a puzzlement to his followers why wealth did not become concentrated solely in a tiny group of people in the advanced societies such as England and Germany. **Lenin** later came along and retrofitted Marxism in a way that made it possible to justify revolutions in less economically advanced societies such as Russia and China.

1848*: THE YEAR OF REVOLUTIONS

Only 1789* and 1989* reverberate in quite the same way as 1848* in the history of modern Europe. One famous historian wrote that is was the turning point in history in which history failed to turn. After 1848 relative social peace reigned until 1917.

Causes:

- Food shortages
- Weakness in factory production
- Low wages, unemployment
- Poor living conditions worsened in cities
- Discontent among peasants
- Nationalism
- Liberal reformism
- Domino effect

FRANCE
Dissatisfaction with corruption and the inefficiency of Louis Philippe's leadership plus a sense of national humiliation in foreign affairs precipitated overthrow of the July Monarchy. Serious conflict broke out between middle class liberals and the workers leading to violence in the **Bloody June Days**. The 2nd Republic marked the triumph of property owners and constitutionalism. The election of Napoleon's nephew (**Louis Napoleon** – r. 1852-70) as President was caused by fear of disorder and search for the return of military glory.

AUSTRIA
Metternich was driven into exile and the incompetent Emperor was replaced by a younger one (**Franz Joseph** – r. 1848-1916). Revolts in various parts of the Habsburg dominions were successfully repressed by the policy of keeping insurgents divided. Perhaps the most serious was the outbreak of nationalism in Hungary repressed by Russian troops called in by Vienna. Nicholas I was happy to oblige. Rural reforms pacified the peasantry and military conquest put down the Italians.

BRITAIN
Chartist (working class movement demanding the vote and other constitutional reforms) protest a flop. Alliance of middle and upper classes with the monarchy held firm.

PRUSSIA
Frederick William IV (r. 1840-61) forced to make some constitutional concessions.

GERMANY

Liberal nationalists call unofficial meeting of the **Frankfurt Parliament**. Plans to unify fall into two categories. The **Grossdeutsch** solution included the Austro-Hungarian empire, thus bringing millions of non-Germans along. The **Kleindeutsch** solution excluded Austria, which left millions of Germans out of the state and made illiberal Prussia the dominant force. The imperial crown was finally offered to the King of Prussia, who declined it because he would be limited by a liberal constitution and have to accept the throne from middle class liberals. Thus, perhaps the last chance for a peaceful unification of Germany was lost.

ITALY

Uprisings in the Austrian north and in the Papal States. Republican nationalist, **Joseph Mazzini** (d. 1872), founder of Young Italy, led a revolt in the Papal States that forced the Pope to flee Rome. Repressed by Austrian intervention. Pius IX returned to the Vatican a confirmed reactionary.

THE CRIMEAN WAR (1853-56)

Often overlooked but important. A conflict between Russia on the one hand and Great Britain, France, and the Ottoman Empire on the other. It was fought mainly on the Crimean peninsula in the Black Sea, hence the name given to the war. Austria stayed neutral, to the indignation of Nicholas I, who had bailed Franz Joseph out of difficulty in Hungary in 1849.

Causes:

- Russian foreign policy was to assert as much power as possible in the Balkans, destroy or subordinate Ottoman authority, gain free passage of shipping through the Dardanelles (and thus permanent warm water ports for commerce, and a naval presence in the Mediterranean.)
- Napoleon III of France was intent on winning military achievements to match his uncle's and win popularity.
- Britain regarded the Mediterranean as their lake, and thus a Russian naval presence was an unacceptable intrusion.
- Ottomans were trying to stave off collapse. They were already "The Sick Man of Europe".
- Technical dispute over religious authority in Jerusalem, really only a pretext.
- Sardinia enters war against Russia to gain leverage with France for unification of Italy.

Great Figures:

- **Florence Nightingale** (d. 1854) – addressed the inadequate medical treatment accorded British soldiers. Helped found the modern nursing profession. One of the first women not a monarch or writer to achieve international fame for work in the public realm.
- **Alexander II of Russia** (r. 1855-81) – succeeded his father, Nicholas I during the war. Negotiated peace and instituted reforms.

Outcomes:

- Implacable enmity by Russia towards Austria due to its failure to come to its aid during the war
- Sardinia gains a place at the negotiating table allowing Count Cavour to work with Napoleon III
- Russia reforms and rearms, becoming much more formidable
- Russia was blocked from acquiring access through the Dardanelles
- Military embarrassments (e.g. charge of the Light Brigade) and extraordinary number of deaths made engaging in continental warfare very unpopular in Britain. Hence it stood aside during the unifications of Italy and Germany, an ill-judged isolationist policy
- Ottomans staggered on for another half century, although they lost most of their Balkan territories in the years to come
- Balance of power preserved

UNIFICATIONS OF ITALY AND GERMANY

Nationalist aspirations for the unification of **Italy** were stimulated during the occupation of Italy by Napoleon I. Movements were repressed during the next few decades by the Congress system and Austria in particular. The attempt by **Mazzini** to establish an Italian republic failed in 1848. **Count Camillo di Cavour**, liberal Prime Minister of Sardinia (also called Piedmont or Savoy), a kingdom in northwest Italy, then organized the gradual conquest of the entire peninsula during the late 1850s and early 1860s. By the time of his death in 1861 all but the Pope's territories around Rome and the *irredenta* (unredeemed) in the northeast retained by Austria had been incorporated into a united Kingdom of Italy under the rule of the Sardinian King.

1. Cavour entered the Crimean War and gained the alliance of Napoleon III, ever on the lookout for military glory and territorial expansion. Cavour promised Nice and Savoy in exchange for military assistance against Austria
2. Cavour provoked war with Austria and gained Lombardy, but the withdrawal of Napoleon's support left Venetia in Austrian hands (1859)
3. Cavour helped the northern duchies of Modena, Parma, and Tuscany to overthrow their rulers and join the new Italy
4. Cavour assisted rabid nationalist **Garibaldi** (d.1882) to invade Sicily and Naples where he overthrew the Bourbon monarchy and marched north towards Rome
5. Cavour blocked Garibaldi's advance on Rome "protecting" the Pope, negotiated absorption of the Kingdom of the Two Sicilies and most of Papal territories into Italy
6. Gained Venetia from Austria during the Six Weeks War in 1867
7. Napoleon III had garrisoned Rome to protect Pius IX's remaining land. He was forced to recall these troops during the war with Prussia in 1870 when all but the Vatican itself was incorporated into Italy.

Thus Cavour, the leader of a small, weak country, was able to overcome opposition from France, the Pope, Austria, and the kings and princes of the Italian states. He also overcame the republicanism of Garibaldi and Mazzini. Britain did not intervene due to its isolationist policy despite its great interests in the Mediterranean.

Outcomes:

- A liberal, constitutional monarchy ruled a united Italian state, though suffrage limited until 1913
- The North conquered the South, and henceforward the North became the beneficiary of public spending and investment at the expense of the South (most emigrants from Italy fled the poverty of the South)
- The Papacy became a hostile prisoner in the Vatican until finally recognizing Italy in 1929; loses prestige
- The *irredenta* remained a festering wound that played a key role in World War I and the rise of Mussolini
- Italy remained weaker economically and militarily than its size suggested, crippled by corruption and an ineffective political structure
- Cavour never got the credit his work deserved, most of the public praise being given to the King

Nationalist aspirations for the unification of **Germany** were stimulated by the occupation by Napoleon I, who combined much of central Germany into a new Kingdom of Westphalia. Metternich and other German princes and kings helped dampen the nationalist movement until 1848, and Frederick William IV of Prussia rejected the imperial crown offered by the Frankfurt Parliament. An economic agreement (*Zollverein*) established by Prussia in 1834 made the advantages of unity more obvious.

The Prussian Prime Minister, **Otto von Bismarck** (d. 1898) a conservative junker and Prussian patriot decided the only way to preserve Prussian power was to conquer the rest of Germany and absorb it into a gigantic Prussian state. Like Cavour, he was a master of *Realpolitik.*

1. Bismarck provoked war with Denmark in alliance with Austria to seize the border duchies of Schleswig-Holstein
2. Bismarck provoked war with Austria, which was defeated rapidly by **von Moltke** (d. 1891) at the battle of **Sadowa** (1867). Austria was knocked out of contention as leader of a united Germany. The Catholic southern German states that allied with Catholic Austria were not punished, but northern Protestant Hanover was seized and the king overthrown
3. Bismarck goaded Napoleon III into war in 1870 (Franco-Prussian War). The pretext involved possible Hohenzollern succession to the Spanish throne (Ems Telegram). Southern German states allied with Prussia against France. Napoleon III was defeated and captured on the battlefield
4. Bismarck persuaded the King of Bavaria, the largest southern Catholic state, to offer the imperial crown to William I, King of Prussia, who became **German Emperor** 1871* (ceremony held in the Hall of Mirrors at Versailles)
5. Harsh peace imposed on humiliated France including heavy reparations and confiscation of two border provinces, **Alsace and Lorraine**. France became a perpetual enemy, thus ensuring the continued loyalty of the southern states to Prussian leadership

Thus Bismarck overcame the opposition of Austria, Denmark, the German Princes and Kings, and France to achieve unification. Russia was persuaded to remain neutral and Britain remained in isolation.

Outcomes:

- German Empire established 1871* headed by Hohenzollern dynasty in a federal state where smaller kingdoms and principalities retained their monarchs but in which Prussian power and the authority of the Emperor (Kaiser) predominated
- Bismarck a national hero who retained tight control over the state until his dismissal in 1890
- German Empire built on military victory
- France deeply aggrieved and sought revenge
- Italy gained Papal states and Venetia
- Austrian weakness offers the Hungarians an opportunity to gain more autonomy in the *Ausgleich* (1867) when the Dual Monarchy was established sharing a ruler, military, and diplomatic corps, but with a separate parliament and domestic government in Budapest
- Napoleon III overthrown and France returned to republican government (Third Republic)
- Bismarck pursued a pacific foreign policy thereafter
- Bismarck established a long-term alliance with Austria, while other states on the periphery increasingly sought security with each other, especially France and Russia, which seemed like encirclement to the Germans and aroused their anxiety
- Bismarck banned the Socialist Party but enacted social legislation to win loyalty of the working class
- Bismarck unsuccessfully pursued vendetta against independent sources of power outside his authority, such as the Catholic church – *Kulturkampf*

EUROPE IN THE SECOND HALF OF THE 19TH CENTURY

The map of Europe in 1871 was simpler in aspect than it ever had been or ever would be in modern times. Four huge empires bestrode the center and east: Russia, Germany, Austria-Hungary, and the Ottomans (most of the Balkans was still technically theirs). In the west Great Britain, France, and Italy controlled most of the territory, along with Spain, Portugal, and the three Scandinavian countries. The only small states were the Benelux countries, Switzerland, Greece, and Montenegro.

FRANCE

- **Second Empire** (Napoleon III) combined progressive economic policies, aggressive foreign policy, and authoritarian institutions. Concessions were made to the working class
- **The Paris Commune** (1871) – city felt betrayed by monarchists in the National Assembly, and anarchists and socialists exploited the chaos of defeat by Prussia to establish a radical regime. Suppressed violently
- **The Third Republic**, although it lasted from 1871 to 1940 was plagued by instability. Orleanists, Bonapartists, Legitimists (Bourbon line), Socialists, Communists, all lacked loyalty to the established political structures. Only the Liberals were pleased, but they distrusted the military and rightly feared reactionary influences (Dreyfus Affair 1894-99).
- Maintenance of the tricolor flag (orig. French Revolution) provoked monarchist antagonism and refusal of the throne by Henry "V", the Bourbon pretender
- Military officers, clergy and aristocracy disaffected
- **Dreyfus Affair** (1894) involving espionage charges against an innocent Jewish officer opened up such serious rifts in French society that the Republic barely survived; Zola, "*J'accuse*"
- The one shared value was hatred for Germany
- French population growth much slower than most other Western countries due to system of land tenure. France lags in the industrial sector, although its empire in Africa and Asia grew large

AUSTRIA

- Austria-Hungary (after 1867) held together by the Habsburg bureaucracy and personal loyalty to **Franz Joseph**
- "Dual Monarchy" after *Ausgleich* 1867
- Composed of many different nationalities (Poles, Germans, Czechs, Ukrainians, Hungarians, Romanians, Croats, Slovenians, Italians, Serbs, etc.) Some of these groups had aspirations for independence (e.g. Poles) while others yearned to be joined with fellow countrymen already independent (e.g. Serbs).
- Competing for territory and influence with Russia as Ottoman authority in the Balkans evaporated
- Hungarian zealots repress other nationalities under their control
- Vienna a center of medical and cultural excellence; the city center was rebuilt on a grand scale; vicious anti-Semitism aroused there

RUSSIA

- **Alexander II** – (d. 1881) was a modernizing, Westernizing Tsar
  - a) emancipates serfs (1861*)
  - b) establishes trial by jury and other legal reforms
  - c) establishes *zemstvos*, local elected councils
  - d) military reforms
  - e) plans constitution limiting the autocracy

- Although serfs are freed from the landlords, the *mir*, a system of shared land tenure tied them to each other; they also were given poor quality land, and had to pay off long-term mortgages to compensate landowners
- Smaller gentry also hurt by the serf abolition program, and most were struggling seriously or bankrupt before the 1917 revolution began
- Secret police and censorship were retained and expanded in the wake of populist and nihilist terror campaigns; numerous attempts made to kill officials, royalty
- Limited industrialization
- Polish rebellion 1863 crushed
- Massive illiteracy and small middle class
- Tsar assassinated by terrorists 1881
- **Alexander III** (r. 1881-94) succeeded his murdered father and instituted aggressive and effective repression; halted reforms
- **Nicholas II** (r. 1894-1917) tried to follow his father's policies but was inept and incompetent. He barely survived an attempted revolution in 1905 after the loss in the Russo-Japanese War. He was forced to grant a parliament (Duma), but renéged on his promises when he could. His minister, **Stolypin**, introduced land reform, but was assassinated in 1909. **Count Witte** fostered further industrialization, which only created a greater threat to autocracy. Trans-Siberian railway.
- Terrible **pogroms** were directed by the state against the Jewish population under Alexander III and Nicholas II

BRITAIN

- **Queen Victoria** (r. 1837-1901) embodied a stricter moral code emanating from the top of society, gloried in the expansion of empire, symbolized stability and grandeur of "Victorian" Britain; Empress of India
- Increased moves towards democracy: 2nd Reform Act 1867, expanded electorate; secret ballot 1872; 3rd Reform Act 1884 moved close to universal male suffrage
- "Tory Democracy" – **Benjamin Disraeli** led the Conservative party towards electoral reform and paternalistic legislation to win votes from the working class – included public health, sanitation, workers housing, and protection for trade unions
- **William Gladstone** led the Liberal Party in reform legislation; with the Education Act (1870) the government took responsibility for elementary schools; competitive exams for the civil service; reformed universities; free trade
- Irish politicians agitated for Irish autonomy **(Home Rule)** and disrupted British politics; Gladstone accepted Home Rule and split the Liberal Party. Home Rule finally granted in 1914, but was deferred by World War I
- House of Lords emasculated by Parliament Act of 1911
- Sun never sets on the British Empire

The European population grew quickly during the second half of the 19th century, literacy spread, and wealth expanded even more rapidly. Industrialization lifted the standard of living and productivity of Western society to incredible heights compared to unindustrialized areas, especially in Africa and Asia but even in comparison to Ireland, Spain, or Russia. Compared with other areas of the world, Europeans in the developed regions married late, had smaller families, lived longer, and accumulated more wealth. Many families practiced contraception.

The **"Second" Industrial Revolution** after 1850 was stimulated by the Bessemer process of steel making, the chemical industry, electrical power to generate machinery, transportation, and eventually lighting. Oil began slowly to replace coal as fuel for ships and the internal combustion engine (i.e. **automobiles** [Daimler 1887] – though these were largely confined to the upper middle classes and above until the 1930s and the middle classes and above until the 1960s). The use of oil also began a system of dependency on foreign sources because except for some found in the Balkans, oil was not produced in Europe until its discovery in the North Sea in the 1970s.

Industrial organization moved to a larger and larger scale, particularly in the coal and steel industries and armaments. This was made possible by the legal reforms establishing protection for shareholders from indebtedness (**Limited Liability** – Ltd.), and the creation of **cartels** (Krupp in Germany, Vickers Armstrong in England, Schneider-Creusot in France). Increased imports of rubber and industrial diamonds from the new colonies further stimulated growth and inventive technologies.

A **consumer economy** developed characterized by sophisticated advertising, department stores, inexpensive luxuries. Mass circulation newspapers and magazines appeared.

Boom/bust cycles still caused serious disruption and mass unemployment.

Child labor and working hours for adults declined. Welfare legislation was introduced in many countries to provide for sickness and injury, pensions, and education.

The draft was introduced or reformed in many countries both to provide the number of troops required for modern mass armies and to bind young people from diverse regions into a single patriotic mass.

The rise of a very large **middle class** in the developed countries created dramatic demand for schools and eventually more universities. The professions expanded rapidly and set standards for admission – teachers, physicians, engineers, etc. The officer corps grew large as armies expanded into multi-million man organizations. Many new occupations of a "white collar" nature such as secretaries, typists, telephonists, clerks, while they did not pay very well, created a **"lower middle class"** separate from factory workers.

Jews were gradually emancipated in most countries, although anti-Semitism was serious in France and Austria, and horrific in Russia.

Aristocrats were challenged in more and more ways, by democracy, promotion by merit, industrial wealth, and a popular press. However, many retained considerable riches and power.

Urbanization continued to progress as more and more people moved from rural areas into cities. Poor housing and sanitation remained, but improvements were made and fewer outbreaks of disease occurred. The centers of many major cities were redesigned and public parks built (Paris under **Baron Haussmann** saw the most radical transformation). Large broad boulevards, museums, subways systems, parks, zoos, and new monuments such as the Eiffel Tower were built. Suburbs expanded.

Women remained dependent on and legally inferior to men. Middle class women did not work and those in the lower classes suffered inferior pay. Most now withdrew from the labor force upon marriage. However, feminism was gathering support, focused largely on gaining the **vote** and **legal equality** for women. New technologies such as electricity and vacuum cleaners created an easier work environment at home.

Feminists agitated with increasing force. **Pankhursts** in Britain. Contraceptive techniques were improved and knowledge about them disseminated more widely.

Emigration from Europe reached a peak in the late 19th and early 20th centuries. Cheap steamboat transportation made it possible for even poor families to travel, often with a father going first, and earning the money to allow his wife and children to follow. People fled political oppression, religious persecution, famine, and poverty. Ireland, southern Italy, and Russia produced the greatest number, but people also sought a new life in proportionally high numbers from Scandinavia, Spain, and Germany. Destinations included North and South America, Asiatic Russia, and Australia.

Socialism flourished in the effluence of raw capitalism. Trade unionism developed, and was effective in helping alleviate working conditions and pay. The spread of male suffrage gave workers a voice, and parliamentary socialist parties worked within constitutional bounds to help the poor. First and Second Internationals met.

Russia:
The terrible conditions of early Russian industrialization were a breeding ground for radical politics. Troops shooting protestors in front of the Tsar's palace in 1905 seriously weakened the bond between the monarch and the people (**Bloody Sunday**) precipitated by loss in Russo-Japanese War. However, the most dangerous opposition to the Tsar developed among Marxist exiles, who split into the more moderate Mensheviks and the extreme radical **Bolsheviks** led by **Lenin**. He attributed the continued success of capitalism in the West to the new imperialism (which provided new sources of investment) and he argued a small band of elite revolutionaries could seize control even of an unindustrialized society and guide it to the Communist utopia (Vanguard of the Proletariat)

Britain:

Radical socialism never took root here. The **Labour Party** representing working class interests operated through constitutional and electoral channels. Socialist intellectuals formed the **Fabian Society**, which advocated a non-revolutionary path to change

France:

Socialism was fragmented in France. The Anarchists refused to enter the political system. Jean Jaurès led the socialist revisionists. Georges Sorel led the Syndicalists (trade unionists) Germany: Although banned from political activity under Bismarck, the socialists were brought into the parliamentary (Reichstag) system under **William II**. The leading Marxist leader **Eduard Bernstein** advocated **"Revisionism"**, a gradualist and peaceful approach to the long-term victory of the proletariat using the existing structure of the state

1. Great Britain ended slavery in its empire in 1833

   (A)   due to a decline in demand for new slaves
   (B)   despite an increase in demand for products grown on slave plantations
   (C)   because the pope and the Roman Catholic church demanded it
   (D)   in order to humiliate Russia
   (E)   because coolies from China had made cheap replacements possible

2.

	Year 1800	Year 1850
Great Britain	620	1290
German States	40	260
France	90	270
Austria	20	100
Belgium	40	70
Russia	20	70
Italy	10	20
Spain	10	20

   This table lists

   (A)   number of warships
   (B)   millions of soldiers
   (C)   1000's of horsepower of steam power
   (D)   square mileage of African colonies
   (E)   millions in growth of population

3. The Crystal Palace erected in Hyde Park in London in 1851 under the direction of Prince Albert

   (A)   was built to exhibit the success of the British industrial revolution
   (B)   was a cathedral to encourage revived religious fervor
   (C)   housed the royal family before Buckingham Palace was built
   (D)   was built to honor the Duke of Wellington
   (E)   housed the first modern swimming pool

4. All of the following were outcomes of the Crimean War fought between 1853 and 1856 EXCEPT

   (A) contributed to Italian independence due to Sardinian participation
   (B) led to British military disengagement from continental affairs for half a century
   (C) the Austrian failure to assist Russia in return for help in 1848 increased the rivalry between these nations in the Balkans
   (D) promoted better medical care for soldiers in the future
   (E) strengthened the Ottoman empire's control over the Balkans

5. In nineteenth-century Britain who among the following were NOT members of the middle classes?

   (A) factory owners
   (B) lawyers
   (C) shopkeepers
   (D) bishops
   (E) physicians

6. The population of Ireland was cut by a quarter during the middle of the nineteenth century as a result of

   (A) routine emigration
   (B) an influenza pandemic
   (C) a potato blight
   (D) acceptance of birth control by the church
   (E) a civil war

7. The establishment of new prison systems and police forces in mid-nineteenth-century Europe reflected

   (A) a response to the upsurge of industrialization, urbanization, and radicalism
   (B) desire of autocratic monarchs to establish police states
   (C) new sympathy for the plight of the poor
   (D) religious revivalist fervor
   (E) need to find jobs for the unemployed

8. Which of the following was not an enemy of Russia during the Crimean War?

    (A)   Great Britain
    (B)   Austria
    (C)   France
    (D)   the Ottoman Empire
    (E)   Sardinia

9. Early legislation restricting child labor in factories in England was hard to enforce for all of the following reasons EXCEPT

    (A)   not enough inspectors
    (B)   owners needed cheap unskilled labor
    (C)   parents desperately needed income
    (D)   children were dependent on parents and employers
    (E)   the courts never upheld the rights of ordinary people

10. Among the causes of unrest within the Habsburg dominions in 1848 were all of the following EXCEPT

    (A)   student unrest
    (B)   aristocratic resurgence among the German nobility
    (C)   Magyar nationalism centered in Budapest
    (D)   Czech liberalism centered in Prague
    (E)   angry peasants

11. In Western Europe the literacy rate during the first half of the nineteenth century exceeded

    (A)   5%
    (B)   10%
    (C)   25%
    (D)   35%
    (E)   50%

12. Nineteenth-century Romanticism emphasized all of the following EXCEPT

    (A)   formal structure
    (B)   imagination
    (C)   emotion
    (D)   heroism
    (E)   personal fulfillment

13. The parliament of German peoples that met in Frankfurt in 1848 was

    (A) dominated by bourgeois liberals
    (B) revived Diet of the Holy Roman Empire
    (C) organized by Prince Metternich
    (D) chose Franz Joseph of Austria as the first Emperor of Germany
    (A) composed of clerical conservatives

14. In the mid-nineteenth century the largest city in Europe was

    (A) Moscow
    (B) London
    (C) Paris
    (D) Berlin
    (E) Vienna

15. The revolution in Paris in 1848 called into question all of the following EXCEPT

    (A) the Orleanist monarchy
    (B) bourgeois capitalism
    (C) gender hierarchy
    (D) the exclusive franchise
    (E) patriotism

Europe, A HISTORY by Norman Davies, © 1993 by Norman Davies.
Used by permission of Oxford University Press, Inc.

16. This map depicts Europe in

    (A)   1800
    (B)   1812
    (C)   1815
    (D)   1832
    (E)   1848

17. "You cannot enter a Gothic church without feeling a kind of awe and a vague sentiment of the Divinity. You were all at once carried back to those times when a fraternity of monks ... met to prostrate themselves before the altar and to chant the praises of the Lord, amid the tranquility and the silence of the night."

This passage was written by a

    (A)   Marxist
    (B)   Utopian socialist
    (C)   Romantic
    (D)   physiocrat
    (E)   Girondist

18. The Reform Ministry of 1830-34 in Britain accomplished all of the following EXCEPT

    (A)   extended the parliamentary franchise
    (B)   defeated France in war
    (C)   abolished slavery in the British empire
    (D)   enacted the New Poor Law
    (E)   restricted working hours for factory children

19. The Reform Act of 1832 in Britain

    (A)   created a standing army for the first time
    (B)   expanded the number of voters
    (C)   abolished the House of Lords
    (D)   replaced William IV with Queen Victoria
    (E)   established a civil service

20. Liberalism was likely to win the most support among which of the following groups?

    (A)   peasants
    (B)   factory workers
    (C)   nobles
    (D)   the bourgeoisie
    (E)   the clergy

21. Factory owners in nineteenth-century industrial cities

    (A)   welcomed workers organizing into unions
    (B)   were ambivalent about the utility of unions
    (C)   tried to block the formation of unions
    (D)   paid workers well enough to that unions were rarely formed
    (E)   ignored unions even after they were formed

22. The July monarchy in France that lasted from 1830 to 1848 was noted for

    (A)   bourgeois liberalism
    (B)   autocratic absolutism
    (C)   ultra-rightest supremacy
    (D)   the White Terror
    (E)   democratic franchise

23. The failure of the British Chartist movement of the 1830s and 1840s was due to

    (A)   failure to gain popular support
    (B)   demands for a republican constitution
    (C)   decision to use violence
    (D)   continued strength and confidence of the aristocracy
    (E)   adoption of their program by the Whigs

24. Wages and living conditions began to improve in fully industrialized countries after

    (A)   1750
    (B)   1775
    (C)   1800
    (D)   1825
    (E)   1850

Chapter XI

The Nineteenth Century - II

1. The worst persecution of the Jews in the late nineteenth and early twentieth centuries took place in

   (A) Prussia
   (B) England
   (C) Spain
   (D) Russia
   (E) the Netherlands

2. Anarchists assassinated all of the following rulers during the late nineteenth and early twentieth centuries EXCEPT

   (A) Tsar Alexander II of Russia
   (B) President William McKinley of the USA
   (C) King Umberto I of Italy
   (D) Empress Elizabeth of Austria-Hungary
   (E) Queen Victoria of Great Britain

3. The establishment of the Third Republic in France in the 1870s

   (A) was universally hailed by the French people
   (B) was due to Napoleon III having no male heir
   (C) was a compromise unsatisfactory to the right
   (D) occurred with the blessing of the Orleanist pretender
   (E) was an army *coup d'etat*

4. Professionalized team sports that emerged during the later nineteenth century were largely due to

   (A) more leisure time and money available to the working class
   (B) royal patronage
   (C) anxiety on the part of the church to fill workers' free time with approved activities
   (D) desire to see violence and cruelty
   (E) interest of women in more exciting activities than sewing and cleaning

5.

ENGLAND AND WALES

1861-69	6.16
1871	5.94
1876	5.62
1890-99	4.13
1900-09	3.30
1910-14	2.82

The figures in the table above refer to which of the following?

(A)   tons of coal in millions
(B)   average family size
(C)   manufacturing productivity rate
(D)   decline in commercial shipping by British ships
(E)   miles of railway per capita

6. The Suez Canal was built by a commercial company with funding from and headquarters located in

(A)   Great Britain
(B)   Ottoman Empire
(C)   Japan
(D)   Germany
(E)   France

7. Electricity made possible all of the following EXCEPT

(A)   telephone
(B)   incandescent bulb
(C)   telegraph
(D)   refrigeration
(E)   ball bearings

8. Germany began to overtake Britain as the industrial leader of Europe in the late nineteenth century for all of the following reasons EXCEPT

(A)   better port facilities
(B)   its industrialists were more entreprenuerial
(C)   German banks were ready to take greater risks
(D)   better scientific and technical schools
(E)   formation of large cartels

9. A British working woman in the second half of the nineteenth century was most likely to be a

    (A) mine worker
    (B) doctor
    (C) secretary
    (D) farmer
    (E) railway conductor

10. All of the following played an important role in the unification of Italy EXCEPT

    (A) Victor Emmanuel II
    (B) Camillo di Cavour
    (C) Giuseppe Garibaldi
    (D) Cesare di Beccaria
    (E) Guiseppe Mazzini

11. Bismarck extended the vote to most adult male Germans because he

    (A) was a passionate democrat
    (B) wanted to copy the English
    (C) was convinced conservative peasants and artisans would outvote middle class liberals
    (D) wanted to counterbalance Russian emigration
    (E) was forced by the Emperor to do so

12. William Gladstone, Liberal Prime Minister of Britain during the second half of the nineteenth century, supported all of the following policies EXCEPT

    (A) extension of the franchise
    (B) spread of public education
    (C) Home Rule for Ireland
    (D) merit exams in the military and civil service
    (E) abolition of the monarchy

13. "In virtue of the new dispositions ... the peasants attached to the soil will be invested within a term fixed by the law with all the rights of free cultivators."

This decree was issued by

(A) Pope Leo XIII
(B) Emperor Napoleon III
(C) Tsar Alexander II
(D) Emperor Franz Josef I
(E) Prince Bismarck

14. Nineteenth-century novelists such as Charles Dickens and Elizabeth Gaskell incorporated all of the following into their books EXCEPT

(A) moral values
(B) contrasts between social classes
(C) miseries caused by industrialization
(D) inequality and inefficiency of the law
(E) communist utopianism

15. Which of the following would NOT have been considered lower middle class?

(A) telephone operator
(B) bookkeeper
(C) bank teller
(D) sales clerk
(E) bricklayer

16. Emperor Napoleon III of France lost his throne due to the

(A) failure of his Mexican adventure
(B) financial crash of 1857
(C) unpopularity of his wife
(D) defeat in war with Prussia
(E) Paris commune

17.   PER CAPITA GNP OF THE EUROPEAN POWERS 1830-1890
                    (in 1960 US dollars and prices)

	1830	1860	1890
Britain	346	558	785
Italy	265	301	311
France	264	365	515
Germany	245	354	537
Russia	170	178	182

Which of the following statements is true about the above table?

(A)   Britain experienced its greatest rise in absolute terms between 1830 and 1860
(B)   Italy was always the poorest of the great powers
(C)   Germany's population was not as well off as Britain's even after full industrialization
(D)   France experienced an economic setback between 1830 and 1860
(E)   Russia's rise in standard of living was rapid after 1860

Hulton Archive/Getty Images

18. The Vienna Opera House, pictured above, opened in 1869. Its construction

(A)   marked the revival of the Gothic style
(B)   was typical of the renewal of major city centers in the second half of the nineteenth century
(C)   showed that patronage of the arts had passed from monarchies to republics
(D)   is an example of the decline in the visual arts in the nineteenth century
(E)   helped to create a new art form called "opera"

19. The "Dual Monarchy" is a term that refers to which of the following pairs of countries?

    (A)   Prussia and Bavaria
    (B)   England and Scotland
    (C)   Austria and Hungary
    (D)   Holland and Belgium
    (E)   Spain and Portugal

20. Establishment of large public parks in urban areas during the second half of the nineteenth century were sponsored by

    (A)   working class self-help cooperatives
    (B)   the Chartists
    (C)   aristocrats anxious to divest urban property due to falling values
    (D)   liberal town councils promoting health and recreation
    (E)   entrepreneurs out to make a profit

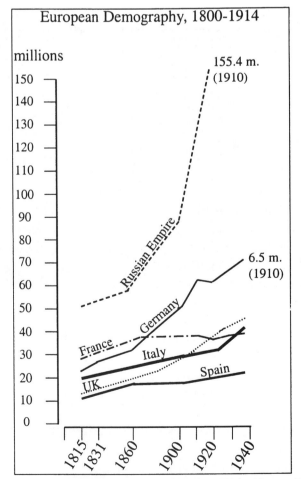

Europe, A HISTORY by Norman Davies, © 1993 by Norman Davies.
Used by permission of Oxford University Press, Inc.

21. All the following statements are true about this graph EXCEPT

   (A) Russia's population expanded the most rapidly
   (B) Britain's population accelerated rapidly during the nineteenth century
   (C) Germany became much larger than Britain
   (D) France remained remarkably stable in size
   (E) Italy was never smaller than Britain

European Railways 1835-1905

Length of the railway (■ = 2000 km)

	Austria	France	Germany	UK	Sweden	Italy	Russian Empire
1835	—	141	6	544			
1855	1588	5037	7826	11,744	—	1207	1049
1875	10,331	19,357	27,970	23,365	3679	8018	19,029
1895	16,420	36,240	46,500	28,986	9756	15,970	37,058
1905	21,002	39,607	56,739	31,456	12,647	17,078	61,085

Europe, A HISTORY by Norman Davies, © 1993 by Norman Davies.
Used by permission of Oxford University Press, Inc.

22. This chart indicates that

   (A) Russia was the most industrialized country in Europe
   (B) Britain always had a greater length of track than any other state
   (C) Italy increased at a greater rate than anywhere else between 1855 and 1875
   (D) proportionate to its size Austria had the largest rail system in 1905
   (E) the acceleration of German industrial growth during the later nineteenth century and after is shown by its railways

23. The conflict between "Slavophiles" and "Westernizers" involved which of the following?

    (A) Russian nationalists resisting the policies of industrialization and integration
    (B) those who wanted a union of all the Slavic states vs. the Poles who wanted to unite with Germany
    (C) Bulgarian versus Roumanian nationalists
    (D) Albanian and Bosnian nationalists who wanted to conquer Greece against those who wanted a federal union within the Ottoman empire
    (E) Followers of the Orthodox leader in Constantinople versus those who acknowledged the pope in Rome

24. During the nineteenth century middle class women did all of the following EXCEPT

    (A) cared for children
    (B) planned meals
    (C) worked in department stores
    (D) supervised the work of servants
    (E) organized social activities

25. The growth of cartels in Europe during the second half of the nineteenth century

    (A) was only permitted in the colonial empires
    (B) replaced limited liability companies
    (C) allowed a few large companies to dominate production and distribution
    (D) was found only in Russia and Austria-Hungary
    (E) was carried out through government ownership

Chapter XII

World Supremacy

THE NEW IMPERIALISM

During the second half of the 19th century, especially between 1880 and 1900, European powers used their military and economic might to impose control on vast portions of Africa and Asia. Although the British and French lost huge empires in the 18th century, they gained even larger ones in the 19th. In some cases, such as China, European power was exercised indirectly, while in Africa a more official colonial presence was established. The British, of course, continued to hold a huge empire in India, and presided over loyal dominions in Canada, Australia, and New Zealand.

As most colonies won independence in the 1940s-70s, views on imperialism both among the colonized and the European intelligentsia were almost wholly negative and condemnatory. Most historians also concluded that only in certain instances did Europeans actually net a profit from imperial control. Often they ruled at a loss. In recent years African, Asian, and European historians have begun to see the process in a less ideological way and noted the benefits as well as the losses and humiliations inherent in the process.

Causes:

- Search for more markets from European manufactured goods
- Search for raw materials: rubber, coco, gold, diamonds, oil, and minerals
- Missionaries sought to convert non-Christian peoples
- "Keeping up with the Joneses" – search for status and desire not to "fall behind"
- Explorers and adventurers desiring to visit uncharted regions
- Need for supply and coaling stations for ships
- Need to secure strategic points in order to protect existing empires (e.g. Suez Canal, Malta, Cape Town, Singapore)
- Search for places to invest capital
- Social Darwinism – sense of racial superiority, paternalism, "White Man's Burden"
- Discovery of quinine made penetration of malarial areas possible for the first time
- Railways, telegraph, the machine gun, steamboats, etc. used to control vast areas cheaply

Outcomes:

- Britain secured a dominant global position not seriously challenged until 1914, and not wholly lost until after World War II; control of the Suez Canal, Malta, and Gibraltar made the Mediterranean a British lake until 1945; fought to suppress Boer control of rich South Africa (1899-1902) – gold, diamonds
- French empire smaller but important to trade and national pride and identity
- Dutch empire did not expand, but discovery of oil in the East Indies sustained power at a higher level than Holland's size would otherwise justify
- Germans got the booby prizes, the pickings left over after the British and French had finished. Heightened German paranoia
- China turned into a warring, corrupt, drug-ridden, helpless giant (though much of this was due to its own culture's inability to cope with modernity – unlike Japan, which industrialized rapidly and became an imperial power in its own right)
- USA began to emerge on the world stage. Defeated Spain in 1898 and began to build its own empire in the Caribbean and Pacific – Panama Canal
- Globalization of the world economy picked up speed. Steam ships, the Suez and Panama canals, the telegraph, trans-oceanic cables, refrigerated ships, etc. extended the reach of the European economy hugely
- The standard of living in Europe continued to rise and the range of consumer products was greatly diversified.
- Even the lowest class workers in Europe were persuaded by their governments that they were superior masters over the colonialized, inferior peoples of Asia and Africa. This diffused social tension at home and created a cross-class shared sense of national mission and solidarity
- Italians feel "left out" and humiliated. Their one major bid to establish an empire led to the only major defeat by an African army of a European one in Ethiopia
- In Africa only Liberia and Ethiopia escaped colonial status
- In Asia only Siam, Persia, and Afghanistan survived free
- The Russians sold Alaska to the USA but retained a gigantic and rich empire in Siberia, which was gradually populated by emigration from European Russia, and expanded southward into the Caucasus towards Afghanistan and India
- Huge improvements in infrastructure: roads, railways, ports, bridges, etc. built. Hospitals, schools opened. Children of native elites educated in Britain and France
- New agricultural techniques and crops were introduced, and famines relieved or eliminated
- Cruel and inhumane treatment of some native peoples by Europeans, especially in Leopold II of Belgium's Congo
- Cruel and inhumane native practices abolished and slavery largely ended

1. One of the reasons Germany began to fear Russia in the period 1900 to 1914 was the

   (A)   Russian alliance with Japan
   (B)   Russian alliance with Austria
   (C)   Russian capture of Constantinople
   (D)   completion of a naval fleet matching Germany's in size
   (E)   rapid rate of Russian industrialization

2. The number of British colonial administrators governing the whole of the Indian empire in 1900 totaled

   (A)   6,000
   (B)   50,000
   (C)   100,000
   (D)   250,000
   (E)   600,000

3. In his book on imperialism Lenin argued that

   (A)   capitalism led to imperialism
   (B)   imperialism was a wholly benign development
   (C)   Marx had predicted imperialism correctly
   (D)   Europe should attack the United States before it was too late
   (E)   imperialism would make Britain permanently safe from revolution

Courtesy of the National Portrait Gallery, London

4. This photograph of Queen Victoria highlights her

   (A)   role as an autocratic ruler
   (B)   enjoyment of the mild English climate
   (C)   role as empress of India
   (D)   position as grandmother of Europe
   (E)   loneliness without her family

5. "We don't want to fight,
    But by jingo if we do,
    We've got the men,
    We've got the ships
    We've got the money too!
    The Russians will not have Constantinople!"

    The above stanza refers to

    (A)   Ottoman control of the Black Sea
    (B)   threats to British interests in the Mediterranean
    (C)   Austrian control of the Crimea
    (D)   German control of Morocco
    (E)   French interests in Algeria and Egypt

6. The harshest rule suffered by any African colony was imposed by

    (A)   Victoria of Britain in Nigeria
    (B)   Leopold II of Belgium in the Congo
    (C)   Nicholas II of Russia in Ethiopia
    (D)   Napoleon III of France in Mali
    (E)   Wilhelm II of Germany in Togoland

7. Victorian India was a multi-cultural and multi-ethnic society in which the most important division lay between

    (A)   Muslims and Hindus
    (B)   princely states and direct British rule
    (C)   language versus ethnic groups
    (D)   Chinese immigrants and the native population
    (E)   rural versus urban areas

8. "All the remaining European culture-bearing peoples possess areas outside our continent where their languages and customs can take firm root and flourish. This fact, so painful to [our] national pride, also represents a great economic disadvantage."

    "Our nation" in the above passage was

    (A)   Russia
    (B)   Germany
    (C)   France
    (D)   Spain
    (E)   Britain

9. Between 1816 and 1850 how many Europeans left their home countries to begin new lives overseas?

   (A)   50,000
   (B)   100,000
   (C)   500,000
   (D)   750,000
   (E)   5,000,000

10. China succumbed to European imperialism in the nineteenth century for all the following reasons EXCEPT

   (A)   poor leadership
   (B)   internal rebellions
   (C)   resistance to technological innovation
   (D)   no previous experience meeting the West
   (E)   unwillingness to trade with Europeans

11. "History shows me one way, and one way only, in which a state of civilization has been produced, namely, the struggle of race with race, and the survival of the physically and mentally fitter race."

   This passage encapsulates the primary idea of

   (A)   Social Darwinism
   (B)   Fabianism
   (C)   Marxism
   (D)   Positivism
   (E)   Existentialism

12. During the nineteenth century the Mediterranean Sea became a "British lake" because all of the following were controlled by the English EXCEPT

   (A)   Egypt
   (B)   Malta
   (C)   Gibraltar
   (D)   Cyprus
   (E)   Sicily

13. Britain and France helped prop up the failing Ottoman Empire during the nineteenth century because

(A)   of increased religious toleration during the Victorian period
(B)   the Ottomans assisted them in keeping Greece from being independent
(C)   romantic feelings about the glories of Constantinople
(D)   fear that Russian power would penetrate into the Mediterranean
(E)   personal regard for Sultan Abdul Hamid II

14. Which country among the following hoped to establish unbroken sovereignty in East Africa stretching from Cairo in Egypt to Capetown in South Africa?

(A)   France
(B)   Spain
(C)   Russia
(D)   Great Britain
(E)   Italy

15. By 1815 Great Britain had accumulated an empire that included what proportion of the world's population?

(A)   one in two
(B)   one in five
(C)   one in ten
(D)   one in twenty
(E)   one in fifty

16. The Russo-Japanese War that took place between 1904 and 1905

(A)   was a serious blow to the authority of Tsar Nicholas II
(B)   was a huge setback for Japanese expansionism
(C)   was the last war fought with sailing ships
(D)   demonstrated Russian military superiority
(E)   allowed China to be divided equally between Russia and Japan

17. Bismarck's attitude towards acquiring colonial possessions for Germany was

(A)   enthusiastic
(B)   total opposition
(C)   indifferent
(D)   embarrassed
(E)   limited interest

18. China was twice defeated in war by a European power which sought to force it to accept imports of opium during the mid-nineteenth century. This country was

   (A) Great Britain
   (B) Germany
   (C) Spain
   (D) France
   (E) Italy

19. European countries were motivated to assert imperial control over countries on other continents during the second half of the nineteenth century by all of the following EXCEPT

   (A) economic profits
   (B) rivalries with other European powers
   (C) missionary zeal
   (D) refocus domestic discontent
   (E) regain territories lost in the eighteenth century

20. Which of the following countries did NOT undergo significant expansion during the imperialist age of the nineteenth century?

   (A) Britain
   (B) Spain
   (C) Russia
   (D) France
   (E) United States

21. European imperialism in Africa was facilitated by all of the following EXCEPT

   (A) discovery of quinine
   (B) invention of the telegraph
   (C) use of steam boats
   (D) advanced rifles
   (E) submarines

No testing material on this page.

Chapter XIII

Intellectual Turmoil

The second half of the 19th century produced some of the supreme intellectual achievements of human history. But it was also a time of darkening visions and cultural confusion. We achieved a greatly enhanced understanding of ourselves, but the price was an increasing fear that the world was irrational, morality all relative, and that we exist in a state of uncertainty. The idea of "progress" still held the field, but some began to doubt. There was a more healthy and open attitude towards sex, and an unhealthy appetite for war.

Great Figures:

- **Charles Lyell** – *Principles of Geology* (1832)
- **Charles Darwin** – published *The Origin of Species* in 1859. His **theory of evolution** changed the way we looked at ourselves. Met fierce resistance from religious critics. Later spawned racist theory called **Social Darwinism**.
- **August Comte** (d. 1857) – positivism – social improvement to be based on collection of facts – growth of social sciences to be helpful to society
- **Herbert Spencer** (d. 1903) – evolutionary ethics, Social Darwinism
- **Theodor Herzel** (d. 1904) – Zionism
- **Pius IX** – (d. 1878) the ostrich approach to modern science – ignore it – *Syllabus of Errors*; Vatican I – Pope is infallible when speaking *ex cathedra* (1870)
- **Leo XIII** – (d. 1903) reconciled science with faith and Scripture – *Rerum Novarum*
- **Gregor Mendel** (d. 1884) – genetics
- **Sir James Frazer** (d. 1941) – anthropology
- **Louis Pasteur** (d. 1895) – Pasteurization, vaccinations
- **Marie Curie** – (d. 1934) isolated radium
- **Pavlov** – (d. 1936) – behavioralism, "conditioning"
- **Max Planck** (d. 1947) – quantum theory of energy
- **Albert Einstein** (d. 1955) – theory of relativity
- **Lord Rutherford** (d. 1937) – nuclear physics
- **Walter Heisenberg** (d. 1976) – uncertainty principle
- **Sigmund Freud** (d. 1939) – psychoanalysis. Human sexual impulses form personality – id, ego, superego. Dreams are the fulfillment of suppressed wishes
- **Friedrich Nietzsche** (d. 1900) – challenged existing morality and values; God is dead; will to power; Christianity the religion of the weak
- **Schliemann** – modern archeology, discovery of ancient Troy
- **Picasso** (d. 1973) – pre-1914 period develops **Cubism**, portrays people in inhuman forms

145

The response to these intellectual developments and world events was increasingly inchoate and pessimistic. The British novelist, Charles Dickens, depicted grim realities. The Russian Count **Tolstoy** in his great novels, especially *War and Peace*, saw mankind as victims of fate. Flaubert and Zola rejected Romanticism in a spirit of harsh realism. Ibsen and Shaw were also not optimistic about the human condition and drew searing portraits of inhumanity. Munch's famous painting of an alienated man holding his head, "The Scream" (1908), symbolized profound despair.

More romantic impulses fueled Wagner's operas and the lyrical beauty of French **Impressionist** paintings.

1. Among the greatest scientific breakthroughs of the late nineteenth and the early twentieth centuries more occurred in which of the following than the others?

    (A) physics
    (B) optics
    (C) astronomy
    (D) medicine
    (E) phrenology

2. In a typical French city in 1840 about half the people attended mass regularly. By 1900 what percentage still did so?

    (A) 16
    (B) 30
    (C) 36
    (D) 41
    (E) 45

3. "Authors of the highest eminence seem to be fully satisfied with the view that each species has been independently created. To my mind it accords better with what we know of the laws impressed on matter by the Creator, that the production and extinction of the past and present inhabitants of the world should have been due to secondary causes, all beings are the lineal descendants of some few beings which lived long ago."

    This passage was written by

    (A) Nietzsche
    (B) Pope Pius IX
    (C) Darwin
    (D) Chateaubriand
    (E) Comte

4. Which of the following is incorrectly paired?

    (A) Darwin and biology
    (B) Spencer and philosophy
    (C) Renan and theology
    (D) Mendel and genetics
    (E) Pavlov and physics

5. Existentialists such as Sartre and Camus argued that

   (A)   faith in God would resolve all the world's problems
   (B)   humans were alone in the universe with no future and no hope
   (C)   terror and violence were healthy and cleansing
   (D)   realism in art is essential if the true nature of man is to be revealed
   (E)   men are superior to women

6. Sigmund Freud theorized that human actions were primarily shaped by

   (A)   the unconscious
   (B)   rational thought
   (C)   religion
   (D)   fear of authority
   (E)   financial greed

© Fotomas/Top Foto/The Image Works

7. This caricature satirizes

   (A)   the founder of the first modern zoo
   (B)   Wihlem I, first Emperor of Germany
   (C)   Kipling's "White Man's Burden"
   (D)   Charles Darwin's theory of evolution
   (E)   the conservatism of Pope Pius IX

8. Charles Darwin's theories were

    (A)   immediately embraced by the Anglican church
    (B)   based on the advances made in genetics
    (C)   renounced by the author later in life
    (D)   used as a basis for racist theories
    (E)   not taught in British universities until the 1950s

9. The Temperance Movement of the later nineteenth and early twentieth centuries was motivated by all of the following EXCEPT

    (A)   the assumption that drunkenness was a sign of moral weakness
    (B)   the threat drunkenness posed to the social order
    (C)   the beer industry's fear that gin was becoming too popular
    (D)   the connection between alcoholism and poverty
    (E)   lower worker productivity

10. The belief that the privileges of the capitalist elite would gradually give way to democratic reform would most likely have been held by

    (A)   an evolutionary socialist
    (B)   a classical economist
    (C)   a Marxist
    (D)   an anarchist
    (E)   a Carlist

11. The *Communist Manifesto* advocated all of the following EXCEPT

    (A)   constitutional monarchy
    (B)   confiscation of landed property
    (C)   heavy income taxes
    (D)   abolition of all inheritance
    (E)   free education for all

Christie's Images, London, UK/Bridgeman Art Library, (C) 2004 Mondrian/Holtzman Trust/c/o Artists Rights Society (ARS), New York

12. This painting is representative of which artistic style?

    (A)   cubism
    (B)   surrealism
    (C)   mannerism
    (D)   abstractionism
    (E)   socialist realism

13. Pope Leo XIII in his encyclical *Rerum Novarum* issued in 1891

    (A)   called attention to social justice and worker victimization
    (B)   abolished the Latin mass
    (C)   condemned progress and liberalism
    (D)   denounced monarchy as a system of government
    (E)   declared open war on Protestantism

14. Which of the following best describes what was unique about Marxism?

    (A)   it was socialist
    (B)   derived from an analysis of industrialization
    (C)   claimed its predictions were inevitable
    (D)   it was anti-clerical
    (E)   argued capitalism was unjust to workers

Claude Monet, French, 1840-1926, Arrival of the Normndy Train, Gare St. Lazare, oil on canvas, 1877, 59.6 X 80.2 cm, Mr. And Mrs. Martin A. Ryerson Collections. 1933.1158, photograph courtesy of the Art Institute of Chicago

15. The creator of this painting was

    (A) trying to convey a first impression of the scene
    (B) portraying the scene in realistic detail
    (C) working for a princely patron
    (D) encouraging Frenchmen to emigrate
    (E) showing how trains had become outmoded

16. The movement for women's rights that developed during the second half of the nineteenth century hoped to change all of the following EXCEPT

    (A) laws concerning ownership of property
    (B) divorce laws
    (C) system of military service
    (D) the franchise
    (E) laws of adultery

17. The mass reading public in the later nineteenth century mainly purchased

    (A) novels
    (B) tabloid newspapers
    (C) poetry
    (D) magazines
    (E) religious tracts

18. Tactics employed by women seeking the vote before World War I included all of the following EXCEPT

    (A)   hunger strikes
    (B)   radio advertising
    (C)   petitions
    (D)   marches
    (E)   destruction of property

19. Which among the following did NOT help to inspire Karl Marx's theories

    (A)   Hegel's philosophy
    (B)   Adam Smith and David Ricardo
    (C)   Utopian socialists
    (D)   factory conditions in Manchester
    (E)   Russian anarchism

20. An anarchist would be most likely to do which of the following?

    (A)   assassinate a king
    (B)   vote for a communist candidate
    (C)   join the police
    (D)   strengthen parliamentary institutions
    (E)   support a dictator

21. This painting by Pablo Picasso is characterized by which of the following?

    (A) realism
    (B) deliberate incompetence
    (C) romanticism
    (D) fragmentation of perception
    (E) impressionism

No testing material on this page.

Chapter XIV

War and Revolution

WORLD WAR I (1914*- 1918*)

The Great War, as it was known until 1939, was the most important formative event of the 20th century. It also killed more people that any other human activity in history up until that time. Its horror was only exceeded by the Second World War, and in the case of France and Britain far fewer soldiers were killed 1939-45 than 1914-18. It is hard to assign blame to any single country or person for the outbreak of this war, although Serbia stands as perhaps the guiltiest, with Germany not far behind. However, even the English concealment of a military agreement with France, which led to German miscalculation, was also a factor.

Long-term causes:

- The Alliance systems that developed after 1871 to provide security eventually became seen as threats and dragged countries uninvolved in the immediate dispute that led to war into the maelstrom. While Bismarck was in office, he was able to structure alliances that retained the balance of power in a way his successors could not
- Imperial rivalries in Africa and Asia created tensions and distrust
- Gradual collapse of the Ottoman Empire created instability and tempted the greedy – "Sick man of Europe"
- Rivalries in the Balkans exacerbated other problems
- Fragility of the Austro-Hungarian empire made leaders overly aggressive to nationalist threats, especially among the southern slavs
- Social Darwinism encouraged the notion that war was healthy and good
- German fears that Russia, when fully industrialized, would overpower all other continental powers, and dictate to Europe – Germany had no natural frontier to protect her on the East
- The rapid creation of a giant Germany and even more speedy industrialization created tensions and anxieties that made for oversensitive responses to perceived threats
- British fears that Germany was rapidly overtaking her in industrial production and world trade. Britain's large population packed into a small island could only survive by industry and trade
- The character of **Kaiser William II** – unstable, paranoid, politically insensitive, aggressive. He created alarm and fear even when no harm was meant
- The character of Tsar Nicholas II, weak, prevaricating, and inept – pressure of Slavophiles

- The "Tirpitz" naval build up in Germany, for which the British could see no purpose except an attack on them. This fear was exacerbated by the invention of the **"Dreadnought"** type of battle-ship by the British, a new technology that was easy to copy and destroyed Britain's historic vast superiority in numbers over other navies
- French desire for revenge against Germany and to regain Alsace Lorraine
- Russian bitterness towards Austria both for its failure to help in the Crimean War and annexation of Bosnia without giving promised support to Russia to open the Dardanelles to Russian ships; supports nationalism, especially in Serbia
- Italian bitterness about failing to reclaim the *irredenta* controlled by Austria
- Serbian desire to create a **"Greater Serbia"** that included Serbs living under Habsburg rule and gaining access to a seaport on the Adriatic
- The spirit of nationalism, which persuaded most Europeans that they were superior to everybody else and had a right to take what ever they wanted if they could get away with it
- Failure of political and military leaders to have adequate options available for mobilization

Short-term Causes:

- Assassination of the Archduke **Franz Ferdinand**, heir to the Austrian throne, June 1914* at Sarajevo in Bosnia. The Serbian government had knowledge of the terrorist threat, encouraged it, and wanted Franz Ferdinand dead because it was feared that his plan for a "Triple Monarchy" giving Slavs autonomy comparable to the Hungarians might succeed in blocking the creation of a Greater Serbia
- Austria sought promises of support from Germany
- Germany issued a **"blank check"**, essentially giving Austria total control over the diplomatic situation and urged Austria to solve the Serbian threat once and for all
- Austrians issued an ultimatum demanding a major surrender of Serbian national integrity
- Serbia sought support from Russia
- Russia threatened to "mobilize" against Austria but the mobilization plan could only be implemented against Austria and Germany together, as it was always assumed any war fought against one would be fought against both
- Russia sought support from France. France issued a "blank check" to Russia
- Germany demanded a halt to Russian mobilization. It had only one **(Schlieffen)** plan, which had to be launched immediately if Russia began to mobilize. This plan was built on the assumption that any war against Russia would be fought against its ally France as well. To cope with the threat of a "two Front" war the Germans intended to defeat France first, swiftly, and then turn on the slower Russia. Only immediate mobilization could make this successful
- The Serbians and Russians refused to back down
- Germany invaded Belgium (the Schlieffen plan involved an indirect surprise attack on France)
- Britain demanded German withdrawal due to an 1830 treaty protecting Belgium, but in reality because a secret military agreement with France required it to lend aid to Paris
- Austria invaded Serbia

- Russia invaded Germany and Austria
- Britain came to the aid of France
- Italy offered to aid Germany and Austria if the *irredenta* was returned. They refused
- The Ottoman Empire entered the war on the side of Germany and Austria
- In 1915 Italy entered the war on the side of the French and British after a promise of the *irredenta* after the war was won
- In 1917 the USA entered the war due to German pursuit of unrestricted submarine warfare ("Lusitania", the Zimmermann Telegram, and not having to ally with the Tsar due to his removal)

Terms/events:

- **Triple Alliance** – Germany, Austria, and Italy
- **Entente Cordiale** – France and Russia (1904)
- **Triple Entente** – France, Russia, and Britain (1907)
- **The Central Powers** – Germany, Austria, Ottoman Empire, and Bulgaria
- **The Allies** – France, Britain, Russia, Belgium, Serbia, Romania, Italy, Portugal, Japan, USA
- Neutrals – Scandinavia, Holland, Spain, Switzerland
- 1st and 2nd Moroccan Crises – German threats and aggression against French interests in Africa (1905, 1911)
- 1st and 2nd Balkan Wars – threats to Ottoman Empire (1911, 1912)
- Battle of the **Marne** (1914) – French and British barely halt the German advance near Paris
- Battle of Verdun – horrific defense by the French 1916
- Battle of the Somme – British/German stalemate 1916
- Battle of **Jutland** (1916) – only major naval engagement of the War. British suffered greater losses, but Germans successfully confined to port thereafter
- The Trenches – many people thought the war would be over quickly. They had not realized that defensive tactics had overtaken offensive ones. A defensive line of trenches was built from the North Sea to Switzerland that remained relatively fixed for five years. Machine guns and barbed wire had made cavalry obsolete and infantry charges ineffective. **The war became one of attrition**
- Mustard gas, airplanes, tanks, flame-throwers, and other new technologies were applied to the stalemate without success. Massive artillery barrages also failed to work
- Lusitania – British ship with American passengers sunk by a German submarine (1915). The Germans ceased unrestricted submarine warfare, but resumed it in 1917 in a desperate gamble that Britain could be starved to defeat before the USA could take an effective part in the war
- Britain survived the submarine onslaught by using convoys
- Britain and France tried to break the stalemate by attacking the Dardanelles, which would knock out the Ottomans and allow them to supply Russia. The attack failed

- Total War – concept of organizing all facets of the state and the economy to win the war; Walter Rathenau of Germany did this very effectively; unprecedented central planning and invasion of private business and life
- Germany tried to break the stalemate by encouraging the collapse of Tsardom and then the Provisional government, especially by sending the Bolshevik Lenin from Switzerland to Petrograd – "sealed train"

Germany surrendered on November 11, 1918*. The Central powers lost because they overextended themselves at the **Treaty of Brest-Litovsk** (1918 with Russia) that involved military occupation of a third of European Russia, starvation and lack of raw materials (the Allied blockade was increasingly effective in a war of attrition), failure of the submarine campaign, and above all collapse of morale within the army in October 1918 (the prospect of fighting against millions of freshly trained, well fed, and well armed Americans finally did them in). In order to avoid the disintegration of the army, which was the only defense the elites had for their property against socialist revolution at home and Communist invasion from Russia, the top generals forced the Kaiser to abdicate and flee to Holland and surrendered to the Allies.

Meanwhile the smaller monarchies in Germany collapsed, and the Habsburg Emperor (who had attempted earlier to achieve a separate peace) was overthrown.

The Russian Revolution

Causes:

- Defeats and suffering due to the war. The strain of fighting Germany and Austria placed too heavy a burden on Russian resources, and it could not be adequately supplied by the Allies because no railway line existed to the ice-free White Sea, and the Black Sea was blocked by the Ottomans
- Tsar **Nicholas II** inept, incompetent, and unworthy of his position. "Bloody Sunday" and the loss of the Russo-Japanese War in 1905 had undermined his authority. When in 1915 he left the capital to take personal command of the army, he
    - a) then had to accept personal responsibility for defeats
    - b) left his wife in charge of the government
- Tsaritsa **Alexandra** a neurotic, unpopular German (seen as a traitor) influenced by a charlatan, Rasputin, who gained ascendancy due to the illness of the heir to the throne, a hemophiliac. Under the monk's influence government ministries went to crooks and incompetents
- Middle class democratic politicians (Kadets) were alienated and distrustful
- Workers in the factories supported radical change
- Food crisis in St. Petersburg precipitated revolt. Troops and Duma failed to support the Tsar, and he was forced to abdicate in March

- New **Provisional Government** established by Lvov and **Kerensky** tried to negotiate with Germany, but found Berlin's demands too greedy. Decision to continue the war and subsequent defeats further weakened morale
- Soldiers ceased to fight and deserted in large numbers
- **Lenin** and the Bolsheviks organized a coup that overthrew Kerensky in November 1917*
- Lenin's leadership was crucial; he was a political genius and utterly ruthless; his assistant Trotsky was also very able; promises "Peace, Land, and Bread"

When the Bolsheviks failed to win the first true democratic elections in Russian history, the legislature was closed and a Communist dictatorship was imposed by force. The Tsar and his wife and five children were murdered. Opposition from monarchists, democrats, Orthodox Christians, and aristocrats was eventually crushed in a civil war. The Red Army was successfully led by **Leon Trotsky**.

Outcomes:

- Romanov monarchy and democratic Provisional government overthrown
- Bolsheviks gain power and gradually destroy all opposition
- Trotsky negotiated peace with Russia at Brest-Litovsk. Russia suffered huge territorial losses, but regained much of the land after German defeat
- Communism became a frightening threat to both conservative dictatorships in central Europe and capitalist democracies in the West
- Stalin took power after Lenin's death in 1924 and established the most brutal dictatorship known to history

The Treaty of Versailles

A peace conference in Paris took place in 1919 without the presence of the Germans or Austrians. The "Big Four," **David Lloyd George** of Britain, **Georges Clemenceau** of France, **Woodrow Wilson** of the USA, and Orlando of Italy met to impose terms on the defeated. This became the "Big Three" after Orlando departed incensed when denied the entire *irredenta*, for which Italy had entered the war in the first place. This was due to one of Wilson's **"Fourteen Points,"** which promised self-determination to oppressed peoples. Lloyd George and Clemenceau were perfectly ready to abandon their promises to Italy in order to win Wilson's agreement to their own agendas. Indeed, they conceded Wilson the **League of Nations** (which they did not value highly) in exchange for his concessions on reparations and territorial adjustments that favored France and Britain.

- **War Guilt Clause** – Germany forced to accept total responsibility for the outbreak of the war

- **Reparations** – Germany forced to pay most of the costs for war damage and for the loans, pensions, education of orphans, etc. – a gigantic sum in gold. In addition much of its merchant fleet was confiscated by the British, and railway freight cars and factory machinery by the French. This was the equivalent of asking a man to run a 100 yard dash and then cutting off his legs. The Saar border region was temporarily annexed by France to compensate for loss of coal production in occupied territories during the war
- **Alsace and Lorraine** were returned to France
- **Poland** was recreated and given territory taken from Germany, Austria, and Russia. A **"corridor"** was cut through Prussia to give the new state access to the port of Danzig, and hence a million Germans were denied self-determination and the German state was in two pieces
- An entirely new state of **Czechoslovakia** was created out of Bohemia and Moravia, formerly part of Austria. In order to give it a defensible natural frontier, the mountainous **Sudetenland** along the German border was given to the new country, and thus two million Germans were denied self-determination
- **Austria** was reduced to a pygmy state too small to support its huge capital at Vienna
- **Hungary** was established as an independent state, largely shorn of its non-Magyar subject peoples, but also with Hungarians placed under the rule of Yugoslavia, Czechoslovakia, and Romania. **Plebiscites** were held to achieve self-determination, but the checkerboard nature of ethnic distribution did not yield clear borders in many instances
- **Yugoslavia** was established as an independent state. This made Serbia the biggest winner of the war and gave them more territory that they had ever anticipated gaining. Many smaller ethnic groups – Albanians, Croatians, Slovenians, Hungarians, Romanians, Italians, Montenegrins, Macedonians, etc. were placed under their rule without regard for self-determination
- **Romania** was almost doubled in size with additions coming mainly from Hungary
- **Bulgaria** was reduced in size
- Greece gained territory
- The **Ottoman Empire** was liquidated. The core became the Republic of Turkey when the Sultan was overthrown soon after the war. Mandates (protectorates) under the League were established in Palestine, Jordan, and Iraq (Britain) and the Lebanon and Syria (France). Britain had promised an Arab throne to the ruler of Mecca for help during the war against the Ottomans (British officer, Lawrence of Arabia, helped lead Arab revolt), but the rising Saudi dynasty drove them out and established an independent Arabia. Hence the Hashemite family were made kings of Iraq and Jordan instead
- Japan was given German territory in the Pacific and China
- Britain gained German territories in Africa
- Finland, Estonia, Latvia, and Lithuania were given independence from Russia
- The **League of Nations** was established to settle international disputes
- The Rhineland was demilitarized

Germany, Poland, Czechoslovakia, and Austria became republics. Hungary was ruled by a Regent who denied the Habsburg pretender the right of return. The Kings of Serbia became rulers of Yugoslavia, and the reigning dynasties survived in Romania, Bulgaria, and Greece.

Wilson's "Fourteen Points" were more honored in the breach than in the letter. The British succeeded in blocking "freedom of the seas", and although the League was established, it failed to have much impact, in part because Russia, Germany, and even the USA were not members.

Russia and Germany were the ghosts at the feast. Neither was represented in the negotiations. Indeed, France, Britain, Japan, and the USA invaded Russia and tried to put down the Communist revolution. Her western borders, though better than those imposed by Germany at Brest-Litovsk, were imposed without consultation and included loss of territory and population.

Germany initially refused to sign the treaty, and only did so when faced with a blockade and starvation. The English economist, John Maynard Keynes called Versailles a "Carthaginian Peace" (excessively harsh) and predicted that German economic weakness would make it impossible for them to pay the ridiculously high reparations. He called this situation very dangerous. He was right. However, it is hard to see how Lloyd George and Clemenceau could have done anything else as the democratically elected leaders of nations that had suffered unprecedented numbers of casualties (one in two Frenchmen between the ages of 18 and 40 was killed or wounded). Only Wilson might have salvaged something, but he was out-maneuvered and placed excessive faith in the League, which he believed could rectify mistakes made in Paris.

The US Senate refused to ratify the Versailles treaty and the USA withdrew into reckless isolationism.

Outcomes of World War I:

- The **Versailles settlement** did not destroy Germany, but left it bitter and revengeful
- The **Russian Revolution** and rise of the USSR
- Use of propaganda greatly developed and refined as a political and military weapon; hatreds encouraged by governments to help win the war make it hard to build peace; "disinformation"
- Collapse of the ancient dynasties. Especially disastrous was the **disappearance of the Habsburg monarchy,** which with all its failings had created an center of stability and peace in central Europe. Now a vacuum existed that great powers would vie to fill. The overthrow of the Ottoman Empire also left a cauldron of troubles in the Middle East
- Collapse of the **old landed elites** – liquidated physically in Russia, discredited in Germany, and put under severe economic stress in Britain. Heavy taxation, loss of sons in the war, a new democratic spirit in the West, lack of servants, and other factors largely eliminated them from the center of affairs and the top of society, although individual figures such as Churchill remained important
- **Women** got the vote, and their work in jobs replacing male soldiers earned them new respect, and the change in skirt lengths was physically liberating. However, many women had to leave the work force and lost their financial independence on the return of the men from the front

- Victorian **morality** was largely abandoned and sexual mores loosened. Old-fashioned values of "honor" and deference seemed outdated or were associated with a discredited social and political system
- **"Total War"** had led to large-scale interventions into economies that did not fully disappear after the war. Heavy taxation was instituted during the war and remained a means of government management thereafter
- Serious **economic dislocations** changed the structure of nations and the world. Britain and Germany lost markets to the USA and Japan. Huge war loans burdened recovery. supporting millions of widows, orphans and the disabled imposed serious financial burdens. Tariffs were increasingly put up to protect home economies
- The **USA** became a world power and Japan became the first Asian power in modern times to be accepted as an equal in treaty negotiations
- Labor unions strengthened and socialists gained mass support and moved towards gaining control of governments
- The Colonial empires of France and Britain survived, though increasingly native peoples challenged European rule. They later also felt service of colonial troops in the war ought to be rewarded, and the ideals of freedom for which the Allies claimed to be fighting ought to apply to them also. It should be noted that Canada, Australia, New Zealand, (and South Africa, Egypt, and India less willingly) followed Britain into the Second World War
- World War I weakened human regard for the value of life. The deaths and maiming of millions of young men under the most inhumane conditions was unprecedented and shattered all previous conceptions of decency and what was allowable. The devaluing of life undermined limits that would help condone even more terrible killing twenty years later
- Disillusion and denial of rationality; Wilfrid Owen; *All Quiet on the Western Front*

1. Austria-Hungary delayed taking action against Serbia in July 1914 after the assassination of the Archduke Franz Ferdinand

   (A) while they awaited German promises of support
   (B) in order to seek an alliance with France
   (C) out of fear of the Ottoman empire
   (D) to give the Serbs more time to get ready
   (E) until everyone was back from vacation

2. Georges Clemenceau's statement that "war is too important to be left to generals" refers to

   (A) the tactical incompetence of the French general staff
   (B) ordinary soldiers ought to be promoted to high positions
   (C) the German generals were the cause of their country's defeat
   (D) civilian control was necessary to conduct overall strategy
   (E) civilians were more patriotic than soldiers

3. "The Serbian Government must cooperate inside their country with the organs of the Imperial and Royal Government in the suppression of subversive movements directed against the integrity of the monarchy."

   This requirement was part of an ultimatum issued in 1914 by

   (A) Austria-Hungary
   (B) Germany
   (C) Russia
   (D) France
   (E) Italy

4. Who among the following was NOT a leader of one of the leading combatant powers during the First World War?

   (A) David Lloyd George
   (B) Paul von Hindenburg
   (C) Sun Yat-sen
   (D) Woodrow Wilson
   (E) Georges Clemenceau

5. The principal reason why the Provisional Government in Russia did not win popular support in 1917 was

    (A)   its decision to make peace with Germany
    (B)   its weak alliance with the Ottoman Empire
    (C)   further setbacks in the war
    (D)   the restoration of Nicholas II to the throne
    (E)   the attack by the Japanese at Port Arthur

6. Which of the following countries became independent as a result of World War I?

    (A)   Norway
    (B)   Portugal
    (C)   Greece
    (D)   Lithuania
    (E)   Egypt

7. Communist uprisings took place in all of the following places at the end of the First World War EXCEPT

    (A)   Munich
    (B)   Berlin
    (C)   Budapest
    (D)   St. Petersburg
    (E)   Paris

8. The Schlieffen Plan developed by Germany before the outbreak of war in 1914

    (A)   included provisions for a secret invasion of England
    (B)   was a plan to support the Boers in South Africa
    (C)   had inducements for Mexico to invade the United States
    (D)   relied on unrestricted submarine warfare
    (E)   resolved the problem of a two front war with France and Russia

9. "We are fighting for the liberty, the self-government, and the undictated development of all peoples, and every feature of the settlement that concludes this war must be conceived and executed for that purpose. Wrongs must be righted and then adequate safeguards must be created to prevent their being committed again."

This passage was written by

(A)   Sultan Abdul Hamid II
(B)   Kaiser Wilhelm II
(C)   President Woodrow Wilson
(D)   Premier Georges Clemenceau
(E)   Prime Minister David Lloyd George

10. In 1917 the Bolshevik leader Lenin offered the Russian people

(A)   Peace, Land, and Bread
(B)   Blood, Sweat, and Tears
(C)   Liberty, Equality, and Fraternity
(D)   Church, Throne, and Law
(E)   Democracy, Prosperity, and Freedom

11.   64, 40, 28, 16

The numbers listed above are for battleships possessed by the following countries in 1914. Which list appears in the correct order of magnitude to match the figures?

(A)   Germany, Great Britain, France, Austria-Hungary
(B)   Great Britain, Germany, France, Austria-Hungary
(C)   France, Germany, Great Britain, Austria-Hungary
(D)   Germany, France, Austria-Hungary, Great Britain
(E)   Great Britain, France, Germany, Austria-Hungary

12. Russia and Germany signed a peace treaty in 1918 at Brest-Litovsk that

(A)   allowed Russia to retain Poland
(B)   gave Germany one third of European Russia
(C)   forced Russia to renounce communism
(D)   led both to attack France
(E)   restored the Tsar to power

13. Which among the following countries was not a combatant in World War I?

   (A) Japan
   (B) India
   (C) Ottoman Empire
   (D) Australia
   (E) Dutch East Indies

14. The theater of war on the Western Front between 1914 and 1918 lay largely in

   (A) Germany
   (B) France
   (C) Holland
   (D) Britain
   (E) Belgium

15. Factors undermining faith in the Tsarist system between 1914 and 1917 included all of the following EXCEPT

   (A) Rasputin's influence within the imperial family
   (B) food shortages
   (C) the alliance with France
   (D) military defeats
   (E) a German empress

16. Popular opinion in Germany, Austria, and Russia largely reacted to the outbreak of war in 1914 with

   (A) horror and aversion
   (B) resigned acceptance
   (C) great enthusiasm
   (D) fear of defeat
   (E) puzzlement and perplexity

17. The Gallipoli Campaign was designed by Winston Churchill to accomplish which of the following?

   (A) get military supplies to Russia
   (B) bring Sweden into the war
   (C) keep Greece out of the war
   (D) block submarines from entering the Mediterranean
   (E) hold Italy as an ally

18. During the First World War the concept of "Total War" was first developed. This term described

   (A) the use of nuclear weapons
   (B) take no prisoners
   (C) the government controls the economy
   (D) the demand for unconditional surrender
   (E) a campaign of racial extermination

19. Emperor Wilhelm II of Germany is best characterized as

   (A) farseeing and statesmanlike
   (B) mature and seasoned
   (C) uncultured and brutish
   (D) unstable and reactive
   (E) democratic and libertarian

20. "The question as to who is to rule the country, i.e., of the life or death of the bourgeoisie, will be decided on either side, not by reference as to the paragraphs of the constitution, but by the employment of all forms of violence."

   This statement was made in 1920 by

   (A) Trotsky
   (B) Briand
   (C) Mussolini
   (D) Dawes
   (E) Keynes

21.   WAR EXPENDITURES 1914-19
                                 (in 1913 billions of dollars)

British Empire	23.0
France	9.3
Russia	5.4
Italy	3.2
USA	17.1
Germany	19.9
Austria-Hungary	4.7
Bulgaria, Turkey	0.1

Which of the following statements is accurate with relation to this data?

(A)   the Central Powers outspent the Allies
(B)   Britain spent the most per year of fighting
(C)   Allied resources were much greater than the Central Powers
(D)   Italy played little part in the war
(E)   Russia had a small army and navy

22. Trench warfare was established along the Western Front early in World War I because

(A)   airplanes allowed most of the fighting to be done in the skies
(B)   improvements in the rifle made snipers the principal combatants
(C)   neither side had cavalry regiments to break holes in the line
(D)   defensive weapons had gained the advantage over offensive ones
(E)   the terrain made it difficult to assemble large armies

23. The United States entered World War I in 1917 for all of the following reasons EXCEPT

(A)   the Russian Revolution
(B)   Woodrow Wilson's belligerent policy
(C)   Anglophilia
(D)   sinking of the Lusitania
(E)   the Zimmermann telegram

24. The Central Powers (Germany, Austria-Hungary and Turkey) had all of the following assets during World War I EXCEPT

    (A) plentiful raw materials
    (B) good internal lines of communication
    (C) the high quality of the German army
    (D) the ability to isolate Russia
    (E) high level of technology and education in Germany

25. Which among the following countries was neutral during World War I

    (A) Great Britain
    (B) Sweden
    (C) Russia
    (D) Ottoman Empire
    (E) France

No testing material on this page.

Chapter XV

Dictatorship and Democracy

THE POST WAR WORLD

The 1920s witnessed a return to prosperity and peace, but the 1930s were dark years both in economic terms and politically. The **Locarno Treaty** 1925 and the Kellogg-Briand Pact 1928 created the illusion that peace might be permanent.

FRANCE

Obsessed by a search for security against Germany. Created an Eastern Alliance system of useless allies. Spent huge sums on defenses along the German border (the **Maginot Line**) that proved equally worthless. Occupied the Ruhr industrial area in Germany to force payments of reparations (1923), a policy that precipitated hyperinflation and even more bitterness in Germany. Unstable political system

GREAT BRITAIN

Full democracy established. **Labour Party** enters government in a coalition. Depressed economy, unemployment and a general strike in 1926. Aspects of the welfare state expanded. Southern Ireland given independence. Military weakness

GERMANY

Democratic **Weimar Republic** established, but much instability. Occupation of the Ruhr leads to hyperinflation that nearly destroyed the middle class. Economy staggered under many burdens

RUSSIA

Lenin instituted modified capitalism (New Economic Program – **NEP**) to restore strength to the economy. KGB (Cheka) set up. Trotsky (who believed the Russian experiment could only succeed if the revolution spread around the world) and Stalin (who argued for "socialism in one country", that is building up the strength of Communism in Russia first) struggled for power. Stalin won. He **collectivized** agriculture and instituted **Five Year Plans** to build up heavy industry first before military and consumer production could begin. Millions were killed, imprisoned or died in famines during the seizure of agricultural land. Prosperous peasants **(kulaks)** were targeted. Slave labor and terror were used to implement the Five Year Plans, millions more died in the labor camps **(gulags)**

ITALY

The humiliation at Versailles and political instability led to the success of **Benito Mussolini,** founder of an anti-capitalist, anti-communist, extreme nationalist party, the **Fascists**. He used street violence, murder of opposing leaders, and a March on Rome to force conventional politicians and the King to give him power. He ruled 1922 to 1943

POLAND

Political instability led to the take-over in 1926 by a dictator, **Marshall Pilsudski**

CZECHOSLOVAKIA

A good industrial base helped create prosperity, and sustained democracy under the leadership of Thomas Masyrak

HUNGARY

Authoritarian rule under Admiral Horthy

AUSTRIA

One-party rule under Dolfuss and then Schuschnigg

YUGOSLAVIA

Ruled by Alexander I until his assassination in France and then the Regent Paul

The Great Depression 1929*-1939

Causes:

* The financial disruption and burdens produced by the war
* Inflated currencies
* Tariff barriers
* Lack of strong economic leadership, Hoover's failure as a President of USA
* Flood of cheap wheat from the Americas to Europe undermined agricultural prices Farmers had to pay more for goods due to rising industrial wages
* Unemployment reduced consumption
* Crisis of production and distribution of goods in the world market, outstripped demand, stagnation
* Crash of the stock market in New York 1929 due to excessive speculation
* Credit crises in European banks 1931

Not everything went wrong during the depression and each country experienced it differently. Technological advancements continued. **Radio** for wireless communication was followed by general broadcasting for the public. This created a new world of entertainment, information, propaganda, and education. TV was born in Britain just before the Second World War. Electricity continued to be spread to rural areas and lightened the lives of millions of farm families. **Synthetics** had been introduced during the war to replace unavailable products. These were improved and expanded. More cheap and attractive goods became available to ordinary people. Automobiles were greatly improved and became less expensive. This promoted the growth of many industries and the building of highways. **Air**

travel increased. Lindbergh flew the Atlantic, and long distance services became available just before the next war. Trans-Atlantic telephone cables were laid, and telephones became more common.

Britain went off the gold standard, erected tariff barriers, cut benefits, and raised taxes. A **National Government** helped lead the recovery, but permanent unemployment arose in some industries. France followed a similar path, although a **Popular Front** of left wing parties under **Leon Blum** tried to extend social benefits. Unemployment was never as serious as in Britain.

Germany suffered seriously during the depression, and the untimely death of a leading statesman, **Gustav Stresemann**, left a vacuum of political leadership.

J. M. Keynes, the economist, advocated (1936) "pump priming" as a solution to the depression – government spending to provide employment and inject money into the economy.

TOTALITARIANISM

The rise of **fascism and communism** changed the face of political and social organization, to say nothing of culture, between 1919 and 1939. In many ways they were similar and in many different. It is perhaps more useful to think of them as opposite ends of an almost closed circle than as on the right and left of a continuum.

Similarities	Differences
State over the individual	C – goal was no government
Totalitarian	F – state is everything
Militaristic	
Secret police/censorship	
Concentration camps	C – goal is internationalist
Individual counts for nothing	F – intensely nationalistic
One party	
Tolerate no opposition	
One leader	C– goal is to promote equality
Cult of personality	F – inequality is seen as natural
Ambitions of world conquest	
Mutual antagonism	C – goal is peace and prosperity
Anti-capitalist	F – war is good, slavery for the
Anti-religious	losers
Propaganda over truth	
Messianic, provide a whole belief system	
Use of modern technology to lie and kill	

Murder millions of people

Utopian

Based on hate

European in origin

Planned economies

Provide full employment

Attempt to solve class conflict engendered by industrialization

Revolutionary

Stalin was the greatest murderer among the three totalitarian leaders. At least 10 million people died as a direct result of his rule, although if Hitler's responsibility for the Second World War is added to the killing of his own people, then his total could be counted as high as 40 million. Mussolini used murder infrequently, and most of the deaths for which he was responsible were due to greed and incompetence. The killings of opponents and the use of terror to build political and economic power were rational, if inhuman in their scale. However, much of the killing, the **Great Purges** in Russia or the **Holocaust** of the Jews, was irrational, counter-productive, the product of madness, paranoia, and immoral, unlimited power.

Mussolini developed the fascist ideology (1919-22). He was outraged by the *irredenta* crisis and feared that socialism would sap the national character. He dreamed of reviving the Roman Empire and resolving the class conflicts aroused by capitalism. He established state control over the economy. He was a gifted speaker and propagandist, but unlike Hitler he was not driven by racism. He worked out a **concordat** with the Church and tolerated the constitution, including his own official subordination to the monarchy (he was legally appointed to office by the King in 1922, though the "March on Rome" was a kind of blackmail). Italy remained economically and military weak. He called himself the Leader, ***Duce***.

Hitler attempted a coup in the early 1920s (was jailed and wrote *Mein Kampf*), but eventually came to power in 1933* by constitutional means. Although his fascist party, the National Socialist Party (Nazi), never won a majority of the votes, in coalition with other right wing groups, he did control a majority of seats in a democratically elected legislature. The President, the old junker Field Marshal von Hindenburg, despised him (Hitler had never been more than a corporal in the army and came from a lower middle class family, the first truly common man to dominate Europe's stage), but really had no option but to appoint him Chancellor. Hitler suspended the constitution quite legally after the Reichstag fire, and when the old aristocrat died, he never held another election. He became the Leader, ***Führer***. Hitler was driven by ambition comparable to that of Napoleon, and possessed political skills of a high order. However, his vision was warped by malignant racism and a fantastic vision of the world that led him to prolong the war so that he could punish his own people for failing him.

Fascism also came to Spain in the aftermath of a bloody civil war 1936-39 between the left (aided by Stalin) and the right (aided by Mussolini and Hitler). The conservative general, Francisco Franco, established a Falange Party, and called himself the Leader, *Caudillo*. However, he turned out to be a better survivor than his mentors. He wisely escaped a military alliance with the Axis, and prepared for the restoration of the monarchy after his death in 1975.

Various dictators in the Balkans also adopted fascism.

1. All of the following are connected with Irish politics EXCEPT

   (A)   the six counties
   (B)   Sinn Fein
   (C)   Dail Eireann
   (D)   Eamon De Valera
   (E)   Ruhr Valley

2. "The three national designations – Serbs, Croats, and Slovenes – are equal before the law throughout the territory of the Kingdom, and every one may use them freely upon all occasions of public life and in dealing with the authorities."

   This statement refers to what country?

   (A)   Yugoslavia
   (B)   Czechoslovakia
   (C)   Poland
   (D)   Bulgaria
   (E)   Romania

3. Hitler used all of the following to gain and maintain power EXCEPT

   (A)   ritual spectacles
   (B)   television
   (C)   campaigning by airplane
   (D)   films
   (E)   radio

4. The winner of the Spanish Civil War that took place between 1936 and 1939 was

   (A)   King Alphonso XIII
   (B)   Miguel Primo de Rivera
   (C)   Francisco Franco
   (D)   Antonio Salazar
   (E)   the Duke de Medinacelli

5. Which of the following was a fundamental component of fascist ideology?

   (A)   anti-communism
   (B)   racial tolerance
   (C)   belief in democratic institutions
   (D)   multi-party system of government
   (E)   non-aggressive foreign policy

6. Authoritarian regimes were established before 1939 in all of the following countries EXCEPT

   (A)   Poland
   (B)   Yugoslavia
   (C)   Bulgaria
   (D)   Czechoslovakia
   (E)   Greece

7. The New Economic Policy (NEP) instituted by Lenin in Russia in the early 1920's

   (A)   was a modified version of the old capitalist system
   (B)   confiscated all private property
   (C)   was an extension of the peace treaty with Germany
   (D)   involved the takeover of Poland and Hungary
   (E)   returned farmland to the peasants

8. "The Final Solution" was the name given to the Nazi policy of

   (A)   invasion of Russia
   (B)   unification of Italy and Germany
   (C)   destruction of democracy everywhere
   (D)   completion of the autobahn system
   (E)   extermination of the Jews

9. "Socialism in one country" was a slogan that referred to

   (A)   the ideological struggle between Trotsky and Stalin
   (B)   the need to build socialism in Germany
   (C)   the conflict between the Bolsheviks and Mensheviks
   (D)   Hitler's call for national rejuvenation
   (E)   the Fabian party in England

10. Stalin conducted a series of "Purges" and show trials during the 1930s. The victims of these activities included all of the following EXCEPT

   (A)   veteran revolutionaries
   (B)   foreign diplomats
   (C)   ethnic minorities
   (D)   senior military leaders
   (E)   Trotskyites

11. Germany was added to the League of Nations in

   (A)   1917
   (B)   1919
   (C)   1926
   (D)   1938
   (E)   never admitted

12. Early in his regime Hitler was faced with the dilemma of choosing to support either one or the other of the following

   (A)   Catholic or Protestant churches
   (B)   the army or the SA
   (C)   reparations or tariffs
   (D)   Poland or Switzerland
   (E)   socialists or communists

13. The Weimar Republic (1918-33) in Germany was weakened by all of the following EXCEPT

   (A)   a president who believed in hereditary monarchy
   (B)   heavy reparations due to the Allies
   (C)   the Great Depression
   (D)   hyper-inflation
   (E)   invasion by the Soviet Union

14. Stalin's Five-Year Plans in the Soviet Union

   (A)   brought an end to Lenin's New Economic Policy
   (B)   concentrated at first on consumer goods
   (C)   failed to industrialize Russia
   (D)   helped workers quickly achieve a higher standard of living
   (E)   opened Russia to capitalist investment

15. The "Kristallnacht" attack of November 9-10, 1938 in Germany involved

   (A)   the assassination of Paul von Hindenburg
   (B)   abolition of all political parties
   (C)   failure to take over Austria
   (D)   destruction of Jewish property
   (E)   massive book burning

16. The Popular Front in France, led by Leon Blum, founded in 1936, was composed of

    (A) fascists
    (B) royalists
    (C) Bonapartists
    (D) leftists
    (E) anarchists

17. All of the following were or became dictatorships EXCEPT

    (A) Soviet Union
    (B) Germany
    (C) Spain
    (D) Hungary
    (E) Sweden

18. The Vichy regime in France that existed between 1940 and 1945

    (A) was totally subservient to Hitler
    (B) led the resistance to fascism
    (C) allied with Great Britain
    (D) declared war on Italy
    (E) was led by communists

19. The inflationary spiral that took place in Germany during the early 1920s was precipitated by

    (A) monarchist attempts to regain power
    (B) French occupation of the Ruhr Valley
    (C) US failure to pay back loans
    (D) British closing of the Scheldt
    (E) Nazi agitation

20.   NATIONAL INCOME OF THE POWERS IN 1937 AND PERCENT SPENT ON
DEFENSE (in billions of dollars)

	National Income	% on Defense
USA	68	1.5
British Empire	22	5.7
France	10	9.1
Germany	17	23.5
Italy	6	14.5
USSR	19	26.4
Japan	4	28.2

Based on the table above, which of the following statements is true?

(A)   the Allies were poorer than the Axis
(B)   the Axis powers all spent a greater percentage of their national income than the
Allies
(C)   Germany spent more money on war preparations than any other country
(D)   Japan was more powerful that the USSR
(E)   the Allies had far greater economic resources than the Axis

21. Which of the following were the "Dominions" loyal to Great Britain in both the First
and the Second World Wars?

(A)   Canada, Australia, and New Zealand
(B)   India, South Africa, and Algeria
(C)   Argentina and Brazil
(D)   Egypt, Palestine, and Iraq
(E)   China and Mongolia

22. All of the following were key battles in the Second World War EXCEPT

(A)   Stalingrad
(B)   D-Day
(C)   Battle of Britain
(D)   Pearl Harbor
(E)   Somme

23. What social background would you expect to find among supporters of a revolutionary party?

    (A)   nobles
    (B)   lawyers, doctors, and civil servants
    (C)   shopkeepers
    (D)   industrial workers
    (E)   business executives

"Which backbone shall I lay out this morning, My lord?"

© *Solo Syndication Ltd.*

24. This cartoon portraying the British Foreign Secretary, Lord Halifax, in 1938 (FO = Foreign Office)

    (A)   is critical of the policy of Appeasement
    (B)   suggests that the aristocracy ought not to meddle in democratic politics
    (C)   looks to Halifax to provide the nation with a strong defense against Hitler
    (D)   supports Halfax for prime minister
    (E)   is critical of Halifax's love of luxury

No testing material on this page.

Chapter XVI

Wars–Hot and Cold

WORLD WAR II 1939*-1945*

Hitler planned to establish a great German Empire stretching across much of Europe dominated by the "Aryan" race. The Scandinavians, British, French, Spanish, and Italians would be his allies or neutral. The Slavic peoples would be slaves. Communism and capitalism would be eliminated. The German people, packed tightly into a small place, would gain **lebensraum** (space to expand) in a gigantic, largely agricultural "utopia". He planned to rectify all the mistakes made at Versailles.

- 1933 – Germany withdrew from the League of Nations
- 1935 – Germany renounces restrictions on rearmament
- 1936 – Rome/Berlin **Axis**
    Germany reoccupies the Rhineland with military forces
- 1938 – **Anschluss** (union) with Austria
    Munich Crisis over reoccupation of the Sudentenland
- 1939* – Germans occupy Prague
    Nazi-Soviet Pact
    Germany invades Poland
    Britain and France declare war

Appeasement

Britain, France, and the USA kept giving in to German, Italian, and Japanese demands or failed to prevent or punish their aggression until 1939 in the case of the France and the UK and 1941 for the USA. The leading "Appeaser" was Prime Minister **Neville Chamberlain** of Britain. Winston Churchill was the leading opponent of Appeasement.

Causes:

- Fear of another war with massive loss of life
- Desire to spend money on social programs rather than rearmament
- Guilt about the mistakes made at Versailles
- Fear of Communism greater than fear of fascism, and Hitler was seen as a force to be used against the USSR. Indeed, the ideal scenario was for the fascists and communists to kill each other off
- Hitler's anti-Semitism accorded with the feelings of many leaders in the West

- USA isolationism. France and Britain did not want to go to war without American support
- Chamberlain's naiveté and failure to grasp that he was not dealing with statesmen but moral gangsters; he "gave away" Czechoslovakia

Making War

Initially, Germany and the USSR split Poland and fighting stopped. The **Phoney War** was a period when Hitler hoped France and Britain would negotiate a peace. In April Germany invaded France, again sweeping around French defenses by going through Belgium. France collapsed quickly: the heart of its people was not ready for another long and bloody war, many of the French were sympathetic to anti-Semitism and fascism, and the leadership of the army was both incompetent and traitorous. A quasi-fascist regime was set up under Marshal Pétain at **Vichy**. Among the military leaders, only **Charles de Gaulle**, whose advice on tank warfare had been ignored, escaped to England to establish a Free French government. The small British army was pushed aside, lost all of its equipment, and barely managed to escape at the last minute by sea at **Dunkirk**. **Winston Churchill** replaced Chamberlain as Prime Minister of Britain, rallied his nation and saved freedom for the world. President **Franklin Roosevelt** grasped the nature of the emergency and established a **Lend-Lease** program circumventing neutrality to help supply the British with war materials.

The Germans sought to achieve air and sea superiority in the English Channel in order to invade Britain. However, the Royal Navy was much stronger than the German fleet and in the **Battle of Britain** in August and September of 1940 the RAF defeated the *Luftwaffe* and blocked the invasion. The invention of **radar** and the superb quality of British airplanes and pilots saved the day.

When it seemed safe, Italy entered the war on the side of Germany (Axis powers) and engaged the British in North Africa and attempted to invade Greece. Both campaigns failed, and Hitler had to deploy troops unexpectedly to salvage the situation. In the end the Axis failed to capture Cairo and the Suez Canal and were driven out of Africa. Yugoslavia and Greece were captured, but at the price of delaying the invasion of Russia, which came in June 1941. Although the Germans reached the suburbs of Moscow, they had too little time before a terrible winter set in to achieve victory. Stalin was saved by British intervention, US entry into the war, and the valor of his people aroused by a patriotic fervor inspired by the brutality and racism of the Nazis. Somewhere between 20 and 30 million Russians died.

The Japanese attack on **Pearl Harbor**, Singapore, the Philippines, and Dutch East Indies in December 1941, provoked at least to some degree by Roosevelt's embargo on oil which would have forced Tokyo to withdraw from its empire in China, allowed the Japanese to get fuel from the Dutch East Indies. Roosevelt was then able to carry the USA into the war in Europe (thanks to a declaration of war by Hitler – one of the great puzzles of modern history, probably attributable to his gross ignorance of the world outside Europe and his racism, which led him to believe the USA was a "mongrel" nation incapable of success in war).

The USA and Britain agreed to fight a defensive war in Asia and an offensive one in Europe, where most of their resources would be invested. Japan was an economic pygmy compared to the Third Reich.

Russia halted the German advance at the bloodiest battle in human history at **Stalingrad** in 1942. Mussolini was overthrown in 1943. North Africa and Italy were invaded by the US and British in 1943, and the **D-Day** invasion of Normandy took place in June 1944.

Germany was defeated in May 1945*. Hitler committed suicide and his officials were imprisoned and some executed after the **Nuremburg Trials**. It was revealed that Germany had organized a massive campaign to murder millions of Jews, men, women, and children, and also gypsies, homosexuals, clergymen, the mentally retarded, the aged, liberals and communists in what became known as the **Holocaust**. Atomic bombs were dropped on **Hiroshima** and Nagasaki in August 1945, and Japan also surrendered.

Making Peace

Churchill, Roosevelt, and Stalin worked closely together (if not always amicably) to coordinate the conduct of the war and the settlement afterwards. At a series of conferences at Washington, Quebec, Casablanca, Tehran, **Yalta**, and **Potsdam** strategy was hammered out and the peace arranged. No formal treaty like Versailles was ever signed to end the Second World War. Roosevelt's failing health perhaps weakened his judgment in making concessions to Russia that Churchill did not want to make. However, in Eastern Europe the reality was that Britain and the USA could do little to restrain Stalin unless they wished to fight a Third World War. At Potsdam the dead Roosevelt was replaced by **Harry Truman**, and Churchill lost an election to **Clement Attlee**.

- Unconditional surrender was demanded by the USA and Britain, as a way of reassuring Stalin they would not make a separate peace. Russia also accepted no conditions
- Germany was divided into four zones (the French were included) and ruled by military force until "denazification" could be completed and a new constitution written. Berlin lay within the Soviet Zone and was itself divided into four zones. The Allied sectors eventually emerged as the democratic Federal Republic (West Germany) while the East became a Soviet satellite state until it merged with the West in 1990
- Poland was reconstituted, and absorbed East Prussia. It quickly fell under Soviet domination
- Finland and Austria retained their independence, but the Soviets held a kind of veto on their foreign policies – "Finlandization" – until 1989
- Estonia, Latvia, and Lithuania were absorbed directly into the Soviet Union
- Hungary, Czechoslovakia, Romania, and Bulgaria fell under Soviet rule in the years immediately after the war.
- Yugoslavia and Albania went communist but were led by resistance figures (**Tito** and Hoxha) unfriendly to Russia
- Italy abolished the monarchy and established an unstable but ultimately successful democracy

- Greece fought a bloody civil war in which the communists were defeated with British and then American (the **Truman Doctrine**) aid
- France established the 4th Republic that proved hopelessly unstable
- Britain survived but was economically eviscerated and spiritually exhausted. It ceased to be a superpower and the empire evaporated soon after the war
- The USA and the USSR emerged as superpowers in a new bi-polar world
- China was liberated from Japanese rule but plunged into a civil war in which the Communist **Mao Zedong** triumphed in 1949
- Japan retained its emperor but had an American devised democratic constitution imposed on it. Japan managed an extraordinarily rapid economic recovery that catapulted it into great economic power status for the first time
- A replacement for the League of Nations, the **United Nations**, was established and proved somewhat more effective than its predecessor in providing a forum for peaceful resolution of disputes
- The inhuman treatment of the Jews and other minorities and the brutality of the Germans in Russia and the Japanese in China left a permanent mark of disgrace on those societies. The need to guard against man's capacity to do evil was rendered self-evident

THE COLD WAR

In 1946 Churchill described an **Iron Curtain** dividing Europe between the Soviet controlled East and the free West. The West formed a military alliance, the North Atlantic Treaty Organization (**NATO**). The US policy developed to counter the Soviet threat was called **"containment,"** constant counter-pressure to the expansive pressure of the USSR.

Causes:

- The Soviets had been excluded from the secret of the Atomic bomb and feared the West might use it unilaterally while they had yet to acquire the technology. Later a similar fear developed in the West about superior Russian missile technology. In part, the bomb dropped on Hiroshima was a message to the USSR that the West was prepared to use nuclear weapons if necessary to preserve freedom (a message sent at the cost of the hapless Japanese)
- The Soviet and democratic ideologies were both aggressive, based on the assumption of total moral ascendancy
- The Russians saw their control of Germany and Poland in particular and Eastern Europe in general as a reasonable strategy to prevent a repeat of the German/Austrian attacks of 1914 and 1941. The West saw a Communist empire in the making
- The West feared Communist parties might win elections in France and Italy, which would lead to an overthrow of democracy and alliance with the Soviet Union. Many resistance heroes during the war were communists, and they did well in elections afterwards
- The West saw signs of a vast Communist conspiracy around the world once Mao achieved power in China – nearly half of humanity was now under red rule. The **Korean War** (1950-53) reinforced conspiracy theories

- The Soviets remained bitter about the failure of the US and UK to launch a second front in Europe in 1942 and 1943, which would have relieved some of the German pressure. The assumption was that the West wanted the stuffing knocked out of the Soviet Union
- Stalin imagined enemies everywhere
- The West was horrified by the brutality of Stalin's rule
- The **Marshall Plan** (1947), even though offered to the Soviets, was seen as a plot to bribe Europeans with American wealth
- The **Berlin Blockade** (1948-49) was an attempt to push the West out of Germany (US response of "airlift")
- **NATO** (1949) was seen as an offensive alliance preparing to attack Russia
- The **Warsaw Pact** was seen as a Soviet offensive alliance preparing to invade Western Europe
- In the end, enormous wealth spread throughout all classes in the West was rightly seen by the Communist leaders as a mortal danger to the long-term survival of Communism

THE POST WAR WORLD

Ironically, the Cold War and the spread of nuclear weapons (first to Britain, then Russia, France, and China) created the idea of mutually assured destruction (**MAD**), which prevented another general war so long as no accidents or another Hitler came on to the scene. Only the **Cuban Missile Crisis** of 1962 seemed to bring the Cold War to a near hot one. Nevertheless, everyone was aware of possible doom. Competition even included war for medals at the Olympic Games.

During the 1960's much cultural innovation and protest against traditional values arrived, largely as a product of pressure from youth, especially college aged students. Everything from the ascent of "the Beatles" to the Civil Rights movement in the American South to the world crisis evoked by the Vietnam War played a role. Clothes, music, political rhetoric, and social structure all changed. Some see the "60s" rebellion as an uprising by privileged youth against boredom, security, and the lack of existential challenge in the post-war capitalist boom. This was clearly not the case in Belfast or Selma, however.

SOVIET UNION
Stalin died in 1953 and his successor, Nikita **Khrushchev** not only condemned his brutality and began to dismantle the gulags but also tried to establish links with the West. His failed agricultural policy and the perception that he was the loser in the Cuban Crisis led to his overthrow in 1963. His successor **Brezhnev** was more brutal and less innovative but also interested in links with the West. The Soviets succeeded in reducing infant mortality, spreading education, achieving more equality. The successes of their Space Program and military prowess distracted attention from the failure of food production and the underlying weakness of the economy

GREAT BRITAIN
Atlee's Labour Party won power in 1945 and proceeded to nationalize major industries, provide more educational opportunities, and establish the National Health Service

(free medical care). Structural weaknesses in the economy, loss of world markets, and continued spending on military forces suitable to its pre-war stature undermined recovery from the war. Powerful labor unions, class conflict, and loss of status as a great power left Britain weakened and by the 1970s in turmoil

FRANCE
The 4th Republic staggered to a collapse in the mid-1950s humiliated by the loss of empire and the on-going conflict in Algeria. De Gaulle was recalled to power and imposed a new constitution with a strong president – the **5th Republic**. The Gaullist, center-right party dominated until student and worker uprisings in 1968 drove the General from power

GERMANY
Konrad Adenauer and Ludwig Erhard led the Federal Republic into the respectable circle of nations and produced an economic "miracle" of recovery. Germany rapidly became the most powerful economy in Western Europe but stayed on a democratic course

ITALY
Became a republic in 1946. The Christian Democrats under De Gasperi staved off the Communists, rebuilt the economy, joined NATO, moved towards economic strength for the first time

EAST GERMANY
The most depraved and unhappy of the Soviet satellites under the crude and craven rule of Stalinists. Berlin Wall built in 1961 to stop everybody from leaving

POLAND
Unrest in 1956 led to a lessening of harsh communist policies under Wladyslaw Gomulka

HUNGARY
Open revolt in 1956 led by Imre Nagy suppressed violently by Russian invasion

CZECHOSLOVKIA
"Prague Spring" followed by Soviet "invasion" and suppression of reform 1968

Decolonization

Great Britain withdrew from India in 1947 and two warring states, Muslim Pakistan and Hindu India emerged. The independence movement had been led by **Gandhi** and **Nehru**. The Dutch left Indonesia in 1949. The French fought against a Communist insurgency in Vietnam led by **Ho Chi Minh** unsuccessfully and were forced to withdraw in 1954. A war in Algeria dragged on until 1961. The USA gave independence to the Philippines in 1946. Thereafter the colonial powers were in full retreat. Britain gave up its African colonies in the 1950s and 60s. The French followed suit. The Portuguese held on a little longer (1975). The disastrous intervention by the British and French at **Suez** in 1956 in which they attempted to resist Egypt's nationalization of the canal was condemned both by the USA and the USSR and discredited remaining imperialist impulses. In South Africa, a post-colonial white regime established *apartheid* and brutally repressed African peoples. A peaceful transition of power was not arranged until 1991. Perhaps the worst suffering due to colonialism occurred in the Belgian Congo, where European rule had been bad, and the African successor governments were even worse. The legacy of Belgian rule in Rwanda, where the most terrible racial violence since World War II broke out in 1994, was equally appalling.

Causes:

- Effective leadership of independence movements by native leaders
- Exhaustion of European powers by the war
- Pressure from the USA to decolonize and threatened withdrawal of aid if they did not
- Spread of education and nationalist aspirations in Africa and Asia
- The British defeat at Singapore by the Japanese convinced colonial peoples they could defeat the Europeans
- Cold War diplomatic and propaganda requirements
- West's realization that it must live up to its own declared values relating to freedom and democracy
- Realization that many colonies cost more than they were worth

International Cooperation

The Bretton Woods Agreement (1944) provided for new currency and banking arrangements, and led to the International Monetary Fund (IMF) and the World Bank. These aided economic recovery and later helped developing nations. The UN established many agencies to promote world health, refugees, education, and children.

The Middle East

During the First World War, the British had attempted to win support against the Ottomans and from Jews in the US and Germany by issuing the **Balfour Declaration** in 1917, which promised support for a Jewish national homeland. Once in control of Palestine, the British did not hinder Jewish immigration, but they also did not help the Zionists. After the war the British were too weak to continue to hold on to their empire and much sympathy for the Jews had been engendered around the world due to the Holocaust. The creation of the state of **Israel** in 1948 was welcomed by many Europeans.

The Arabs, however, viewed this event with horror and bitterness that has never been assuaged. Repeated wars have ensued. The Europeans have tried to balance their need for oil (which comes largely from Arab states), and their support for democracy in Israel, which has a largely European Jewish population. The irreconcilable differences in the Middle East were exploited during the Cold War, led to a huge surge in terrorism, use of oil as a political weapon by the producing states (OPEC) that ignited serious inflation and economic downturns during the 1970s in the West. The terrorist Palestinian movement, the **PLO**, was led by Yasser Arafat.

Further complications ensued in 1991 when Iraq attacked Kuwait (Arab) and Israel. A Western/Japanese coalition led by the USA freed Kuwait and punished Iraq in the **Gulf War**, but the latter continued as a rogue state and base for terrorism. Russian weakness made it possible for the West to become more aggressive in attacking Iraq, but liberal ideologies weakened support for further battles. US and Britain invaded Iraq again in 2003 and toppled Hussein regime.

The European Union

Jean Monnet of France worked quickly after the war to establish an economic system that would tie Germany, France, and the Benelux countries so tightly together that integration would make future war impossible. The European Coal and Steel Union was the result of this work (1952). Later more economic links and more countries were included leading to the **Treaty of Rome** in 1957 which established a six-nation free trade area, the European Economic Community (**EEC**) or Common Market. In 1967 the next step was to begin a movement towards political union, which led to the European parliament at Strasbourg and the rise of the European Community (**EC**). A treaty of Union was signed at Maastricht in 1991 (**EU**). This organization now regulates laws, issues passports, and has established a common currency (**Euro**). Some countries such as Denmark and Britain have been reluctant followers. Sweden came in late, and Norway not at all. Many of the former Soviet states will enter the Union in 2004. Turkey is pressing for entry.

The Welfare State

After the war most Western democracies committed heavily to reforms to equalize society in all its basic functions: the workplace, parenthood, medical care, education, recreation, vacations, and housing. Government care from "cradle to grave." This was paid for by heavy taxation that at some levels could reach over 90%. Inheritance taxes also increased. However, after many initial successes, governments found that nationalizing some industries made them inefficient and over reliant on subsidies, so privatization began to restore them to the controls of the marketplace. Also, very high taxation tended to drive businesses elsewhere and throttle entrepreneurship and dynamism on the job. Most countries have been forced to retreat when the price of the welfare state became too high to allow capitalism to flourish.

Intellectual Currents

- **Existentialism**, especially associated with Camus (d. 1960) and **Sartre** (d. 1980), in the tradition of Nietzsche and Kirkegaard, painted a bleak picture of the human condition, we are alone and "condemned to be free." They emphasized taking action.
- Organized religion weakened further, and regular religious attendance diminished to a tiny minority in most Western countries.
- Deconstructionists focused on the biases and class and cultural assumptions in the texts detached from the creative force of artists.
- Increasing tolerance for homosexuals.
- Postmodernism in the arts embraced contemporary popular and commercial culture.

- Rock dominated the music scene and homogenized culture.
- **Vatican II** (1962) liberalized Catholic practice and theology. Latin mass abandoned. **John Paul II** (1978) charted a more conservative course. The first non-Italian elected to the Papacy in modern times. His Polish origins made him an influential force in the breakdown of Soviet power in Eastern Europe.
- Artists' and composers' visions of their role in society were fragmented and chaotic. Styles proliferated, many eschewed beauty, realism was reviled, primitivism, cacophony, and abstraction prevailed. The desire to shock became rampant.
- Television and radio largely devoted themselves to popular culture. Professional athletics became big business.
- Big science was well funded, and research universities produced many breakthroughs in medicine, biology, and physics. DNA was identified at Cambridge (1952) and slowly decoded. Organ transplants became possible. The "pill" transformed sex life. "Dolly" the sheep cloned. Human genome mapped.
- Social science became more influential and respected.

Women's Liberation

Women built on the achievements of earlier feminists and the work of authors such as **Simone de Beauvoir** (*The Second Sex*, 1949) made the case that discrimination against women went far deeper than political and legal issues. Women had accepted their fate too passively. Women were encouraged to enter into the workforce in much larger numbers and to demand equal wages and rights to promotion. The work at home must be more equally divided. Special account needed to be taken of the impact of motherhood on careers and marriages. Leadership roles in politics and business were slow to come, but progress was made. Mediterranean cultures found it harder to adjust, and conservatively interpreted Islam remained a major impediment.

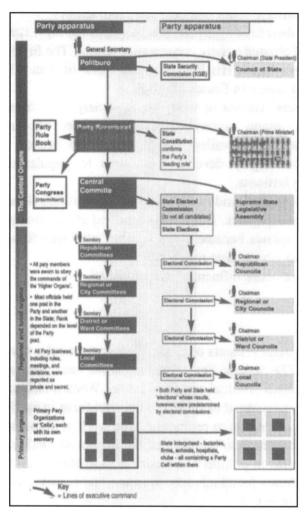

Europe, A HISTORY by Norman Davies, © 1993 by Norman Davies.
Used by permission of Oxford University Press, Inc.

1. This chart illustrates the governmental structure of what country?

   (A)   Germany
   (B)   France
   (C)   Italy
   (D)   USSR
   (E)   Great Britain

2. "We are economically oppressed: in jobs we do full work for half pay, in the home we do unpaid work full time. We are commercially exploited by advertisements, television, and the press; legally we often have only the status of children."

This passage was written by a

(A)   Polish peasant in 1885
(B)   British feminist in 1969
(C)   Nigerian rebel 1935
(D)   Russian dissident 1973
(E)   Bosnian muslim 1988

© *Solo Syndication Ltd.*

3. This cartoon entitled "On Target" published in 1963 portraying President De Gaulle of France as a submarine which has just torpedoed Britain's attempt to join the Common Market implies he

(A)   hoped NATO would come to the rescue
(B)   wanted to destroy NATO as well as keep Britain out of Europe
(C)   watched over European security with care
(D)   welcomed the American rather than British leadership of Europe
(E)   placed excessive emphasis on the French navy

4. Pope John XXIII (1958-63) called the Second Vatican Council to

(A)   modernize and update Catholic practices
(B)   reassert papal control over the church
(C)   condemn Protestant liberalism
(D)   make a concordat with the Soviet Union
(E)   revive conservative values

5. Which among the following countries was not behind the "Iron Curtain" under Soviet control?

   (A) Czechoslovakia
   (B) Poland
   (C) Romania
   (D) Greece
   (E) Bulgaria

6. "We must wait ever vigilant, applying pressure when needed and make sure every move made by the USSR is met with a counter move."

   This statement summarizes the key elements of

   (A) the containment policy pursued by the United States
   (B) the financial plan conceived by George Marshall
   (C) the recommendation of the French communist party to De Gaulle
   (D) Mao Zedong's statement against Stalin
   (E) Poland's foreign policy under Gomulka

7. The most important contribution to popular culture made by Britain during the 1960s and 1970s was in

   (A) athletics
   (B) cinema
   (C) music
   (D) literature
   (E) graphic arts

8. All of the following were moments of high tension between the East and the West during the Cold War EXCEPT

   (A) Berlin airlift
   (B) Cuban missile crisis
   (C) Prague spring
   (D) Hungarian revolt
   (E) fall of the Berlin wall

9. The Truman Doctrine (1947) stated that

(A) the United States would provide support for countries threatened by communism
(B) the Monroe Doctrine was still valid
(C) the US would overthrow Castro
(D) Scandinavia was in the Russian sphere of influence
(E) American aid would be cut off to Eastern Europe

10.

DEFENSE EXPENDITURES OF THE POWERS 1948-1970
(in billions of dollars)

	USA	USSR
1948	10.9	13.1
1950	14.5	15.5
1955	40.5	29.5
1960	45.3	36.9
1965	51.8	62.3
1970	77.8	72.0

Which of the following statements is true about this table?

(A) the USSR consistently outspent the USA
(B) spending was about equal
(C) the greatest increase for the US was between 1950 and 1955
(D) the Viet Nam War had little effect on US spending
(E) increases reflected the tensions of the Cold War

11. The gradual rise in the standard of living in Europe during the 1950s

(A) led to civil war
(B) weakened electoral support for the communist party
(C) allowed the Soviets to expand their influence
(D) was confined to Scandinavia and Iberia
(E) led to the dismantling of the welfare state

12. Western European welfare states usually enacted all of the following reforms EXCEPT

(A) nationalization of major businesses
(B) free health care
(C) free university education
(D) guaranteed jobs
(E) old age pensions

13. Which two countries laid the foundation for peace and prosperity in the post-World War II era by reaching out to cooperate with each other?

    (A)   Russia and Great Britain
    (B)   Italy and Poland
    (C)   France and Germany
    (D)   Russia and Germany
    (E)   France and the USA

14. Decolonization took place after World War II for all of the following reasons EXCEPT

    (A)   pressure from the United States
    (B)   weakness of European economies
    (C)   successful indigenous leadership
    (D)   German leadership
    (E)   living up to the ideals for which the war was fought

15. "Comrades, quite a lot has been said about the cult of the individual and about its consequences. [It has been] ... the source of a whole series of exceedingly serious and grave perversions of Party principles, of Party democracy, of revolutionary legality."

    This passage comes from

    (A)   Nixon's debate with Khrushchev in the American kitchen
    (B)   Khrushchev's denunciation of Stalin
    (C)   Churchill's attack on De Gaulle
    (D)   Harold Wilson's criticism of Margaret Thatcher
    (E)   Willie Brandt's challenge to Konrad Adenauer

16. After World War II which of the following settlements was imposed on Germany?

    (A)   the monarchy was restored
    (B)   it was divided into four sectors of occupation
    (C)   membership in the UN Security Council
    (D)   total occupation by the USSR
    (E)   decentralized into 150 small states

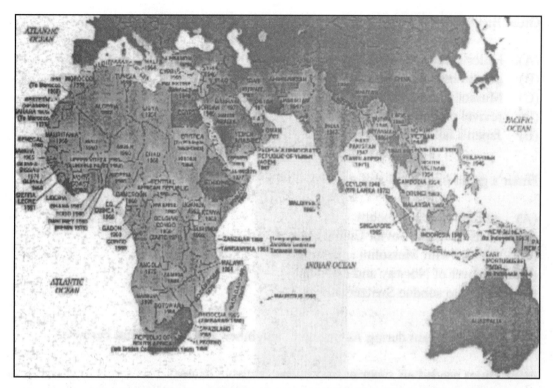

Map: from A HISTORY OF MODERN EUROPE: FROM THE RENNAISANCE TO THE PRESENT by John Merriman. Copyright © 1996 by John Merriman. Used by permission of W. W. Norton & Company, Inc.

17. This post-war map shows which of the following?

    (A) the decolonization process
    (B) the Arab League
    (C) NATO
    (D) Soviet satellites
    (E) where and when AIDs was first identified

18. Which of the following was NOT a World War II conference among Allied leaders?

    (A) Casablanca
    (B) Tehran
    (C) Yalta
    (D) Potsdam
    (E) Nuremburg

19. Great Britain, the United States, and Russia won World War II because of

    (A) Hitler's tactical mistakes
    (B) greater industrial capacity
    (C) Mussolini's incompetence
    (D) revival of the French national spirit
    (E) Japan's failure to reach Australia quickly

20. Hitler's greatest political and strategic blunder was the

    (A) murder of Ernst Roehm
    (B) invasion of the Soviet Union
    (C) alliance with Mussolini
    (D) takeover of Norway and Denmark
    (E) failure to subdue Switzerland

21. The Battle of Britain during August and September 1940 was crucial because

    (A) Hitler needed air superiority over the English Channel
    (B) it distracted Hitler's forces away from the Russian front
    (C) the British were able to sink the Bismarck
    (D) it saved France
    (E) it followed up on the D-Day victory

22. The Gaullist Party in France

    (A) wanted a Gallican church
    (B) were all former Vichy supporters
    (C) were mainly socialists
    (D) were royalists
    (E) supported the Fifth Republic

Imperial War Museum

23 This painting of a London street in 1941 shows

(A)   the dangers of gas lighting technology
(B)   aerial bombardment of civilians
(C)   anti-church rioting
(D)   problems with urban crowding
(E)   a communist uprising

24.   AVERAGE ANNUAL RATES OF GROWTH OF OUTPUT PER CAPITA

	1948-1962
USA	1.6
Belgium	2.2
France	3.4
West Germany	6.8
Italy	5.6

The statistics in the table above show that

(A)   Germany had the largest economy in the world
(B)   Italy had a larger economy than France
(C)   the USA had a smaller economy than the combined European one
(D)   Belgium surpassed Britain in the rate of growth
(E)   former Axis powers recovered more rapidly than the Allies

© Solo Syndication Ltd.

25. This cartoon published in 1944 portrays Hitler

    (A)   as a still powerful force at the bargaining table
    (B)   on the verge of military defeat
    (C)   as hopeful that a new strategy will defeat Russia
    (D)   as childish and whimsical
    (E)   as dangerous when cornered

Chapter XVII

Contemporary Europe

THE COLLAPSE OF COMMUNISM 1989*-1991

The Cold War rumbled on with ups (*détente*) and downs. Space and arms races frightened everyone. Cuba, Vietnam, and Afghanistan were the most notable open points of conflict. The Prague Spring in 1968, was put down by a Soviet invasion, and the Solidarity Movement led by Lech Walesa in Poland besmirched the reputation of the Russians around the world and at home in ways previous protest movements had failed to do

Causes:

- Russia stagnated and drifted during Brezhnev's last years and the deaths of his two immediate successors from old age were embarrassingly symbolic of atrophy
- Communist ideology was wrong about human motivation. The system lacked incentives, deterred entrepreneurship, and failed to produce enough food due to collectivized agriculture
- The Russian birthrate was declining and that of ethnic minorities rising. The latter would soon outnumber the former in total population and many were restive under Russian rule. Deep nationalistic aspirations were a serious danger as was the revival of Islamic faith in the southern regions
- *Détente* between China and the USA (1972) weakened the notion of monolithic communism and the USSR felt threatened
- Conquered peoples in the Baltic republics and Eastern Europe were pressing for freedom
- The war in Afghanistan was unsuccessful and increasingly unpopular at home
- The cost of competing with Western military technologies, especially "Star Wars", which threatened to make the USA invulnerable to a nuclear attack, was getting beyond the capacity of the USSR to pay
- Middle class professionals and managers were increasingly resentful of their exclusion from decision making
- George Orwell's *Animal Farm* and *1984* (1949) had made it difficult for communist propagandists to convince educated people that totalitarian rule had any redeeming value
- Solzhenitsyn's documentation of the history of repression destroyed any remnants of moral authority the Soviet Union retained
- Central planning could not produce an adequate and balanced range of consumer goods. Housing was inadequate. The population was increasingly aware that Westerners had created a much richer material culture

- The new leader, **Mikhail Gorbachev** (1985-1991) instituted reforms (*glasnost* – openness; *perestroika* – decentralization of the economy) that did not go far enough and antagonized the old guard. He still believed in communism
- Elections in Poland and the "velvet" revolution in Prague led by Vaclav **Havel** destroyed the underpinnings of communist power in the East
- Gorbachev's failure to use force to impose order in the Baltic Republics and to make Hungary close the border it opened with Austria led to political and population movements that gained a momentum that could not be stopped
- Berlin Wall demolished
- The failed *coup* attempt against Gorbachev in 1991 destroyed the credibility of the old leadership, and placed the dynamic, if erratic, **Boris Yeltsin** in power

Outcomes:

- The Cold War came to an end
- Russia went into a deepening economic and demographic crisis
- Russia took faltering steps towards democracy and the free market
- Gorbachev ousted and held responsible for Russian loss of prestige and empire
- Baltic states gained independence
- East and West Germany reunified
- Czechoslovakia, Hungary, Romania, Bulgaria, Albania and Poland gained freedom (Czechoslovakia broke into the Czech Republic and Slovakia)
- Yugoslavia broke apart in the 1990s. The resulting civil wars produced independent states of Croatia, Slovenia, and Macedonia. Bosnia-Herzegovina and Kosovo were torn apart and required international intervention to pacify
- Ukraine, Moldova, and Belarus broke away from Russia and took important military and economic assets with them
- Islamic republics in the south and Georgia and Armenia in the Caucasus also gained independence
- Radical decline in the already poor standard of living took place in Russia. Alcoholism rose dramatically, and the average age of mortality dipped fast
- The USA became the only superpower
- War in Chechnya
- Land reform finally enacted (2002)

CONTEMPORARY EUROPE

GREAT BRITAIN
Britain emerged out of its economic and social crisis of the 1970s with a yank of the neck by Prime Minister **Margaret Thatcher** (1979-90). She crushed the unions and Argentina (Falklands War). She reversed economic decline and changed the spirit of the nation. However, her policies caused deep antagonism and ideological blindness induced her fall. The success of the Conservatives led to the remaking of the Labour Party (New Labour) by **Tony Blair**, who renounced socialism as the fundamental principle of the party. In the late 1990s he led the movement for devolution (parliaments for Scotland and Wales), helped

tame the Northern Irish crisis, and moved towards greater integration with Europe while continuing a special relationship with Washington.

FRANCE

The Gaullists were defeated in 1981 by the Socialists under **François Mitterrand**. He proved to be a moderate reformer, worked effectively on European integration, and cooperated with a Gaullist prime minister (*cohabitation*). The Gaullists regained the presidency in 1995. Although the communists and neo-fascists are largely marginalized, fringe groups in profound disagreement with the existing constitution remain prevalent.

RUSSIA

Yelstin failed to make effective economic reforms which led to a breakdown. **Vladimir Putin** elected President in 2000 and restored a sense of purpose and order. He has made some effective reforms and finally pushed through the right to buy and sell agricultural land. He has been cooperative with the West while Russia was weak, but he is a former KGB agent with no time for a free press and also a deeply committed nationalist.

GERMANY

Chancellor **Helmut Kohl** organized reunification in 1990. This has proved costly and a less happy marriage than expected. The East's economy was so bad that even the dynamism of the West has struggled to achieve prosperity and repair the damage of 45 years of misrule. The socialist Chancellor Schröder is charting a newly independent foreign policy and sees the EU as a counter-balance to US power.

ITALY

Serious terrorist outbreaks in the 70s dissipated. The economy has prospered, but the lengthy rule of the Christian Democrats, kept in power because the only alternative was Communism, led to widespread corruption in the political system. Finally alternative parties have gained office, including the present center-right government.

YUGOSLAVIA

Ethnic antagonisms re-emerged after Tito's death in 1980. The upheavals elsewhere in the Balkans unleashed civil war. Croatia and Slovenia became independent in 1991. The worst fighting took place in Bosnia. The UN and NATO intervened in 1994. Serbian leader **Slobodan Milosevic** continued to foster ethnic trouble and terror until overthrown after NATO bombing in 1999-2000. He is now on trial for war crimes at The Hague.

Ordinary people's lives have been greatly transformed in recent years. Divorce has become common and unmarried childbirth routine. One-parent families proliferate and in most two-parent families both parents work outside the home. Manufacturing jobs have declined, and more and more people work in the service or technology sectors. Small farms are disappearing. More and more people go on to higher education. Drug use proliferated. Concern about "dumbing-down" of education.

Present problems include making the transition to the euro (€) successful, immigrants and refugees, right-wing resurgence (neo-Nazis), festering terrorism in the Basque region of Spain and possibly reviving in Northern Ireland, deciding who and what rate should new members be allowed to enter the EU and NATO. Will the EU be able to make credible and determined joint responses to foreign policy crises? (So far, no). With the USA as the only superpower, there is a tendency to pull against its lead. The information economy and the Internet have transformed business, recreation, education, and all forms of technology. The long-term economic troubles of capitalism in Japan, environmental damage (especially global warming), and the terrorist attacks of September 11, 2001 leave cause for heavy anxiety. So too does the disparity between the rich and poor in the world (especially unrestrained population growth in Asia and AIDs in Africa), and the dispersal of more easily accessible weapons of mass destruction.

1. Boris Yeltsin gained early popularity during his rise to power in Russia by accomplishing which of the following?

   (A) defying a Communist coup attempt
   (B) executing Gorbachev
   (C) leading a coup against Brezhnev
   (D) declaring war on China
   (E) rebuilding the Berlin Wall

2. How many nationalities were included within the borders of the Soviet Union before 1991?

   (A) 3
   (B) 6
   (C) 12
   (D) 25
   (E) 92

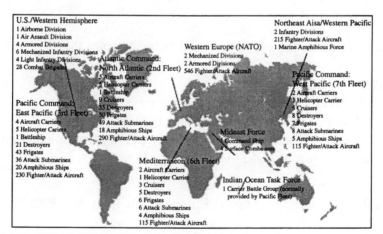

From THE RISE AND FALL OF THE GREAT POWERS by Paul Kennedy, copyright © 1987 by Paul Kennedy.
Used by permission of Randon House, Inc.

3. This map shows the military force deployments of

   (A) Britain in 1914
   (B) France in 1942
   (C) Russia in 1970
   (D) USA in 1987
   (E) China in 1990

4. Prime Minister Margaret Thatcher of Great Britain instituted all of the following reforms EXCEPT

(A)   lower taxes
(B)   limits on social welfare
(C)   restriction on unions
(D)   privatization of state-owned industries
(E)   abolished the state-run health system

	Life Expectancy at Birth	Adult Literacy	GDP per head
USSR	70	99%	$6000
Greece	76	93%	$5500
Austria	74	99%	$12,386
Belgium	75	99%	$13,140
W. Germany	75	99%	$14,730
Norway	77	99%	$15,940
Sweden	77	99%	$13,780

5. The set of statistics above, compiled in the 1980s, indicates that

(A)   the higher the life expectancy the richer the country
(B)   income is directly correlated with literacy rates
(C)   Western Europe is more prosperous than the East
(D)   communist countries have lower per capita GDPs than capitalist ones
(E)   Belgium is the best place to live

6. The most difficult challenge facing the European Union in the 1990s has been

(A)   establishing a parliament
(B)   issuing common passports
(C)   negotiating trade agreements
(D)   drafting a human rights charter
(E)   establishing a common foreign policy

7. Which among the following is in correct chronological order?

   (A)   reunification of Germany, Gorbachev takes power, Yeltsin becomes President of Russia, Czechoslovakia split in two

   (B)   Gorbachev takes power, reunification of Germany, Yeltsin becomes President of Russia, Czechoslovakia split in two

   (C)   Yeltsin becomes President of Russia, reunification of Germany, Gorbachev takes power, Czechoslovakia split in two

   (D)   Czechoslovakia split in two, Yeltsin becomes President of Russia, Gorbachev takes power, reunification of Germany

   (E)   Gorbachev takes power, Yeltsin becomes President of Russia, reunification of Germany, Czechoslovakia split in two

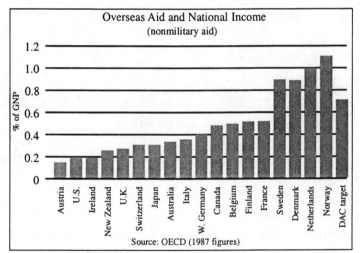

From PREPARING FOR THE TWENTY-FIRST CENTURY by Paul Kennedy, copyright © 1993 by Paul Kennedy. Used by Permission of Random House, Inc.

8. The graph above indicates that

   (A)   Scandinavians are more generous than other nations

   (B)   Europeans are less likely to give much aid compared to the United States

   (C)   Europe gives away more money than the United States

   (D)   only European countries give overseas aid

   (E)   overseas aid is a waste of money

9. The final collapse of the communist party in the Soviet Union in 1991 was triggered by

   (A)   Yeltsin's murder

   (B)   Reagan's election

   (C)   a failed *coup*

   (D)   invasion by Ukraine

   (E)   a major famine

© Les Gibbard, The Guardian

10. The above cartoon suggests what about the relationship between Great Britain and the United States in the 1980s?

    (A)   they were equal partners
    (B)   the US assumed Britain owed a debt to Washington for help in the Falklands War
    (C)   Margaret Thatcher was the dominant partner
    (D)   President Reagan's experience as an actor allowed him to gain the upper hand
    (E)   Britain and the United States were enemies

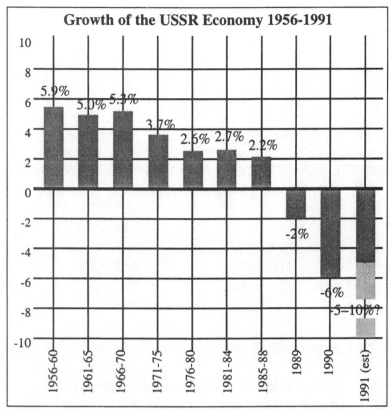

Copyright © 1993 by Paul Kennedy. Reprinted by permission of Random House, Inc.

11. Which of the following statements is true about the above graph?

   (A)   the Soviet economy never increased its rate of growth

   (B)   the Soviet economy was always in negative growth

   (C)   the Soviet economy never grew at a rate greater than the rest of Europe

   (D)   the Soviet economy went into a tailspin in the 1970s

   (E)   Gorbachev's reforms were unable to slow the decline of the Soviet economy

12. "There is great thirst for mutual understanding and mutual communication in the world.
...And if the Russian word 'perestroika' has easily entered the international lexicon, this
is due to more than just interest in what is going on in the Soviet Union. Now the whole
world needs restructuring, ie. progressive development, a fundamental change."

The author of the above passage was

   (A)   Yuri Andropov

   (B)   Konstantin Chernenko

   (C)   Mikhail Gorbachev

   (D)   Leonid Brezhnev

   (E)   Nikta Khrushchev

13. The conflicts in Bosnia and Kosovo during the 1990s led to the break up of

    (A)   Austria
    (B)   Czechoslovakia
    (C)   Yugoslavia
    (D)   Greece
    (E)   Roumania

14.   NUMBERS OF SCIENTISTS AND ENGINEERS PER MILLION
OF POPULATION 1989

Japan	3548
USA	2685
Europe	1632
Latin America	209
Asia (not Japan)	99

The above table indicates that

    (A)   European science is inferior to that practiced in Japan
    (B)   Europe has more scientists than anywhere else
    (C)   Europe has proportionately fewer scientists and engineers than Japan
    (D)   Europe has only one-third the number of scientists and engineers as Japan
    (E)   Europe invests less in educating scientists and engineers than elsewhere

15. Terrorist movements were active in all of the following places during the 1970s and 1980s EXCEPT

    (A)   Finland
    (B)   Northern Ireland
    (C)   the Basque country
    (D)   Italy
    (E)   Germany

16. The Roman Catholic church suffered from declining allegiance in Europe during the last three decades for all of the following reasons EXCEPT

    (A)   denunciation of birth control
    (B)   clerical celibacy
    (C)   refusal to admit women to the priesthood
    (D)   reluctance to address homosexual scandals
    (E)   election of a non-Italian pope

17.   SHARES OF GLOBAL EXPORTS OF COMPUTERS 1980-89

1980	1989
USA (39%)	USA (24%)
W. Germany (12%)	Japan (18%)
UK (10%)	UK (9%)
France (9%)	W. Germany (7%)
Italy (7%)	Taiwan (6%)

The above table indicates that

(A)   Italy remained behind France in computer exports throughout the period
(B)   German computer production declined
(C)   European exports were being overtaken by Asian competition
(D)   Europeans were losing the lead in software production
(E)   European exports exceeded those from the US in 1980

18. The "Green Party" of the 1980s can best be described as

(A)   militant environmentalists
(B)   Irish nationalists
(C)   right wing conservatives
(D)   aggressive monetarists
(E)   pro-war

19. All of the following countries gained their independence after the collapse of the Soviet Union 1989-91 EXCEPT

(A)   Estonia
(B)   Turkey
(C)   Kazakistan
(D)   Belarus
(E)   Ukraine

20.   SHARES OF THE GROSS WORLD PRODUCT 1960-1980

	1960	1970	1980
Japan	4.5	7.7	9.0
EEC*	26.0	24.7	22.5
United States	25.9	23.0	21.5
USSR	12.5	12.4	11.4

*European Economic Community

All of the following statements about the above table are true EXCEPT

(A)   Japan did not have as large an economy as the EEC
(B)   Europe was consistently more productive than the USA
(C)   the USSR and USA constantly declined in their shares
(D)   the USSR and USA declined at the same rate
(E)   Japan constantly grew in their share

21. Which of the following countries had the highest GDP per capita in 1992?

(A)   Portugal
(B)   Switzerland
(C)   Spain
(D)   Czech Republic
(E)   United Kingdom

22. The most violent uprising leading to the overthrow of a communist regime in the period
    1989-91 took place in

(A)   USSR
(B)   Czechoslovakia
(C)   Hungary
(D)   Ukraine
(E)   Romania

© *Les Gibbard, The Guardian*

23. This cartoon published in the 1980s suggests that the Northern Irish (Ulster) question

    (A)   was causing a rift between the British and the French
    (B)   was proving impossible to solve
    (C)   would lead to civil war in Britain
    (D)   might prove helpful in digging the Channel Tunnel
    (E)   was showing that the Irish were more powerful than the British

24.   KILOS OF COAL EQUIVALENT AND STEEL USED TO PRODUCE
                    $1000 OF GDP (1979-80)

	Coal	Steel
Russia	1490	135
Hungary	1058	88
Britain	820	38
West Germany	565	52
France	502	42

Which of the following statements is true about the above table?

    (A)   France was expanding their steel production
    (B)   the Hungarian economy was the weakest
    (C)   Germany had the most efficient steel industry
    (D)   Russia had the second most efficient steel industry
    (E)   the French were more efficient in their use of coal than the British

Europe, A HISTORY by Norman Davies, © 1993 by Norman Davies.
Used by permission of Oxford University Press, Inc.

25. This map shows Europe in

    (A)   1939
    (B)   1945
    (C)   1955
    (D)   1988
    (E)   1992

Document Based Question (DBQ)

(Reading time 15 minutes; writing time – 45 minutes)

Directions: The following question is based on the accompanying Documents 1-12. (Some of the documents have been edited for the purpose of this exercise.)

This question is designed to test your ability to work with historical documents. Write an essay that:

- Has a relevant thesis and supports that thesis with evidence from the documents.
- Uses a majority of the documents.
- Analyzes the documents by grouping them in as many appropriate ways as possible. **Does not simply summarize the documents individually.**
- Takes into account both the sources of the documents and the author's points of view. You may refer to relevant historical information not mentioned in the documents.

QUESTION: Describe and analyze the social, economic, and political considerations which induced some Englishmen, including aristocrats, to press for the passage of the 1832 Reform Bill.

<u>Historical background</u>: During the eighteenth and early nineteenth century momentum for reform of Parliament grew. Conservative governments (Tory) resisted changes to the electoral system. Seats in the House of Commons were divided between counties (where the electorate was dominated by large landowners) and boroughs, a few of which had large numbers of eligible voters, but most (called rotten boroughs) were small and easily controlled by wealthy proprietors. These proprietors were aristocrats (who also composed the membership of the hereditary House of Lords) and some merchants. Many cities that had recently become manufacturing centers were unrepresented while many remote rural villages sent representatives to the Commons. A Whig (liberal) government came to power in 1830, and after a long struggle but with the support of some Tories enacted the Great Reform Act of 1832. The Act extended the franchise to most professional and business people, eliminated many rotten boroughs, and gave seats to big industrial cities such as Manchester and Birmingham.

Borough Electorates in the unreformed House of Commons

1-100 electors	77 seats
101-300 electors	36 seats
310-1,000 electors	46 seats
1,000 plus electors	43 seatsy

Document 1

Source: William Cobbett, radical journalist, *Cobbett's Political Register*, newspaper, 1816

With what indignation must you hear yourselves called the Rabble, the Mob, the Swinish Multitude.... As to the cause of our present miseries, it is the enormous amount of the taxes, which the government compels us to pay for the support of its army, its placemen, its pensioners, etc. and for the payment of the interest on the debt.... The remedy consists wholly and solely of such a reform in the Commons or People's House of Parliament, as shall give to every payer of taxes a vote at elections, and as shall cause the Members to be elected annually.

Document 2

Source: T. L. Wooler, radical journalist, *The Black Dwarf*, journal, 1819

An Englishman is not at liberty to drink spirits, unless he can pay six or seven and twenty shillings a gallon. If wheat could be imported for twenty shillings a bushel, Parliament would not let it enter our ports without a 60 shilling tariff. We pay a one hundred percent duty on tea. If you are rich, you can buy anything. If you are poor, you are miserable thanks to the exactions of the landowners and rich merchants who control seats in Parliament.

Document 3

Source: Viscount Althorp, Whig MP*, letter to a political ally, J. C. Gotch, 1821

I am not afraid of those who attempt to stir up trouble amongst the poor, for they have no power to do any harm, but I am very much afraid of the excuse they will give to those who wish to establish despotism, and I really and sincerely believe such a design is in existence. No man can now gravely assert that the House of Commons have any pretensions to say that they express the feelings of the country. If there is a grain of English spirit left petitions for reform of Parliament will come from every parish in the kingdom.

*Member of the House of Commons

Document 4

Source: Viscount Milton, Whig MP, "Address on the Corn Laws", pamphlet, 1825

The landed gentlemen of England ought to be at the head of everything liberal, and prepared to sacrifice their own interests to promote the general welfare of the country. Was it for them to use their power to pass tariffs through Parliament in order to enrich themselves at the expense of their fellow subjects? He blushed for the order to which he belonged when he thought of the Corn Laws and the arguments used in the House of Commons to maintain them. We stand on a noble eminence; we occupy a station in the public eye, which has been conceded to us by the affections and by the favour of successive generations. Let us beware how we teach men to scan too minutely the value of our claims and the reasonableness of their favour.

Document 5

Source: Earl of Winchelsea in a letter to the Duke of Richmond, both Ultra-Tory (extreme conservative) members of the House of Lords, 1829

When I see how the owners of rotten boroughs were willing to support the government in its outrageous decision to grant Roman Catholics the right to vote, I know our only recourse is parliamentary reform. The mass of the people are loyal to the Church of England and hostile to the pretensions of papists and dissenters. The security of our Protestant monarchy and constitution must be put in the hands of the people or we will soon be mere slaves of the Pope.

Document 6

Source: Thomas Attwood, banker, article in the *Birmingham Argus*, newspaper, 1829

The very serious losses to which the trade of Birmingham has been exposed...might have been greatly diminished, if not entirely prevented, had we been so fortunate as to have possessed two faithful representatives in Parliament during these last thirty or forty years.

Document 7

Source: Marquess of Tavistock, Whig landowner, diary, 1829

If I am to retain popularity with my tenants and laborers on my estates and to keep the votes of the farmers for my nominees for the county seats in Bedfordshire, I must abandon my rotten boroughs and all semblance of participating in corrupt or illegitimate manipulation of rotten boroughs. Acting thus I can appear generous and upright in the eyes of the people.

Document 8

Source: Henry Hunt, radical agitator, speech to a rally of working men in Manchester, 1830

When the Tories charge the Whig ministers of intending to make a democratic House of Commons, the latter say, "No, we are going to keep the power out of the hands of the rabble." Their policy is to get one million of the middle classes, the shopkeepers and those people, to join the higher classes, to preserve property and privilege.

Document 9

Source: Lady Georgina Stuart-Wortley to Lady Harrowby, Tory aristocrats, letter, 1830

The revolution in France in July of this year, which overthrew the King and the aristocracy, was a warning to us all. What folly if we do not learn the lesson that obdurate refusal to meet just grievances only antagonizes the masses and arouses a dangerous spirit.

Document 10

Source: Charles Greville, Tory aristocrat and courtier, diary, 1830

Now that this Reform issue has served the Whigs purposes so well and defeated the Tory Government, some of the former would like to put it aside and take time to consider what they should do. It is a hundred to one that they are not really going to do more than throw a few scraps to mollify the people for the time being.

Document 11

Source: Thomas Babington Macaulay, Whig MP and historian, speech in a debate in the House of Commons, 1831

We exclude from all share in the government vast masses of property and intelligence – vast numbers of the middle classes – those who are most interested in preserving tranquility and who know best how to preserve it. We do more. We drive over to the sin of revolution those whom we shut out of power. The happiness of the people cannot be promoted by a form of government in which the middle classes place no confidence.

Document 12

Source: J.L. Marks, cartoon, 1832

© The British Museum

No testing material on this page.

Free-Response Questions (FRQ's)

1. Assess the degree to which the Renaissance was primarily an episode in the history of art.

2. "The Renaissance was a rehearsal for the Enlightenment." Assess the validity of this statement.

3. Compare and contrast the rise of Spain in the fifteenth and sixteenth centuries and Germany in the nineteenth.

4. To what degree was controversy about the ceremony of the "mass" central to the Reformation.

5. Compare and contrast the characters and achievements of Ignatius Loyola (1491-1556) and Maximilien Robespierre (1758-1794).

6. Discuss the outcomes of the Thirty Years War (1618-1648). Which was the most important?

7. What are the most reliable sources used by historians to study the role of women in the seventeenth century?

8. The English Civil War (1640-1649) is sometimes called the "Puritan Revolution." Is this the best name for it?

9. Assess the successes and failures of the absolutist monarchy of King Louis XIV of France (1643-1715).

10. "Modern science (as it developed in the seventeenth and eighteenth centuries) sprang from the shift by which urban and industrial values replaced those appropriate to a mainly agrarian society." Assess the validity of this statement.

11. "Not a single reform has ever been completed in Russia." Assess the validity of this statement in light of Russian history from the reign of Peter the Great (1682-1725) to the present.

12. The first industrial revolution that took place in Britain during the eighteenth and early nineteenth century was primarily the result of social and political factors not economic ones. Discuss.

13. In what ways did women's roles in pre-industrial society reflect men's opinions of what they should be?

14. Did Napoleon I (1801-1815) further the ideals of the French Revolution of bury them?

15. "Karl Marx (1818-1883) was the last 'philosophe'." Assess the validity of this statement.

16. Classical liberalism of the nineteenth century differs markedly from twentieth-century liberalism. Analyze their similarities and differences.

17. Analyze the factors that made Britain a great power in the nineteenth century.

18. Discuss the positive and negative aspects of European imperialism in Africa between 1880 and 1914.

19. Compare and contrast the characters and achievements of Count Camillo di Cavour (1810-1861) and Prince Otto von Bismarck (1815-1898).

20. Assess the strengths and weaknesses of Imperial Russia between the reigns of Alexander I and Nicholas II (1801-1917).

21. It was unfortunate to incorporate the War Guilt Clause blaming Germany for causing World War I into the Treaty of Versailles. But was it unfair?

22. In what ways did World War I change European thought and culture?

23. Compare the regimes established by Napoleon I (1801-1815) and Adolf Hitler (1933-45). Were they more alike or different?

24. Why has the European Union been successful?

25. Did the United States "win" the Cold War or the Soviet Union lose it?

Sample Examination I

Section I

Three hours and five minutes are allotted for this examination: 55 minutes for Section I, which consists of multiple-choice questions, and 130 minutes for Section II, which consists of the DBQ and two free response essays.

This section should be completed in 55 minutes.

from *A HISTORY OF MODERN EUROPE: FROM THE RENNAISANCE TO THE PRESENT by John Merriman.*
Copyright © 1996 by John Merriman. Used by permission of W.W. Norton & Company, Inc.

1. This map depicts Europe at what date?

   (A)   1300
   (B)   1500
   (C)   1650
   (D)   1700
   (E)   1750

223

2. Among the following which was the only city state to survive the Italian Renaissance with its wealth and power intact?

(A)   Florence
(B)   Venice
(C)   Milan
(D)   Naples
(E)   Genoa

3. King Louis XIV of France used what criteria to appoint officials called indendants to administer local areas?

(A)   loyalty to the crown
(B)   noble birth
(C)   university degrees
(D)   foreign birth
(E)   support for the Enlightenment

4. "God has given to every people its ruler. The royal power is absolute. All the state is in him."

The author of this quotation was

(A)   Bishop Bossuet on Louis XIV
(B)   Tony Blair on Elizabeth II
(C)   Voltaire on Frederick the Great
(D)   Tolstoy on Stalin
(E)   Hitler on Hindenburg

5. Aside from emphasis on which of the following, Protestantism did little to change the traditional place of women in society.

(A)   having children
(B)   acting as grandparents
(C)   companionate marriage
(D)   housekeeping
(E)   keeping pets

6. Martin Luther made close alliances with a number of sovereign princes within the Holy Roman Empire because

(A) he wanted political power for himself
(B) the pope urged him to do so
(C) he sought reconciliation with Charles V
(D) he was related to them by marriage
(E) he feared extreme demands made by the peasantry

7. The Catholic counter reformation enunciated the following policy after the important Council of Trent.

(A) total surrender to Luther's demands
(B) reaffirmed Catholic doctrine
(C) compromise with John Calvin
(D) declaration of war on schismatic Spain
(E) that there should be two popes

8. A majority of the people accused of witchcraft in the seventeenth century were all of the following EXCEPT

(A) from rural areas
(B) rich
(C) women
(D) single
(E) poor

9. Oliver Cromwell emerged as the the central leader of the parliamentary cause during the English Civil War because he

(A) was loyal to the king
(B) restored Catholicism
(C) was helped by Cardinal Richelieu
(D) was a successful military commander
(E) was willing to grant Ireland independence

10. The principal cause for the decline of the Dutch Republic in the later seventeenth century was

(A) poor leadership
(B) wars with France
(C) a hidebound aristocracy
(D) alliance with Britain
(E) rivalry with Russia

11. Which of the following countries was rapidly rising in power and influence during the eighteenth century?

    (A)   Ottoman Empire
    (B)   Sweden
    (C)   Prussia
    (D)   Spain
    (E)   Poland

Priest who runs the cathedral

12. Canon law is concerned with which of the following?

    (A)   torts
    (B)   democratic legislatures
    (C)   the military
    (D)   royal families
    (E)   the church

13. The most significant achievements of the Scientific Revolution fell into which of the following categories?

    (A)   astronomy
    (B)   biology
    (C)   geology
    (D)   epistemology
    (E)   chemistry

14. The Scottish academic and philosophe, Adam Smith, extolled the virtues of which of the following?

    (A)   command economies
    (B)   accumulating more colonies
    (C)   concentrating on amassing large gold reserves
    (D)   monarchical government
    (E)   *laissez-faire* economics

15. "Deism" is a term used to describe the religious thinking of several leading philosophes of the Enlightenment. It describes a religion

    (A)   in which kings were gods on earth
    (B)   in which God was the creator but not actively in control
    (C)   in which God is dead
    (D)   that was polytheistic
    (E)   that is strictly Roman Catholic

16. Feudalism decayed in Western Europe during the later Middle Ages because of all the following reasons EXCEPT

  (A) the spread of itinerant merchants
  (B) urbanization
  (C) new military technology
  (D) invention of steam power
  (E) the black death

17. Parliaments or "estates" in early modern Europe served which of the following functions?

  (A) universal democratic representation
  (B) conducting foreign policy
  (C) protecting local or regional privileges
  (D) choosing prime ministers
  (E) acting as war councils

18. Which of the following countries were the principal commercial rivals in international trade during the seventeenth century?

  (A) France, Britain, and the United Provinces
  (B) France, Spain, and Italy
  (C) Spain, Portugal, and Italy
  (D) Britain, the United Provinces, and Russia
  (E) The United Provinces, Sweden, and Portugal

19. The House of Orange ruled in the Netherlands from the sixteenth to the eighteenth century as

  (A) hereditary monarchs
  (B) absolute dictators
  (C) French puppets
  (D) elected officials
  (E) naval commanders only

20. By ending clerical celibacy and monastic life, the Protestant Reformation put greater emphasis on which of the following?

  (A) warfare as the noblest profession
  (B) accumulation of wealth as more important that Christian conduct
  (C) papal authority
  (D) the family as the center of life
  (E) entertainment and sexual abandon

21. Among the following royal dynasties which one consistently produced monarchs of outstanding ability and success during the seventeenth and eighteenth centuries?

    (A) England
    (B) France
    (C) Savoy
    (D) Spain
    (E) Brandenburg-Prussia

22. During the Reformation radical Protestants opposed all of the following religious practices EXCEPT

    (A) transubstantiation
    (B) worship at altars
    (C) use of incense in ceremonies
    (D) sermons
    (E) decorations with stained glass

23. The Kingdom of Spain was unified into a single state in 1469 when

    (A) the monarchs of Castile and Aragon married
    (B) Philip V conquered the south
    (C) Portugal broke away as an independent state
    (D) a war was fought with Great Britain
    (E) a plebiscite was held

24. The founding father of humanism, Petrarch, initiated which of the following?

    (A) advocating atheism
    (B) searching monastic libraries for forgotten manuscripts
    (C) denouncing the use of venacular language
    (D) doing scientific experiments
    (E) calling women equal to men

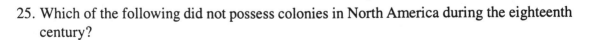

25. Which of the following did not possess colonies in North America during the eighteenth century?

    (A) Portugal
    (B) Great Britain
    (C) Russia
    (D) Spain
    (E) France

26. From the mid-eighteenth century the Western European population did which of the following?

    (A)   stayed steady

    (B)   suffered a small decline

    (C)   steady and substantial growth

    (D)   showed a small increase

    (E)   rapidly declined

27. All of the following contributed to significant advances in the study of astronomy during the sixteenth and seventeenth centuries EXCEPT

    (A)   mountaintop observatories

    (B)   the telescope

    (C)   scientific measurement

    (D)   application of mathematics

    (E)   systematic observation

28. By the mid-sixteenth century European cartographers had

    (A)   mapped Japan and Indonesia

    (B)   mapped Australia and New Zealand

    (C)   achieved a clear picture of both Atlantic coasts

    (D)   reached the North Pole

    (E)   traced the source of the Nile

Courtesy of Houghton Mifflin Company

29. In this drawing of Louis XVI, Benjamin Franklin, and George Washington, the King of France is depicted as

    (A) a cruel imperialist
    (B) the liberator of America
    (C) indifferent to the fate of the Americas
    (D) an enemy of freedom
    (E) incompetent

30. Although Enlightenment thinkers were often creative and original contributors to knowledge, the key component to their contribution was

    (A) the popularization of science
    (B) astrology
    (C) drama and poetry
    (D) the extermination of witches
    (E) advocacy of republican opinions

31. The Royal Society and the Academy founded by Charles II of England in 1662 and Louis XIV of France in 1666 respectively were intended to promote

    (A) science
    (B) religion
    (C) commerce
    (D) war
    (E) genealogy

32. The term "Newtonian Synthesis" is used to describe

    (A) Newton's religious views
    (B) the discoveries leading to an understanding of gravity
    (C) the joint work of Newton and Locke
    (D) the sciences of ballistics and optics combined
    (E) Newton's writings about the New World

33. The English philosopher and father of the Enlightenment, John Locke, believed that

    (A) we are born "hardwired" to think in certain ways
    (B) revolutions are never necessary or successful
    (C) the scientific method can be applied to the study of human activity
    (D) custom should be valued over reason
    (E) universal suffrage is essential for good government

34. One of the main reforms carried of by Enlightened despots during the eighteenth century was

    (A) codifying the laws
    (B) strengthening the church
    (C) avoiding war at all costs
    (D) granting more power to the nobility
    (E) closing universities

35. Who among the following was most closely connected with the concepts of the "social contact" and the "general will"?

    (A) Louis XIV
    (B) Thomas Hobbes
    (C) Lorenzo de Medici
    (D) Rosa Luxenburg
    (E) Jean Jacques Rousseau

36. "Let others wage war. You, happy _____ , marry to prosper."

    Among the following countries, which is being referred to in the above epigram?

    (A) Venice
    (B) Great Britain
    (C) France
    (D) Austria
    (E) Russia

37.

	1690	1760	1814
A	400,000	330,000	600,000
B	30,000	195,000	270,000
C	73,000	40,000	25,000

Correctly identify which countries possessed armies of these sizes between 1690 and 1814.

    (A) A France B Prussia C United Provinces
    (B) A Prussia B France C United Provinces
    (C) A France B United Provinces C Prussia
    (D) A United Provinces B France C Prussia
    (E) A Prussia B United Provinces C France

38. Which among the following was not a middle class occupation during the nineteenth century?

(A) senior military officer
(B) banker
(C) industrialist
(D) university professor
(E) lawyer

39. All of the following were associated with Queen Victoria (reigned 1837 to 1901) EXCEPT

(A) propriety and high moral standards
(B) the imperial crown of India
(C) elaborate and high decorated architecture
(D) grandmother of many European monarchs
(E) equality for women in the political sphere

40. The German Chancellor, Otto von Bismarck, enacted a major welfare program for the working class

(A) to outflank the socialists
(B) at the behest of Emperor Wilhelm I
(C) to satisfy military recruitment quotas
(D) to undermine the aristocracy
(E) out of religious convictions

41. The French "Third Republic" (1871-1940) was characterized by

(A) lack of an empire
(B) continuous wars
(C) religious tolerance
(D) political instability
(E) dictatorship

42. During the nineteenth century the status of the professions (law, medicine, clergy, etc.) was

(A) declining
(B) about the same as in the eighteenth century
(C) rising
(D) ignored by the rest of the bourgeoisie
(E) merged with the lower middle class

43. Which among the following was not incorporated into the unified Kingdom of Italy during the 1860s?

   (A)   Savoy
   (B)   Rome
   (C)   Naples
   (D)   Venetia
   (E)   Tuscany

44. Emperor Napoleon I accomplished or enacted all of the following EXCEPT

   (A)   suppressed and censored the press
   (B)   made peace with the Roman Catholic church
   (C)   placed his brothers on foreign thrones
   (D)   codified the laws
   (E)   never lost a battle

45. The Crimean War (1853-56) was fought by Great Britain, France, and the Ottoman Empire against what enemy?

   (A)   Prussia
   (B)   Russia
   (C)   Austria
   (D)   Italy
   (E)   Spain

46. President Woodrow Wilson hoped above all else to accomplish which of the following at the peace conference at Versailles in 1919?

   (A)   found a League of Nations
   (B)   restore the Tsar of Russia to the throne
   (C)   maintain the integrity of the Austro-Hungarian Empire
   (D)   create an alliance system to surround Germany
   (E)   sustain colonial empires

47. Emperor Napoleon III was

   (A)   elected president of France in 1848
   (B)   Napoleon's son who died before he could ascend the throne
   (C)   ruled in the early twentieth century
   (D)   abdicated in order to make way for a democratic republic
   (E)   insisted that France pursue a pacifist foreign policy

From CITIZENS by Simon Schama, copright © 1989 by Simon Schama. Used by permission of Alfred A. Knopf, a division of Random House, Inc.

48. This drawing of 1794 entitled "Robespierre guillotining the executioner" suggests

   (A)   more people should be executed
   (B)   the Terror was out of control
   (C)   the Terror was helping France
   (D)   guillotines were breaking down
   (E)   the guillotine should be made a French export

49. Occupations among the lower middle classes in the nineteenth century would have included all of the following EXCEPT

   (A)   skilled laborer
   (B)   café owner
   (C)   minor official
   (D)   school teacher
   (E)   small shopkeeper

50. Which pair of countries supported the fascist general Francisco Franco during the Spanish Civil War 1936-39?

    (A)   France and Britain
    (B)   USA and Poland
    (C)   Greece and Denmark
    (D)   Germany and Italy
    (E)   Russia and Turkey

51. Which among the following was one of the most important achievements of British Prime Minister Margaret Thatcher in the 1980s?

    (A)   appeased foreign aggressors
    (B)   pulled Great Britain out of the European Union
    (C)   sided with Europe against the United States
    (D)   extended the benefits of the welfare state
    (E)   reversed nationalization of businesses enacted in the 1940s

52. During the nineteenth century middle class women took part in all of the following EXCEPT

    (A)   cared for their children
    (B)   supervised servants
    (C)   became doctors and lawyers
    (D)   supported philanthropic organizations
    (E)   arranged social activities

53. Belgium was established as an independent country in

    (A)   1585 in a revolt against Philip II of Spain
    (B)   1640 during the Thirty Years' War
    (C)   1789 as a result of the French Revolution
    (D)   1831 in a revolt against the Netherlands
    (E)   1918 at the Treaty of Versailles

54. "Separate spheres" is a term used by historians to describe

    (A)   divisions between activities acceptable for men and women
    (B)   imperialism in Africa as opposed to Asia
    (C)   the division of powers between monarchs and legislatures
    (D)   balloon ascents
    (E)   the division between working class and nobles

55. I knew a simple soldier boy
    Who grinned at life in empty joy,
    Slept soundly through the lonesome dark,
    And whistled early with the lark.

    In winter trenches, cowed and glum,
    With crumps and lice and lack of rum,
    He put a bullet through his brain,
    No one spoke of him again.

    This poem refers to which of the following conflicts?

    (A)   Thirty Years War
    (B)   War of the Spanish Succession
    (C)   Napoleonic War
    (D)   World War I
    (E)   Cold War

Map: 1815-1860, from *A HISTORY OF MODERN EUROPE: FROM THE RENNAISANCE TO THE PRESENT* by
John Merrimn. Copyright © 1996 by John Merriman. Used by permission of W.W. Norton & Company

56. This map the areas of which of the following?

    (A)   industrialization
    (B)   a Lutheran majority
    (C)   the possessions of Queen Victoria
    (D)   areas affected by nationalist uprisings
    (E)   areas where women were granted the franchise

57. The reign of Tsar Nicholas II of Russia (1894-1917) was marked by

    (A) failure to implement meaningful reforms
    (B) military victories
    (C) enlightened and tolerant treatment of minorities
    (D) rejection of foreign alliances
    (E) continuance of reforms begun by Alexander II

58.

ETHNIC GROUPS	POPULATION
Germans	12.0
Magyars	10.1
Czechs	6.6
Poles	5.0
Ukrainians	4.0
Romainians	3.2
Croats	2.9
Serbs	2.0

The above list is of populations in which of the following places?

    (A) Holy Roman Empire
    (B) Balkan peninsula
    (C) Ottoman Empire
    (D) Russian Empire
    (E) Austro-Hungarian Empire

59. During the nineteenth century middle class families in Western Europe would have engaged in all of the following activities EXCEPT

    (A) visit museums
    (B) take foreign tours
    (C) emigrate to the United States
    (D) read novels
    (E) promenade in public parks

60. Which among the following were important medical advances that took place in the nineteenth century?

    (A) blood transfusions and antibiotics
    (B) Pasteurization and anesthetics
    (C) Bone scans and bypass surgery
    (D) Vaccinations for small pox and sulfa drugs
    (E) Amputations and transplants

61. The opening of the Suez Canal in 1869 was of vital importance to which great power?

    (A) Austria-Hungary
    (B) Germany
    (C) Great Britain
    (D) Spain
    (E) Russia

62. One of the most important policies pursued by Austria's Chancellor Prince Metternich between 1815 and 1848 was

    (A) encourage the unification of Germany under Prussian leadership
    (B) suppress nationalistic movements in Germany
    (C) reject all foreign alliances
    (D) create an empire in Africa
    (E) establish an independent Poland

63. Japan was able successfully to resist submission to European imperialism because of the

    (A) strength of its feudal system
    (B) openness of Japan to foreign contacts in the sixteenth and seventeenth centuries
    (C) success it had in playing one enemy against another
    (D) rapid adaptation to Western technology
    (E) skill of samurai warriors

64. World War I had a devastating impact on aristocratic society for all of the following reasons EXCEPT

    (A) the younger generation was killed in the trenches
    (B) extremely high taxation was imposed
    (C) servants disappeared
    (D) they were banned from politics
    (E) the rise of democratic values

65. In 1850 the middle classes formed the greatest proportion of the population in which of the following countries?

    (A) Great Britain
    (B) Germany
    (C) Austria-Hungary
    (D) Russia
    (E) Ottoman Empire

66. During the first half of the nineteenth century major European cities experienced which of the following?

    (A)   shrank in size
    (B)   built over all remaining open land within city limits
    (C)   rejected new emigrants
    (D)   were abandoned by monarchs who took up residence in the countryside
    (E)   became overcrowded

67. The Zollverein founded in 1834

    (A)   was a customs union led by Prussia including most of the German states
    (B)   unified Austria and Germany
    (C)   separated Austria and Hungary
    (D)   led to the separation of Southern and Northern Ireland
    (E)   was the name of the Catalonian independence movement

68. The potato blight of 1845

    (A)   was first discovered by Charles Darwin
    (B)   affected crops only in the Mediterranean region
    (C)   led to famine in Ireland and on the continent
    (D)   produced mass emigration from Spain
    (E)   led German farmers to convert all agricultural production to wheat

69. Place the following list of events in eighteenth and nineteenth-century France in the correct chronological order.

    (A)   First Empire, First Republic, July Monarchy
    (B)   First Republic, First Empire, July Monarchy
    (C)   July Monarchy, First Empire, First Republic
    (D)   July Monarchy, First Republic, First Empire
    (E)   First Republic, July Monarchy, First Empire

70. The electoral franchise in Great Britain was doubled in size by the Great Reform Act of 1832. This change was made by which of the following?

    (A)   imposed by France after Britain's military defeat
    (B)   Marxist revolutionaries
    (C)   Whig aristocrats
    (D)   a military junta
    (E)   the Duke of Wellington

71. Nineteenth-century liberals believed in which of the following ideas?

    (A)   state sponsored religion and mercantilism
    (B)   absolute monarchy and no constitutions
    (C)   anti-nationalism and pro-democracy
    (D)   power shared between a hereditary nobility and the monarch
    (E)   *liassez-faire* and the vote for property owners

72. Who among the following monarchs was murdered by Communist revolutionaries?

    (A)   Franz Joseph of Austria-Hungary
    (B)   Queen Victoria of Great Britain
    (C)   Wilhelm II of Germany
    (D)   Nicholas II of Russia
    (E)   Louis Philippe of France

73. Rank the following cities in order of the size of their populations in 1800 from largest to smallest.

    (A)   Paris, Berlin, London
    (B)   London, Paris, Berlin
    (C)   Berlin, Paris, London
    (D)   London, Berlin, Paris
    (E)   Berlin, London, Paris

74. The emergence of mass politics in the later nineteenth century was made possible by all of the following EXCEPT

    (A)   extension of the franchise
    (B)   steam driven printing presses
    (C)   labor unions
    (D)   radio
    (E)   secret ballot

75.

INDEX OF INDUSTRIAL PRODUCTION (1958=100)

	1938	1952	1959	1963	1967
United States	33	90	113	133	168
West Germany	53	61	107	137	158
France	52	70	101	129	155
Italy	43	64	112	166	212
Britain	67	84	105	119	133
Sweden	52	81	106	140	176
Japan	58	50	120	212	347

Which of the following countries enjoyed the greatest rate of industrial growth between 1938 and 1967?

(A)   West Germany
(B)   United States
(C)   Japan
(D)   Britain
(E)   Italy

76. The industrial revolution in Britain during the later eighteenth and early nineteenth centuries

(A)   involved the intensification of forms of production that already existed
(B)   introduced many new domestic cleaning devices
(C)   required little capital investment
(D)   created few new jobs
(E)   took place mainly in London

77. The Berlin Wall was torn down in 1989 because

(A)   Russia ordered it to be removed
(B)   Hungary opened its border with Austria
(C)   The United States threatened to use nuclear weapons
(D)   NATO destroyed it with tanks
(E)   East Germany voted to join West Germany

78. All of the following are aspects of the twentieth-century "Welfare States" EXCEPT

    (A)   nationalization of industries
    (B)   free medical care
    (C)   old age pensions
    (D)   assigned employment
    (E)   free university education

79. Numerous applications for membership in the European Union have recently come from which of the following regions?

    (A)   Scandinavia
    (B)   the Mediterranean region
    (C)   the central region
    (D)   Iberia
    (E)   the east

80. What issue has the European Union had the greatest difficulty finding a common policy?

    (A)   foreign affairs
    (B)   trade regulations
    (C)   human rights
    (D)   industrial standards
    (E)   passports

Section II

Part A

(Reading time 15 minutes; writing time – 45 minutes)

Percent of Section II score – 45

Directions: The following question is based on the accompanying Documents 1-13. (Some of the documents have been edited for the purpose of this exercise.)

This question is designed to test your ability to work with historical documents. Write an essay that:

- Has a relevant thesis and supports that thesis with evidence from the documents.
- Uses a majority of the documents.
- Analyzes the documents by grouping them in as many appropriate ways as possible. **Does not simply summarize the documents individually.**
- Takes into account both the sources of the documents and the authors' points of view.

You may refer to relevant historical information not mentioned in the documents.

QUESTION: Analyze the ways in which various people viewed the causes of the terrorist campaign in Northern Ireland between 1969 and 1999.

Historical Background: The English completed the conquest of Ireland in 1649 by which time most of the land owned by the native Roman Catholic population had been redistributed to Protestant British settlers. In 1922 Ireland attained independence except for Ulster, the six counties in the north where Roman Catholics were in a minority. Northern Ireland remains a part of the United Kingdom. A local assembly dominated by Protestants (Unionists), Stormont, governed the province until a terrorist campaign led by the Irish Republican Army (Nationalists) in the 1970s and 1980s provoked direct rule from London and occupation by the British army. Protestant "Loyalists" fought back, inspired by the oratory of their hero, the Rev. Ian Paisley. Peace negotiations followed an IRA cease-fire in the mid-1990s.

Document 1

Source: Edward Warnock, Unionist Member of Parliament, letter to Terence O'Neill, Prime Minister of Northern Ireland, 13 November 1968.

If ever a community had a right to demonstrate against the denial of civil rights, Derry is the finest example. A Roman Catholic and Nationalist city has for three or four decades been administered (and none too fairly administered) by a Protestant and Unionist majority secured by a manipulation of the Ward boundaries for the sole purpose of retaining Unionist control.

Document 2

Source: Lord Cameron, British official, Government Report on Disturbances in Northern Ireland, 1969.

A rising sense of injustice and grievance among large sections of the Catholic population has arisen in respect to: (1) inadequacy of housing; (2) unfair methods of allocation of houses built; (3) a growing and powerful sense of resentment and frustration among the Catholic population at the failure to achieve either acceptance on the part of the Government of any need to investigate these complaints or to provide and enforce a remedy for them; (4) resentment, particularly among Catholics, as to the existence of the Ulster Special Constabulary as a partisan and paramilitary force exclusively recruited from Protestants.

Document 3

Source: Les Gibbard, political cartoon in a British newspaper, 11 September 1969.

© Les Gibbard, The Guardian

Document 4

Source: British Army intelligence report, 1972

The IRA gunmen are usually unemployed, working-class Catholics, some of whom would probably have been ordinary criminals if it were not for the Nationalist movement. They were mostly young, under 23, and the greatest single factor in their joining the IRA was past or present membership by a member of their family.

Document 5

Source: Harold Wilson, British Prime Minister, television broadcast, May 25, 1974.

British parents have seen their soldier sons vilified and spat upon and murdered. British taxpayers have seen the taxes they have poured out, almost without regard to cost, going into Northern Ireland. They see property destroyed by evil violence and are asked to pick up the bill for rebuilding it. All this has been caused by people who spend their lives sponging off welfare programs and British democracy and then systematically assault democratic methods. Who do these people think they are?

Document 6

Source: Opinion poll, Northern Ireland, 1978.

CHOICE OF NATIONAL IDENTITY FOR CATHOLICS

British	Irish	Ulster	Other
15%	69%	6%	10%

CHOICE OF NATIONAL IDENTITY FOR PROTESTANTS

British	Irish	Ulster	Other
39%	20%	32%	9%

Document 7

Source: John Conroy, American journalist living in a Catholic neighborhood in the Northern Irish city of Belfast, diary, 1980.

My neighbors were haunted by the living, haunted by the dead, haunted by myths and legends and history. The conflict defines their lives. Men and women say they are Catholic, describing not their churchgoing habits but their political beliefs: they are Irish, not British. And their lot grows worse each year. They are ruined by alcohol, unemployment, and despair.

Document 8

Source: Philip Schlesinger, American scholar, *Social Research*, 1981.

The IRA's assassination of Lord Mountbatten, a member of the British royal family, in 1979 was widely interpreted by the British press as irrational, as an act of "evil men" (*Daily Mail*), "wicked assassins" (*The Sun*), "psychopathic thugs" (*Daily Express*), "murdering bastards" (*Daily Star*), as "cowardly and senseless" *(Financial Times)*, and as the product of "diseased minds rather than political calculation." (*Daily Telegraph*).

Document 9

Source: Seamus Finucane, IRA terrorist, press interview after the assassination of his brother by Protestants, 1989.

We lived through fifty years of misrule by Stormont, all the bigotry, the gerrymandering and sectarian killings. I can remember my brother John going for jobs and once they heard you were a Catholic: "Ah don't call us, we'll call you." We were always at the tail end of things. But I knew that the IRA were our defenders, looking after our interests, fighting for our rights. There was a great sense of anger.

Document 10

Source: The Earl of Kilmorey, British Minister for Northern Ireland, newspaper article, 4 April 1990.

Over the last eight years the economy of Northern Ireland is, for the first time this century, growing as fast as the rest of the United Kingdom. There is no reason why over the next ten years it should not do even better and that is bad news for the IRA.

Document 11

Source: Mairtin Muilleoir, City Councilor for Belfast and IRA supporter, funeral oration for a young terrorist killed by the British Army, June 1991.

The English have been killing people in County Tyrone for hundreds of years, they have been killing Irish people in these fields for over a thousand years, but we will teach them the lesson that no matter how many people they kill – and it is always open season on Nationalists, they can kill us in our beds, they can kill us in the streets, they can kill us in the fields but we will continue on.

Document 12

Source: Wall painting in a Catholic neighborhood, Belfast, 1991.

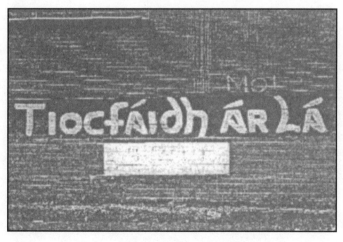

Queen's University, Belfast

"Our day will come." (translation)

Document 13

Source: Kevin Toolis, Irish journalist, *Rebel Hearts*, 1995.

As a philosophy, Irish Republicanism is the unqualified belief that a United Ireland is an intrinsic good, and the demand for Irish national self-determination so pressing, so overwhelming, that this goal must be pursued at all costs but principally and immediately by force of arms.

Section II

Part B

Group 1

(Suggested planning and writing time – 35 minutes)

Percent of Section II score – 27 1/2

Directions: You are to answer ONE question from the three questions below. Make your selection carefully, choosing the question that you are best prepared to answer thoroughly in the time permitted. You should spend 5 minutes organizing or outlining your answer. In writing your essay, <u>use specific examples to support your answer</u>.

2. What was the most significant long-term outcome of the Protestant Reformation?

3. Compare and contrast the impact on British society of the English Civil War (1641-49) and the Glorious Revolution (1688-89).

4. "Successful eighteenth-century states were those where the central government achieved a satisfactory relationship with its aristocracy." Assess the validity of this statement.

Group 2

(Suggested planning and writing time – 35 minutes)
Percent of Section II score – 27 1/2

Directions: You are to answer ONE question from the three questions below. Make your selection carefully, choosing the question that you are best prepared to answer thoroughly in the time permitted. You should spend 5 minutes organizing or outlining your answer. In writing your essay, <u>use specific examples to support your answer</u>.

5. Analyze the benefits and costs of the changes brought to urban life by the advance of industrialization in nineteenth-century Britain.

6. Analyze the significance of the Crimean War (1853-56).

7. Analyze the similarities and differences between communism and fascism.

No testing material on this page.

Sample Examination II

Section I

Three hours and five minutes are allotted for this examination: 55 minutes for Section I, which consists of multiple-choice questions, and 130 minutes for Section II, which consists of the DBQ and two free response essays.

This section should be completed in 55 minutes.

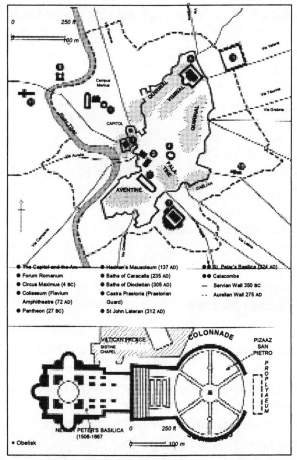

Europe, A HISTORY by Norman Davies, © 1993 by Norman Davies.
Used by permission of Oxford University Press, Inc.

1. This map portrays which of the following cities?

   (A)   Rome
   (B)   Paris
   (C)   London
   (D)   Athens
   (E)   Vienna

2. The Eastern Orthodox Church held the allegiance of most of the population in which of the following areas

   (A)   Russia and the Balkans
   (B)   Italy and Switzerland
   (C)   Egypt
   (D)   Poland
   (E)   Spain and Bohemia

3. "Brandish your swords.... You cannot meet a rebel with reason. Your best answer is to punch him in the face until he has a bloody nose."

   The statement above, which refers to a peasant revolt, was made by

   (A)   William Penn
   (B)   Menno Simons
   (C)   Emelian Pugachev
   (D)   Martin Luther
   (E)   Giuseppe Garibaldi

4. "Vernacular" is a term particularly characteristic of the Renaissance period that was used to describe

   (A)   the frame of the human skeleton
   (B)   local language
   (C)   mercenary warfare
   (D)   early printing presses
   (E)   the flow of blood to the heart

5. Which of the following passages was written by Machiavelli?

   (A)   "Loyalty to a small city is a foolish diversion of human devotion."
   (B)   "It is much safer to be feared than to be loved."
   (C)   "Only through prayer can man achieve his full measure of virtue."
   (D)   "In diplomacy honesty is the best policy."
   (E)   "Civilization reached its lowest point during the Roman Republic."

6. Charles I helped to precipitate the English Civil War by doing all of the following EXCEPT

(A) marrying a Catholic
(B) imposing taxation of questionable legality
(C) antagonizing the Scottish Calvinists
(D) supporting Archbishop Laud
(E) favoring the bourgeoisie over the nobility

Tate Gallery, London/Are Resource, NY

7. This painting illustrates the

(A) dangers of overpopulation
(B) affectionate relations between children and parents
(C) importance of athletics in the eighteenth century
(D) rigidity of the French Court
(E) suffering of the Irish poor

8. Both Tsars Ivan the Terrible and Peter the Great attempted to

(A) retain Moscow as their capital
(B) subordinate the boyars as a service nobility
(C) travel to the West
(D) convert to Catholicism
(E) build a fleet

9. The Renaissance began to wane in Northern Italy because of the

   (A)   French invasion of 1494 and the warfare that ensued
   (B)   invention of the printing press
   (C)   cessation of trade
   (D)   discovery of fewer Classical texts
   (E)   re-conquest of the city states by the Papacy

10. The Reformation leader, John Calvin, believed strongly in and

   (A)   advocated that only priests could interpret the scripture
   (B)   encouraged education so that everyone could read scripture
   (C)   welcomed the discoveries of the scientific revolution
   (D)   emulated the educational practices of the Jesuits
   (E)   encouraged study of Latin so that continued use of the Vulgate would be
         possible

11. All of the following were terms used to denote nobilities EXCEPT

   (A)   hidalgo
   (B)   junker
   (C)   grandee
   (D)   peer
   (E)   kulak

12. "In order to reunite more effectively the wills of our subjects and to remove all future
    complaints, we declare that all those who profess the Reformed religion are capable of
    holding ... all public positions, honors, offices, and duties whatsoever."

    The quotation above comes from

   (A)   Treaty of Augsburg
   (B)   Orders of the Council of Trent
   (C)   Edict of Nantes
   (D)   Peace of Westphalia
   (E)   Bull of Pope Gregory XIII

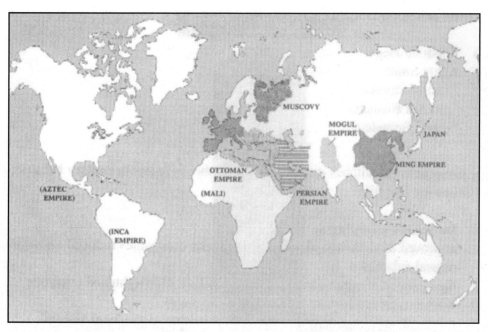

From THE RISE AND FALL OF THE GREAT POWERS by Paul Kennedy, copyright © 1987 by Paul Kennedy.
Used by permission of Randon House, Inc.

13. The date of this map is

    (A)   twelfth century
    (B)   fourteenth century
    (C)   sixteenth century
    (D)   eighteenth century
    (E)   twentieth century

14. The Protestant Reformation encouraged all of the following changes in the status of women EXCEPT

    (A)   more companionate marriage where partners respected each other
    (B)   more grounds for divorce if husbands violated the laws of marriage
    (C)   nunneries as a means of escape from wife battering
    (D)   more sensitivity by husbands to the needs of wives
    (E)   better education for women so that they could read the Bible

15. Charles I of England was forced to call Parliament into session even though he did not want to because only it could

    (A)   grant new taxes
    (B)   conduct foreign policy
    (C)   free prisoners
    (D)   change the religious settlement of Elizabeth I
    (E)   appoint Cromwell Lord Protector

16. An early and important advocate of *laissez-faire* was

    (A) Friedrich Hegel
    (B) Adam Smith
    (C) Friedrich Engels
    (D) Otto von Bismarck
    (E) Eduard Bernstein

17. The persecution of witches came to an end in the seventeenth century because of all of the following EXCEPT

    (A) the scientific revolution
    (B) improved medical knowledge and insurance companies reduced vulnerability to natural calamities
    (C) the violence of witch hunts became excessive and frightened everyone
    (D) women were elevated to a more respected status
    (E) rulers saw persecution of witches as threatening to the legal system

By courtesy of the National Portrait Gallery

18. This eighteenth-century portrait is intended to convey

    (A) the vice of pride
    (B) the tyranny of absolutism
    (C) the absurdity of elaborate dress
    (D) the majesty of kingship
    (E) republics are better than monarchies

19. The great central and south American native civilizations collapsed after the arrival of Europeans for all of the following reasons EXCEPT

    (A) epidemics such as smallpox
    (B) internal divisions
    (C) European use of horses
    (D) Spanish and Portuguese naval warfare
    (E) belief that the conquistadors were gods

20. The philosophes of the Enlightenment acknowledged their debt to

    (A) the scientific revolution
    (B) the wars of religion
    (C) the Romantic poets
    (D) Savonarola
    (E) the Anabaptists

21. RELATIVE SHARES OF WORLD MANUFACTURING OUTPUT 1750-1900

	1750	1800	1830	1860	1880	1900
UK	1.9	4.3	9.5	19.9	22.9	18.5
France	4.0	4.2	5.2	7.9	7.8	6.8
Germany	2.9	3.5	3.5	4.9	8.5	3.2
Italy	2.4	2.5	2.3	2.5	2.5	2.5
Russia	5.0	5.6	5.6	7.0	7.6	8.8
USA	0.1	0.8	2.4	7.2	14.7	23.6

All of the following statements about the above table are true EXCEPT

    (A) Britain retained the largest share of output throughout the period
    (B) France and Russia had similar levels of output until 1900
    (C) Italy remained the weakest economic power
    (D) the USA accelerated rapidly after 1860
    (E) Britain accelerated most rapidly between 1800 and 1860

22. Napoleon's greatest error of judgment was his

    (A) decision to become Emperor
    (B) marriage to an Austrian Archduchess
    (C) invasion of Russia
    (D) enactment of the Civil Code
    (E) overthrow of the Directory

23. Emperor Joseph II of Austria failed in his attempt to reform his country because he

    (A)   lacked the ruthlessness to create a secret police force
    (B)   failed to win the support of the nobility
    (C)   was unwilling to dissolve the monasteries
    (D)   failed to abolish the robot
    (E)   agreed with his mother's opinion

Rare Books Division, The New York Public Library
Astor, Lenox and Tilden Foundations

24. This painting completed in 1800 entitled "Voltaire Instructing the Infant Jacobinism" was created by the English artist James Gillray. The scene

    (A)   draws a direct connection between the Enlightenment and "The Terror" during the French Revolution
    (B)   shows that Voltaire was overwhelmed by the forces of the Church
    (C)   portrays Voltaire as the voice of reason trying to stand up to irrational hatred
    (D)   reveals that Robespierre was a dwarf
    (E)   refers to Voltaire's ambition to become King of France

25. All of the following were innovations in the eighteenth-century agricultural revolution that took place in England EXCEPT

   (A)   crop rotation
   (B)   introduction of new crops
   (C)   enclosure
   (D)   new breeding techniques
   (E)   mechanized harvesting equipment

26. The mass of the population in England in 1750 was composed of

   (A)   factory workers
   (B)   peasants
   (C)   landless laborers
   (D)   middle class
   (E)   servants

27. "The only serious organization principle for the active workers of our movement should be the strictest secrecy, the strictest selection of members, and the training of professional revolutionaries."

The author of the passage above was

   (A)   Lenin
   (B)   Cavour
   (C)   Franco
   (D)   Bernstein
   (E)   Sartre

28. The "Concert of Europe" was a term used to describe

   (A)   the rise of music in eighteenth-century France, Italy, and Spain
   (B)   the grand alliance between England, the United States, and France against Austria
   (C)   the system of alliances established by the Congress of Vienna
   (D)   the Napoleonic Empire
   (E)   enlightened absolutism in the second half of the eighteenth century

29. In 1792 Mary Wollstonecraft

    (A)   wrote the first book in Britain demanding that women have the right to vote
    (B)   denounced the French Revolution
    (C)   called for Fabian tactics to be used in achieving a communist society
    (D)   first advocated abortion
    (E)   renounced marriage as demeaning to human beings

30. "From Nature doth emotion come, and moods
    Of calmness equally are Nature's gift."

    These lines were written by a

    (A)   Lutheran
    (B)   Newtonian
    (C)   Romantic
    (D)   Marxist
    (E)   Fascist

31. Otto von Bismarck deliberately chose to humiliate his recently defeated enemy by proclaiming the creation of the German Empire in 1870 at

    (A)   Versailles Palace near Paris, France
    (B)   Hofburg Palace, Vienna, Austria
    (C)   Buckingham Palace, London, England
    (D)   St. Paul's Church, Frankfurt, Germany
    (E)   The Winter Palace, St. Petersburg, Russia

32. The Suez Canal built by the French during the reign of Napoleon III connected the

    (A)   Mediterranean and the Black Sea
    (B)   Atlantic and Mediterranean
    (C)   Mediterranean and the Red Sea
    (D)   Mediterranean and the Adriatic
    (E)   North and Baltic Seas

33. The Elector of the German state of Hanover became prominent in 1714 because he

    (A)   ascended the British throne
    (B)   defeated Louis XIV in personal combat
    (C)   converted to Catholicism
    (D)   lost a war against Prussia
    (E)   was elected Holy Roman Emperor

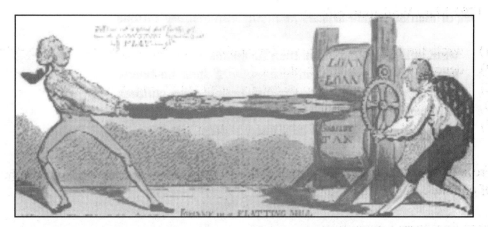

Yale Center for British Art, Paul Mellon Collection

34. This cartoon of 1796 portrays the emblematic Englishman, John Bull

    (A)   ground down by poverty
    (B)   suffering from heavy taxation
    (C)   made to give up British territory
    (D)   trying on newly fashionable clothes
    (E)   experimenting with new technology

35. The Polish Diet in the seventeenth and eighteenth centuries was ineffectual because

    (A)   merchants and nobles were always deadlocked
    (B)   of the strong central monarchy
    (C)   one veto could end the session
    (D)   members were poorly educated
    (E)   the nobility was not adequately represented

36. Economic and social life among the mass of the people under the *ancien régime* of the eighteenth century still primarily focused around

    (A)   the harvest
    (B)   the stock market
    (C)   colonial trade
    (D)   parliamentary elections
    (E)   military service

37. Wives of merchants and artisans in eighteenth-century Europe

    (A)   were totally dependent on their husbands
    (B)   were important partners in business with their husbands
    (C)   were expected only to cook and clean and raise children
    (D)   never remarried if their husbands died
    (E)   rarely gave birth to more than two children

38. All of the following were common characteristics of the ancien régime in eighteenth-century Europe EXCEPT

    (A)   aristocratic elites
    (B)   state religions
    (C)   guilds
    (D)   feudal dues
    (E)   large factories

39. "We have three questions to ask and answer. First, what is the Third Estate? Everything. Second, what has it been heretofore in the political order? Nothing. Third, what does it demand? To become something therein."

    The author of this statement wrote the passage during the

    (A)   third Partition of Poland
    (B)   French Revolution
    (C)   Revocation of the Edict of Nantes
    (D)   St. Bartholomew's Day massacre
    (E)   Glorious Revolution

40. In the mid-nineteenth century the largest category of female occupations in Western Europe were to be found in

    (A)   domestic service
    (B)   factories
    (C)   agriculture
    (D)   office work
    (E)   weaving

Europe, A HISTORY by Norman Davies, © 1993 by Norman Davies.
Used by permission of Oxford University Press, Inc.

41. The unusual configuration of this map

    (A)   is intended to emphasize the importance of the Ottoman Empire
    (B)   shows the conquests of Louis XIV
    (C)   makes us look freshly at the East and the West
    (D)   illustrates the British control over the Mediterranean
    (E)   demonstrates the centrality of Scandinavia to modern history

42. Italy achieved unification in the 1860s for all of the following reasons EXCEPT

    (A)   skillful leadership by Count Camillo di Cavour
    (B)   military victories of Giuseppe Garibaldi
    (C)   failure of Great Britain to intervene
    (D)   military support from Napoleon III
    (E)   statesmanship of Pope Pius IX

43. The Civil Constitution of the Clergy enacted during the early stages of the French Revolution

    (A)   was enthusiastically embraced by the Church
    (B)   left the lower clergy unaffected
    (C)   restored Church lands confiscated in 1789
    (D)   expanded the power of the state over religion
    (E)   was strongly supported by the King

© English Heritage Photographic Library

44. This design of an eighteenth-century English nobleman's house embodies what qualities that the aristocracy admired?

    (A)   American rusticity, grace, and freshness
    (B)   Prussian discipline, frugality, and military spirit
    (C)   Islamic geometric, abstract, and Moorish designs
    (D)   Roman strength, order, and balance
    (E)   Egyptian simplicity, mystery, and rigor

45. The most serious force undermining religious faith in the nineteenth century was

    (A)   Darwin's theory of evolution
    (B)   Bismarck's *Kulturkampf*
    (C)   the Falloux law
    (D)   Gladstone's education reform
    (E)   the encyclical *Rerum Novarum*

46. Woodrow Wilson's Fourteen Points included all of the following EXCEPT

    (A)   abolition of all monarchies
    (B)   freedom of the seas
    (C)   a league of nations
    (D)   self-determination
    (E)   open diplomacy

47. The most common cause of urban riots in the eighteenth century was

    (A)   bread shortages
    (B)   foreign policy issues
    (C)   partisan politics
    (D)   class warfare
    (E)   guild rivalries

48. The three thinkers most closely related to advances in methodology during the scientific revolution were

    (A)   Copernicus, Brahe, and Kepler
    (B)   Brahe, Vesalius, and Harvey
    (C)   Bacon, Galileo, and Descartes
    (D)   Harvey, Galileo, and Newton
    (E)   Newton, Bacon, and Copernicus

49. The most notable characteristic of the scientific revolution of the seventeenth century was the

    (A)   emphasis on empirical data and observation
    (B)   breakthroughs in medicine which reduced the death rate
    (C)   major advances in the engineering of firearms
    (D)   new insights into genetic codes
    (E)   application of steam power to pumping water

50. A monarch called a "politique" practiced which of the following

    (A)   terror and deceit
    (B)   democratic politics
    (C)   live and let live
    (D)   extreme uniformity
    (E)   religious conformity

Europe, A HISTORY by Norman Davies, © 1993 by Norman Davies.
Used by permission of Oxford University Press, Inc.

51. This map shows the boundaries of European states in

(A)   1848
(B)   1866
(C)   1914
(D)   1939
(E)   1945

52. Louis XIV of France used all of the following methods to assert his absolute power EXCEPT

   (A)   appointed intendants as provincial officials who owed loyalty to him
   (B)   made great nobles hold his nightshirt when he went to bed
   (C)   built the great palace at Versailles
   (D)   spent long hours examining official papers
   (E)   supported the Jansenists of the Port Royal community

53. "The utmost the Prime Minister has been able to gain for Czechoslovakia and in the matters which were in dispute has been that the German dictator, instead of snatching his victuals from the table, has been content to have them served to him course by course...."

This passage makes reference to which of the following?

   (A)   the Peace of Augsburg
   (B)   the Edict of Nantes
   (C)   the Munich Agreement
   (D)   the Truman Doctrine
   (E)   the Treaty of Rome

54.   PERCENT OF POPULATION LIVING IN URBAN AREAS 1890-1938

	1890	1910	1920	1938
Britain	29.9	34.9	37.3	39.2
Germany	11.3	20.0	35.7	30.2
France	11.7	14.4	15.1	15.0
Russia	3.6	6.4	3.1	20.2

Based on the information provided above, which of the following statements is accurate?

   (A)   France showed consistent growth in its urban population
   (B)   Russia experienced the greatest surge in urban population between 1890 and 1910
   (C)   Britain was the most urbanized country
   (D)   Germany surpassed Britain in urban growth
   (E)   France and Germany had similar patterns of urban growth

55. Which reform carried out by Catherine the Great of Russia was MOST characteristic of Enlightened Absolutism?

   (A) defeat of the Ottoman Sultan in the Crimea
   (B) restoration of hereditary noble ranks
   (C) partition of Poland
   (D) revision of the legal code
   (E) censorship of books

56. Which European country began to overtake Britain as an industrial power towards the end of the nineteenth century?

   (A) Russia
   (B) Italy
   (C) France
   (D) Germany
   (E) Austria-Hungary

57.   NORWEGIAN EXPORTS TO GERMANY 1905-1945
                              (in millions of kronor)

                              1905   24
                              1910   33
                              1915   120
                              1920   42
                              1925   61
                              1930   66
                              1935   42
                              1940   125
                              1945   10

   These figures indicate

   (A) the impact of the World Wars on the Norwegian economy
   (B) that the great depression did not affect trade
   (C) Germany exported more to Norway than vice versa
   (D) the impact of the second industrial revolution
   (E) Norway exported more to France than it did to Germany

58. The Kellogg-Briand Pact signed in 1928

   (A)   pledged to renounce war as an instrument of national policy
   (B)   was the peace treaty between the Allies and Austria-Hungary
   (C)   established the League of Nations
   (D)   was a naval agreement concluded in Washington
   (E)   provoked the Japanese into invading Manchuria

Reunion des Musees Nationaux/Art Resource, NY

59. This painting is related with which of the following?

   (A)   Nazi propaganda
   (B)   Pablo Picasso
   (C)   Impressionism
   (D)   Art Nouveaux
   (E)   Charlie Chaplin

60. After a prolonged struggle for independence and a civil war, Southern Ireland in the 1920s was

   (A)   an independent nation with not connection to Britain
   (B)   a British colony
   (C)   loosely connected with Britain
   (D)   a protectorate of Germany
   (E)   allied with Russia

61. The Weimar constitution in post-war Germany

    (A)   placed the Chancellor above the President
    (B)   abolished the Reichstag
    (C)   produced stable, long-lived governments
    (D)   was vulnerable to pressure from extremists
    (E)   established communism

62. The country most successful in resisting Soviet control under Stalin and Khrushchev was

    (A)   Poland
    (B)   Yugoslavia
    (C)   Bulgaria
    (D)   Hungary
    (E)   Czechoslovakia

63. According to Winston Churchill at the outset of the Cold War in 1946 an Iron Curtain was falling across Europe from

    (A)   the Baltic to the Adriatic
    (B)   the North Sea to the Bay of Biscay
    (C)   the Black Sea to the Red Sea
    (D)   Suez to Gibraltar
    (E)   the Mediterranean to the Atlantic

64. Socialism may be described as

    (A)   an attempt to create economic equality by government action
    (B)   a call for violent overthrow of the capitalist system
    (C)   an anti-democratic response to the breakdown of the old rural economy
    (D)   a philosophy suitable only for small economic units
    (E)   an avoidance of nationalization of industry at all costs

65. Published long before he was able to gain power, Hitler laid out all of the following policies in his book, *Mein Kampf*, EXCEPT

    (A)   Germany's need for expanded territory
    (B)   the necessity for remilitarization
    (C)   a call for the restoration of the monarchy
    (D)   anti-Semitism
    (E)   a desire to crush communism

66. Who among the following was NOT involved in extending understanding of nuclear physics?

    (A)   Albert Einstein
    (B)   Gregor Mendel
    (C)   Ernest Rutherford
    (D)   Max Planck
    (E)   Werner Heisenberg

67. Which of the following pairs of imperial power and colony does NOT match?

    (A)   Italy and Sudan
    (B)   Great Britain and Egypt
    (C)   Belgium and Congo
    (D)   France and Algeria
    (E)   Portugal and Angola

68. Which of the following countries did NOT fight in North Africa during World War II?

    (A)   United States
    (B)   United Kingdom
    (C)   Italy
    (D)   Russia
    (E)   Germany

69. The bombing of London during the Battle of Britain in 1940

    (A)   caused few casualties
    (B)   stiffened morale against Germany
    (C)   destroyed all British air defenses
    (D)   was aimed only at military targets
    (E)   destroyed the entire city

70. Vatican II, initiated by Pope John XXIII in 1962, was a reform movement within the Roman Catholic Church that

    (A)   encouraged ecumenical relations with other religions
    (B)   abolished the papacy
    (C)   reasserted conservative values
    (D)   helped end the Cold War
    (E)   elected a non-Italian pope

71. The Middle East became a central area of conflict after World War II for all of the following reasons EXCEPT

    (A) oil
    (B) Israel
    (C) Suez Canal
    (D) proximity to Indo-China
    (E) the Cold War

72. Fertility rates among women in Western Europe have declined since the 1950s due to all of the following EXCEPT

    (A) more women in the work force
    (B) higher educational levels
    (C) availability of contraceptive devices
    (D) legalized abortions
    (E) higher infant mortality

73. The Berlin Wall was built in 1961 to

    (A) prevent West Germans from fleeing east
    (B) prevent East Germans from fleeing west
    (C) create a united Berlin
    (D) protect West Germany from the Warsaw Pact
    (E) enlarge the Berlin zoo

74. Who among the following was NOT a president of France during the Fifth Republic?

    (A) Georges Pompidou
    (B) Francois Mitterand
    (C) Francisco Franco
    (D) Charles de Gaulle
    (E) Valery Giscard d'Estang

75.

Russia	16,000,000
Poland	5,600,000
France	350,000
Czechoslovakia	215,000
Great Britain	92,000
Germany	780,000
Italy	152,000

This list of civilian deaths occurred during which war?

(A) World War I
(B) World War II
(C) War of the Spanish Succession
(D) Napoleonic Wars
(E) Seven Years War

76. All of the following dates when independence was granted from colonial rule are correct EXCEPT

(A) India 1947
(B) Indonesia 1949
(C) Angola 1975
(D) Ethiopia 1990
(E) Hong Kong 1997

77. Which among the following was one of the most important results from the United States' engagement in Vietnam during the 1960s and 1970s?

(A) deflation in the US economy
(B) student protests and questioning of authority
(C) US alliance with China
(D) British withdrawal from NATO
(E) successful conclusion of the Cold War

78. Allies of the Soviet Union in the post-war period included all of the following EXCEPT

(A) Cuba
(B) Poland
(C) South Africa
(D) Hungary
(E) Bulgaria

79. Which of the following countries was neutral in both the First and Second World Wars?

   (A)   Great Britain
   (B)   the Netherlands
   (C)   Portugal
   (D)   Sweden
   (E)   Russia

80. Gorbachev's policy of *perestroika* instituted in the Soviet Union during the 1980s was intended to

   (A)   decentralize the economy and allow greater private initiative
   (B)   restore a full command economy
   (C)   restore Stalinism
   (D)   abolish the Communist Party
   (E)   increase the Russian birthrate

Section II

Part A

(Reading time 15 minutes; writing time – 45 minutes)
Percent of Section II score 45

Directions: The following question is based on the accompanying Documents 1-13. (Some of the documents have been edited for the purpose of this exercise.)

This question is designed to test your ability to work with historical documents. Write an essay that:

- Has a relevant thesis and supports that thesis with evidence from the documents.
- Uses a majority of the documents.
- Analyzes the documents by grouping them in as many appropriate ways as possible. **Does not simply summarize the documents individually.**
- Takes into account both the sources of the documents and the authors' point of view.

You may refer to relevant historical information not mentioned in the documents.

QUESTION: Identify and analyze the issues that motivated those who believed Captain Dreyfus should stand convicted of treason against the French Republic.

Historical Background: In December 1894 Captain Alfred Dreyfus, an officer on the General Staff of the French Army and a middle class Jew, was convicted of passing secret information to Germany. Subsequent revelations suggested that he was innocent and had been framed. Documents were forged and facts proving his innocence were concealed in order to sustain an impression of his guilt. The nation became deeply divided by the issue. After a barbarous period of imprisonment a second trial in 1899 upheld the original verdict, but Dreyfus was pardoned and eventually returned to active duty.

275

Document 1

Source: Count Henri Victor de Rochefort, aristocratic military officer, article in the newspaper *L'Intransigent*, 1894

The traitor Dreyfus has not hesitated to make a complete confession. He knows that the German-loving government who rule us have decided to give him a laughable sentence which will be followed promptly by a full pardon. Those in power who wish to maintain his innocence point out that Captain Dreyfus could have had no hope of monetary gain because he was from a wealthy merchant family.

Document 2

Source: Count von Münster, German Ambassador to France, in a report to Prince von Hohenlohe-Schillingfürst, German Chancellor, 1894

The French smell espionage everywhere. The columns of the newspapers in Paris are once again filled with adventurous spy stories and fantastic assertions about the organization of foreign espionage. A heated campaign against foreigners has been let loose, especially against Germans and Italians. Their organizations, consulates, even their embassies are designated as nests of espionage.

Document 3

Source: Article in *Civilità Cattolica*, the official newsletter of the Jesuit Order in France, 1898

Dreyfus is a Jew. Of 260 billions that constitute the wealth of France, the Jews possess 80. They direct home as well as foreign policy. The abandonment of Egypt and the Suez Canal to the British was the work of these Jews, who corrupt the press and parliament. The Jew was created by God to serve as a spy wherever treason is in preparation. Ethnic solidarity ties Jews together across national boundaries. They are never loyal citizens.

Document 4

Source: Emile Zola, a novelist, "A Letter to France", pamphlet, 1898

Public opinion is made up largely of these lies, of these far-fetched and stupid stories, which the reptile press scatter broadcast every day. There are certain newspapers which never publish anything but mud. They drag on their existence with low sales, howling and lying about Dreyfus in order to increase their circulation.

Document 5

Source: Georges Clemenceau, journalist and politician, speech, 1898

As a radical, I can understand why many socialists, themselves the victims of so much injustice, fail to denounce the attack on Dreyfus, which is another act of arbitrary power this time visited upon a member of the bourgeoisie, a class they hate.

Document 6

Source: Jean Jaurès, socialist deputy to parliament, speech 1898

Whether Dreyfus is guilty or innocent, I don't care. But I am concerned about tyranny of the sword. The military courts should not be able to trample on the legal safeguards of citizens, under whatever pretext, be it Jewry, the flag, the nation, or what you will.

Document 7

Source: periodical *Le Pere Peinard*, 1898 "The New Siamese Twins"

Labadie Collection, University of Michigan

Document 8

Source: Maurice Palèologue, French Envoy to the Vatican, report to the Ministry of Foreign Affairs, 1898

At the Vatican they avoid committing themselves on Dreyfus's guilt, but they let slip no opportunity of expressing pity for poor France, which they believe is now discovering to its cost the ordeals and perils to which a nation exposes itself when it allows itself to fall into the hands of Freemasons, atheists, revolutionaries, and Jews.

Document 9

Source: Charles Maurras, journalist, article in the *Gazette de France*, a royalist newspaper, 1898

There are special, unwritten laws, both higher and more rigorous and more extensive than those understood only by the common man. Even forgery may be morally justified for reasons of state, the national interest, the strength and honor of the army. Whether Dreyfus is innocent or guilty, one must not compromise, one must not, for one man, for one single man, risk the life and safety of a people.

Document 10

Source: General Gabriel de Pellieux, letter to his mother, 1899

When Dreyfus finally sees that his position has become untenable, he will repeat his confession and name his accomplices. And that is just what the Jews fear. This race, which introduced us to the cult of the Golden Calf, carries immorality and dishonor to the limit. We, who know he is guilty, fight a good battle, but one without danger, for our enemies are cowards.

Document 11

Source: Paul Nèroulède, aide to the Duke of Orléans, pretender to the French throne, an open letter, 1899

The unexpected death of the President of France is the moment for Frenchmen to resume again the traditions of her history and greatness. We must restore the monarchy if we are to revive national honor, protect the Church and the other institutions precious to our country, especially the army, and above all to exterminate the dangerous liberals and radicals who rally around the traitor Dreyfus. Frenchmen! To your posts! Long live France! God save the King!

Document 12

Source: M. Zakrevsky, judge, Russian High Court, letter to *The Times of London*, 1899

Unable in her vanity and thirst for prestige to accept her humiliating defeat by Germany in 1870, France has gradually cut herself adrift from the great liberal traditions of human dignity which the Declaration of the Rights of Man had embodied. She has drifted into anti-semitism, into anti-protestantism, into oppression of the weak, into brutal militarism, and, finally, into the Dreyfus Affair.

Document 13

Source: Captain Alfred Dreyfus, interview with the *New York Herald*, 1899

I think that at the beginning, up to the time of the court martial of 1894, the officers in charge of the investigation genuinely believed that I was guilty. But once the trial began, it was different. I am certain that from that moment, as they felt they had made a mistake, they were afraid of being accused of carelessness, or worse, and they began to forge false evidence to make sure the people believed I was guilty and the army's honor was unblemished.

Section II

Part B

Group 1

(Suggested planning and writing time – 35 minutes)
Percent of Section II score – 27 1/2

Directions: You are to answer ONE questions from the three questions below. Make your selection carefully, choosing the questions that you are best prepared to answer thoroughly in the time permitted. You should spend 5 minutes organizing or outlining your answer. In writing your essay, <u>use specific examples to support your answer</u>.

2. Discuss the major outcomes of the economic transformation that took place in Europe during the sixteenth century.

3. Describe and analyze the increasing secularization of European culture during the eighteenth century.

4. Compare and contrast the economic theories of mercantilism and *laissez-faire*.

Group 2

(Suggested planning and writing time 35 minutes)
Percent of Section II score – 27 1/2

Directions: You are to answer ONE questions from the three questions below. Make your selection carefully, choosing the questions that you are best prepared to answer thoroughly in the time permitted. You should spend 5 minutes organizing or outlining your answer. In writing your essay, <u>use specific examples to support your answer</u>.

5. Compare and contrast Spain in the seventeenth century and France in the eighteenth century in their role as great powers.

6. "1848 was the turning point at which Europe failed to turn". Assess the validity of this statement.

7. It has been argued that one of the greatest mistakes made in the aftermath of World War I was the break up of the Austro-Hungarian Empire. Analyze the arguments for and against this decision.

Acknowledgements

- **Chapter 5**
  Page 56 Question 12.
  Copyright © 1987 by Paul Kennedy. Reprinted by permission of Random House, Inc.

- **Chapter 8**
  Page 85 Question 2
  From <u>Documents Western Civilization</u>, Volume II (since 1550), 3rd edition by SPIELVOGEL © 1997. Reprinted with permission of Wadsworth, a division of Thomson Learning: www.thomsonrights.com. Fax (800) 730-2215.

  Page 86 Question 6
  From <u>Documents Western Civilization</u>, Volume II (since 1550), 3rd edition by SPIELVOGEL © 1997. Reprinted with permission of Wadsworth, a division of Thomson Learning: www.thomsonrights.com. Fax (800) 730-2215.

- **Chapter 11**
  Page 133 Question 17.
  Copyright © 1987 by Paul Kennedy. Reprinted by permission of Random House, Inc.

- **Chapter 14**
  Page 168 Question 21.
  Copyright © 1987 by Paul Kennedy. Reprinted by permission of Random House, Inc.

- **Chapter 15**
  Page 180 Question 20
  Copyright © 1987 by Paul Kennedy. Reprinted by permission of Random House, Inc.

- **Chapter 16**
  Page 193 Question 2.
  Quoted in Marsha Rowe et al., <u>Spare Rib Reader</u> (Harmondsworth, 1982), p. 574

  Page 195 Question 10.
  Copyright © 1987 by Paul Kennedy. Reprinted by permission of Random House, Inc.

  Page 199 Question 24.
  Copyright © 1987 by Paul Kennedy. Reprinted by permission of Random House, Inc.

• **Chapter 17**

Page 206 Question 5

Copyright © 1987 by Paul Kennedy. Reprinted by permission of Random House, Inc.

Page 210 Question 14.

Copyright © 1987 by Paul Kennedy. Reprinted by permission of Random House, Inc.

Page 211 Question 17.

Copyright © 1987 by Paul Kennedy. Reprinted by permission of Random House, Inc.

Sample Examination I

Page 236 Question 55.

"Suicide in the Trenches", from COLLECTED POEMS OF SIEGFRIED SASSOON by Siegfried Sassoon, © 1918, 1920 by E.P. Dutton. Copyright 1936, 1946, 1947, 1948 by Siegfried Sassoon. Used by Permission of Viking Penguin, a division of Penguin Group (USA) Inc.

Page 244 DBQ Document 1.

"The Longest War", by Mulholland, Marc (2002), pp. 54, 89, & 120. Reprinted by permission of Oxford University Press.

Page 244 DBQ Document 2

"A History of Northern Ireland", by Thomas Hennessey. Reprinted by permission of Gill & Macmillan Ltd.

Page 245 DBQ Document 4.

"The Longest War", by Mulholland, Marc (2002), pp. 54, 89, & 120. Reprinted by permission of Oxford University Press.

Page 245 DBQ Document 5.

"The Longest War", by Mulholland, Marc (2002), pp. 54, 89, & 120. Reprinted by permission of Oxford University Press.

Page 245 DBQ Document 6

"A History of Northern Ireland", by Thomas Hennessey. Reprinted by permission of Gill & Macmillan Ltd.

Page 246 DBQ Document 7

"Belfast Diary", by John Conroy (1995), Used by permission of Beacon Press, Boston.

Page 246 DBQ Document 8

"War & Words", Bill Roston & David Miller (1996), Pale Publications, Belfast

Page 246 DBQ Document 9
From <u>Rebel Hearts</u>: Journeys Within the IRA's Soul, by Kevin Toolis, published by Picador and St. Martin's.

Page 247 DBQ Document 10
<u>Battling for Peace</u>, by Richard Needham (1996), reprinted by permission of Blackstaff Press, Belfast.

Page 247 DBQ Document 11.
From <u>Rebel Hearts</u>: Journeys Within the IRA's Soul, by Kevin Toolis, published by Picador and St. Martin's.

Page 248 DBQ Document 13
From <u>Rebel Hearts</u>: Journeys Within the IRA's Soul, by Kevin Toolis, published by Picador and St. Martin's.